His Word

ISBN-13: 978-1979747424
ISBN-10: 1979747423

Published by The Jenkins Institute

thejenkinsinstitute.com

Professional editing: Kathy Jarrell
Logo design: Philip Jenkins
Interior layout: Joey Sparks

With Thanks

"Your word is a lamp to my feet and a light to my path..." (Psalm 119:105)

"His divine power has granted to us all things that pertain to life and godliness, through the knowledge of him who called us to his own glory and excellence." (2 Peter 1:3)

"So faith comes from hearing, and hearing through the word of Christ." (Romans 10:17)

Thank you for picking up this little book. There are a number of ways you can use it, and our dream is that it will aid you in your walk with God. We were blessed to aid with last year's One Word Study (onewordstudy.com). That study blessed tens of thousands of lives as individuals studied a great Bible word each day and as congregations were united in a common study. While this project is not the same, it has the same focus and goals.

We believe there is no "WORD" as significant as Christ, The Word (John 1). So this project will walk us through the word of Christ. We believe nothing will affect your spiritual life like time spent in the Word of God. We also believe that the God who loves people has protected His Word through the ages, and that any person can pick up His Word and learn how to please Him. Because of these convictions, we determined to focus on that Word this year.

Our greatest desire is that your journey through the Word will increase your love for the "WORD." *"In the beginning was the Word, and the Word was with God, and the Word was God. He was in the beginning with God...And the Word became flesh and dwelt among us, and we have seen his glory, glory as of the only Son from the Father, full of grace and truth"* (John 1:11–22, 14).

As you study privately or in a Bible class, or in a congregation-wide effort, we want you to know we are praying for you. Thank you for joining us on a journey through the Word. One chapter a day, five chapters a week, 260 chapters will take you through the New Testament.

We are so very thankful for the 50-75 teachers, preachers, writers, editors, and proofers who have helped make this come to life. This is no two person project. We are thankful for Kathy Jarrell for her proofreading and Joey Sparks for his formatting and organization. Their efforts helped make this project a reality.

"...Christ in you, the hope of glory" (Colossians 1:27).

Jeff and Dale Jenkins
TheJenkinsInstitute.com

Contents

Week One	Bill Watkins	Matthew 1–5	1
Week Two	Bart Warren	Matthew 6–10	7
Week Three	Charles Abernathy	Matthew 11–15	13
Week Four	Steve Baggett	Matthew 16–20	19
Week Five	Keith Olbricht	Matthew 21–25	25
Week Six	Jeff & Dale Jenkins	Matthew 26–28 Mark –1–2	31
Week Seven	Travis Bookout	Mark 3–7	37
Week Eight	Chris McCurley	Mark 8–12	43
Week Nine	Bryan McAlister	Mark 13–16 Luke 1	49
Week Ten	Joey Sparks	Luke 2–6	55
Week Eleven	Chuck Monan	Luke 7–11	61
Week Twelve	David Salisbury	Luke 12–16	67
Week Thirteen	Michael Moss	Luke 17–21	73
Week Fourteen	Doug Burleson	Luke 22–24 John 1–2	79
Week Fifteen	Buddy Johnson	John 3–7	85
Week Sixteen	Cecil May, Jr.	John 8–12	91
Week Seventeen	Steve Bailey	John 13–17	97
Week Eighteen	Ed Gallagher	John 18–21 Acts 1	103
Week Nineteen	Russ Crosswhite	Acts 2–6	109
Week Twenty	Jason Moon	Acts 7–11	115

Week Twenty-One	Kevin Langford	Acts 12-16	121
Week Twenty-Two	Keith Parker	Acts 17-21	127
Week Twenty-Three	James Hayes	Acts 22-26	133
Week Twenty-Four	Tim Gunnells	Acts 27-28 Romans 1-3	139
Week Twenty-Five	Barry Throneberry	Romans 4-8	145
Week Twenty-Six	Ralph Gilmore	Romans 9-13	151
Week Twenty-Seven	Jacob Hawk	Romans 14-16 1 Corinthians 1-2	157
Week Twenty-Eight	Matthew Morine	1 Corinthians 3-7	163
Week Twenty-Nine	Robert Hatfield	1 Corinthians 8-12	169
Week Thirty	Terry Edwards	1 Corinthians 13-16 2 Corinthians 1	175
Week Thirty-One	Gantt Carter	2 Corinthians 2-6	181
Week Thirty-Two	Justin Guin	2 Corinthians 7-11	187
Week Thirty-Three	Wayne Jones	2 Corinthians 12-13 Galatians 1-3	193
Week Thirty-Four	Mike Vestel	Galatians 4-6 Ephesians 1-2	199
Week Thirty-Five	Jay Lockhart	Ephesians 3-6 Philippians 1	205
Week Thirty-Six	Kurt Montooth	Philippians 2-4 Colossians 1-2	211
Week Thirty-Seven	Denny Petrillo	Colossians 3-4 1 Thessalonians 1-3	217
Week Thirty-Eight	David Morris	1 Thessalonians 4-5 2 Thessalonians 1-3	223
Week Thirty-Nine	Andy Connelly	1 Timothy 1-5	229

Week Forty	Anthony Warnes	1 Timothy 6 2 Timothy 1–4	235
Week Forty-One	Logan Cates	Titus 1–3 Philemon Hebrews 1	241
Week Forty-Two	Austin Johnson	Hebrews 2–6	247
Week Forty-Three	Richard Harp	Hebrews 7–11	253
Week Forty-Four	Drake Jenkins	Hebrews 12–13 James 1–3	259
Week Forty-Five	Kevin Kasparek	James 4–5 1 Peter 1–3	265
Week Forty-Six	Paul Shero	1 Peter 4–5 2 Peter 1–3	271
Week Forty-Seven	Robert Johnson	1 John 1–5	277
Week Forty-Eight	Craig Evans	2 John 3 John Jude Revelation 1–2	283
Week Forty-Nine	Tommy Haynes	Revelation 3–7	289
Week Fifty	Barry Grider	Revelation 8–12	295
Week Fifty-One	Kirk Brothers	Revelation 13–17	301
Week Fifty-Two	Neal Pollard	Revelation 18–22	307

Week One
Matthew 1-5

Bill Watkins

Monday
There's a Place for Me

Matthew's gospel is, more than all of the rest, written in rabbinical form. The emphasis on teaching is more important than chronology. The emphasis on how Christ fulfills the actual wording of Old Testament prophecies stands out throughout the book. For those to whom it was originally written, it was a thoroughly convincing account of the life, works, and teachings of Jesus. For that reason, Matthew begins with this wonderful genealogy.

This account differs from Luke's genealogy, because it shows Jesus' LEGAL ancestry through Joseph. Luke's genealogy apparently shows Jesus' PHYSICAL ancestry through Mary. Together, they show that both legally and physically, Jesus was the Son of David who was prophesied.

What interests me, however, is the checkered and diverse story of the ancestry of Jesus. There were several women mentioned—Tamar, who committed adultery with her own father-in-law—Rahab, who was a prostitute before becoming the wife of Salmon—Ruth, who was a foreigner—and though she is not mentioned by name, Bathsheba, who the text describes, not as the wife of David, but the wife of Uriah, whom David had killed.

There were great people of faith in the line of Jesus. There was Abraham, the father of the faithful, and there were Isaac and Jacob, the patriarchs. There were great kings—David, Jehoshaphat, Hezekiah, and Josiah.

And there were terrible sinners—Ahaz and Manasseh and others. Even some of the great were a mix of righteousness and sin. Abraham and Isaac lied, David committed adultery and murder, Solomon was seduced away from God in spite of his wisdom — and on and on it goes.

What's the point?

In the genealogy of Christ, there were women and men, Jews and Gentiles, rich and poor, good and bad, famous, infamous, and unknowns. The genealogy is a message that there is room for everyone, not only in the genealogy of Christ, but in the Kingdom of Christ.

Today, I will...be less judgmental of others and more thankful that there is room for me in Christ!

Tuesday
God Has Plans for the Whole World

Today's Scripture Matthew 2:1-2

Sometimes forgotten in all the trappings of a holiday story, are the incredible, astounding implications of the first paragraph of Matthew 2. We've heard the legend for so long, that we often fail to actually understand the real story. In two verses, God explodes the idea that He was a regional God with only national interests.

"Now after Jesus was born in Bethlehem of Judea in the days of Herod the king, behold, wise men from the east came to Jerusalem, saying, 'Where is he who has been born king of the Jews? For we saw his star when it rose and have come to worship him.'" (Matthew 2:1-2)

Wait, what!? Who were these "wise men?" What part of the east did they come from? Why are they called wise men at all? We, to this day, can only guess at who they were or where they came from. There are compelling theories, but no real facts to inform us.

And what "star" did they see when it rose? What was the star? Why were they looking for it?

And why did they associate the rising of the star with the birth of the "king of the Jews?" Why did they feel the need to "come to worship him?"

Clearly, these wise men were not Israelites. There is no indication that they had ever read the Hebrew Scriptures. And even if they had, there is no such prophecy in the Old Testament that predicts and connects the rising of a star with the birth of a king.

The implications are astounding. God has always been concerned for all people. He has always been involved in the lives and nations of the whole world.

God loves everyone wants them to be saved. When you spread the gospel, remember that you are going to people on whom God is already working.

Today, I will...lift my vision to everyone God loves and seek to bring them closer to Him.

Wednesday
God's Beloved Son

"And when Jesus was baptized, immediately he went up from the water, and behold, the heavens were opened to him, and he saw the Spirit of God descending like a dove and coming to rest on him; and behold, a voice from heaven said, 'This is my beloved Son, with whom I am well pleased.'" (Matthew 3:16-17)

Jesus once asked the Pharisees, "What do you think about the Christ?" It's a good question.

What you think about him will determine your destiny. Jesus said, *"Unless you believe that I am He, you will die in your sins"* (John 8:24)

So who is He really?

He's not the same person as the Holy Spirit, because the Spirit of God descended like and dove and came to rest on Him. He's not the same person as God the Father, because the voice that everyone heard came from "heaven" and not from below.

He is nothing less than the very Son of God. As we have already noted in chapters one and two of Matthew, Jesus is the prophesied Savior, born of the seed of David and of God, born of a virgin, worshipped by wise men, and protected by his parents and by heaven. He is the one whom God loves and the one with whom He is well-pleased.

How do you respond when someone mistreats your child? You are angry and protective and ready to do battle, if necessary, to defend the offspring that you love.

Guess what? That's the way that God feels as well.

How you treat the Son is how you treat the Father. Jesus said, *"The Father judges no one, but has given all judgment to the Son, that all may honor the Son, just as they honor the Father. Whoever does not honor the Son does not honor the Father who sent Him."* (John 5:22-23)

Today, I will...honor the beloved Son of God by prayer, praise, study, and obedience.

4

Thursday

Fighting the Devil Like Jesus

"Then Jesus was led up by the Spirit into the wilderness to be tempted by the devil. And after fasting forty days and forty nights, he was hungry. And the tempter came and said to him, 'If you are the Son of God, command these stones to become loaves of bread.' But he answered, 'It is written, "Man shall not live by bread alone, but by every word that comes from the mouth of God." Then the devil took him to the holy city and set him on the pinnacle of the temple and said to him, 'If you are the Son of God, throw yourself down, for it is written, "He will command his angels concerning you," and "On their hands they will bear you up, lest you strike your foot against a stone." Jesus said to him, 'Again it is written, "You shall not put the Lord your God to the test." Again, the devil took him to a very high mountain and showed him all the kingdoms of the world and their glory. And he said to him, 'All these I will give you, if you will fall down and worship me.' Then Jesus said to him, 'Be gone, Satan! For it is written, "You shall worship the Lord your God and him only shall you serve."' Then the devil left him, and behold, angels came and were ministering to him." (Matthew 4:1–11)

Today, I want to leave you with a short, but important, thought. Jesus fought the devil in a way you and I can fight him.

Jesus is the Son of God. He has all the power that he needs to send Satan away. He could evict demons with a word!

But he didn't do that, because we can't do that. He did what we can do.

He used Scripture. With each temptation, He responded with, "It is written!" It worked for him and it will work for us.

Today, I will...study the Scriptures and use them to defeat Satan.

5

Friday
We Are Blessed

Today's Scripture Matthew 5:3-11

"Blessed are the poor in spirit, for theirs is the kingdom of heaven. Blessed are those who mourn, for they shall be comforted. Blessed are the meek, for they shall inherit the earth. Blessed are those who hunger and thirst for righteousness, for they shall be satisfied. Blessed are the merciful, for they shall receive mercy. Blessed are the pure in heart, for they shall see God. Blessed are the peacemakers, for they shall be called sons of God. Blessed are those who are persecuted for righteousness' sake, for theirs is the kingdom of heaven. Blessed are you when others revile you and persecute you and utter all kinds of evil against you falsely on my account." (Matthew 5:3-11)

When Jesus spoke the Sermon on the Mount, he would have spoken in Aramaic. The form of his teaching is in Aramaic as well. This tells us something important.

If you have a Bible in which certain words are in italics it is because those words have been added to the text to help supply meaning – they were not in the original text. It you have such a Bible, you will note that the verb is missing from each of the beatitudes. In the original text, there was no are.

If you go to the Hebrew Bible, you will note that Psalm 1:1 does not read, "Blessed is the man who does not walk in the counsel of the ungodly." It reads, "O the blessedness of the man who does not walk in the counsel of the ungodly." The writer is not saying that we will be blessed someday if we do not walk in the counsel of the ungodly. He is saying that we are blessed at the moment that we do not.

I believe that is the import of Christ's words here in Matthew five. It's not that we will be blessed one day – we are blessed now as we obey these words.

Today, I will...be blessed by believing and obeying Christ's words.

Week Two
Matthew 6 – 10

Bart Warren

Monday
Secret Christianity

In this section of the Sermon on the Mount, we read about how the Lord expects His disciples to be giving, praying, and fasting (Matthew 6:2, 5, 16). The question is not "if" we will give, pray, and fast but "how and why" do disciples go about these disciplines?

An unusual emphasis is placed upon doing these things in secret (Matthew 6:4, 6, 18). Christians are to influence others for good, right (Matthew 5:14-16)? How can this be done in secret?

When the Lord speaks of doing things "in secret" He does not mean, "don't let anyone know that you are a Christian." No, we must be seen. We must be distinct. We must go and change the world by bringing others to Christ!

When Jesus speaks of doing things in secret He is talking about motivation. Do we want to be seen by others? Or do we sincerely desire to express love and devotion to God? Jesus is saying, "When you give, pray, or fast... do it because you love me."

My giving is done "in secret" because I do not want my peers looking at me. I want to look at God and say, "thank you." This is personal between my Lord and me. When I give, I show myself that my blessings come from God. When I give, I show God how thankful I am for what He has done.

My praying is done "in secret" because I want the attention of God, not the attention of men. The Bible is clear that some approaches are effective while others are not (cf. Luke 18:1-14). My prayer is offered from a position of humble dependence on the One who sees and knows all.

My fasting is done "in secret" because I need to be reminded that I depend upon God for my blessings, not self or others (cf. Deuteronomy 8:3; Matthew 4:2-4; Acts 13:2-3; 14:23).

Today, I will...remember that I give, pray, and fast because I love Him, not because I want to impress others.

Tuesday
Do Unto Others

Matthew 7 contains the conclusion of the Sermon on the Mount as Jesus stresses the importance of obedience. It is not enough to simply hear what He says; everyone must actually do what He says (7:21-27). We will focus on the first part of the chapter. Two of Jesus' most well-known (and often misunderstood and misapplied) commands are found in this section of Scripture that we are reading today.

"Judge not, that you be not judged." (Matthew 7:1)
"So whatever you wish that others would do to you, do also to them." (Matthew 7:12)

These two statements are bookends to a powerful lesson from Jesus. Have you even seen someone confronted regarding behavior that was deemed inappropriate and heard him or her respond, "You can't judge me"? We all have. Some of us may even have defended our own actions with those words.

To appeal to Matthew 7:1 in this way is woefully inadequate and irresponsible. God actually demands that we identify that which is evil, sinful, etc. (1 Thessalonians 5:21; Ephesians 5:11; Romans 16:17; et. al.). There is evil (as well as good). There is wrong (as well as right). To recognize something as evil is NOT what Jesus condemns.

It is **hypocritical judging** that is condemned. Judging is demanded. Hypocrisy is condemned.

But let us proceed with caution: Simply condemning someone else does not make us righteous. Let us lovingly look for opportunities to teach and to encourage. This is what I would want for someone to do for me.

Let us be real about our own failures and sin. Let us be genuine about our need for grace. We must show mercy in order to receive mercy. In other words, what is condemned in 7:1-5 is judgment that does not include mercy. Do we not long to be judged by a God of mercy and grace? (cf. Matthew 18:33, 35; James 2:13)

Today, I will...seek to be patient, understanding, and merciful. In so doing I will treat others the way I would want to be treated.

Wednesday
If You Will

Jesus has "wowed" the audience with His teaching (Matthew 7:28). Now huge crowds are following Him (8:1). The question becomes: What are the individual members of the audience willing to do? Will they be moved to obedience by the message? Will they be awed by the powerful miracles and thus submit to the One with authority over all time, space, and matter? Consider the example of the leper.

The man makes his way to Jesus and bows before Him. He says, "Lord, if you will, you can make me clean."

Jesus responded: "I will; be clean."

How often have you paused to reflect upon the lengths to which Jesus was willing to go in order to make us clean?

He was willing to forego the glory of Heaven (Philippians 2:6-8; John 17:5). He was willing to be humiliated and hated (Isaiah 53:3). He was willing to die for us (Isaiah 53:12; 1 Peter 2:24). Oh, how He loves us!

Specifically, in this encounter with the leper, Jesus demonstrates His willingness to touch the unclean. Lepers were seen as repulsive and were considered outcasts. They were seen as cursed by God (Lev 13:46). According to passages such as Leviticus 5:3, to touch the one who is unclean is to become unclean.

Jesus did not have to physically touch this man. As is seen in the very next recorded miracle (the paralyzed servant of a centurion—Matthew 8:8, 13), Jesus can simply speak and heal whoever needs to be healed. Jesus chose to touch a man who likely had not had social or physical contact in a long time.

Have you ever felt untouchable? Have you ever stood unclean before God? He is willing to take our shame, filth, and sin upon Himself and to make us clean.

Today, I will...be humbled and inspired by remembering what Jesus was willing to do for the unclean. In light of this, I am willing to display great faith. I am willing to step forward and reveal an unclean life that is in need of restoration.

Thursday
Do You Believe?

Today's Scripture Matthew 9:27-31

As we read through chapter 9, we see that Jesus continues to perform powerful miracles and calls disciples to follow Him. In verses 27-28, some blind men were pleading with Jesus to be merciful to them and to restore their sight. His question to them was this: "Do you believe that I am able to do this?" They said, "Yes, Lord."

Through the pages of Scripture, Jesus continues to ask us this question today.

Do you believe that you can be forgiven (Matthew 9:1-8)? Actually feeling forgiven can be difficult for some. Try as we may, some of us just do not feel forgiven. However, Christ said that He wanted this paralyzed man to know that He had authority to forgive sin (9:6). Jesus healed the physical infirmity of the man so that all might know that He had the power and authority to heal spiritual infirmity.

This man could know when and how he was healed. Today, we too can know when and how we are spiritually healed (Acts 2:38; 22:16; Colossians 1:13-14; 2:12; 1 John 1:7, 9; et. al.).

Do you believe that there is work to do (Matthew 9:9, 35-38)? Jesus called Matthew to follow because there was much work to be done. There were many souls to be saved. He told His disciples, "The harvest is plentiful, but the laborers are few" (9:37). The problem is not with the harvest—the world is lost and dying. There are potential converts everywhere we go. The problem is that there is a lack or workers. There are too few willing to share the good news.

Do you believe that Jesus rules over death (Matthew 9:18-26)? A little girl had died. Jesus said not to worry. The people laughed at Him. He took the girl by the hand and she arose. Jesus is the giver of life (John 10:10; 20:30-31; Ephesians 2:4-5). Jesus is the conqueror of death (Romans 10:9; 1 Thessalonians 4:14). What have we to fear (Hebrews 2:15)?

Today, I will...show Jesus I believe by living with bold and courageous faith.

Friday
Called

Today's Scripture Matthew 10:32-39

The chapter for today contains what we know as "Jesus calling the Twelve." He takes these ordinary men and gives them an extraordinary task. He calls them to take the life-changing message of the Gospel to a lost and dying world. Starting with these few men, the world would soon be turned upside down (Acts 17:6).

We are called through the gospel (2 Thessalonians 2:14), but we are still called. We are called to make a decision (Matthew 10:32-33).

We often quote this passage in relation to Gospel Plan of Salvation. After one has heard and believed the message preached, they must repent, confess, and be immersed in water (Acts 2:38; Romans 10:9-10). However, here in Matthew 10, the emphasis is on more than a one-time acknowledgment or profession of the Lordship of Jesus.

It is about a decision to live for and to stand with Jesus no matter what. The disciples had been told they would be treated shamefully just for being identified with Him (Matthew 10:17-23).

Will we continue to stand with Christ even when others will not? Will we be courageous enough to be identified with Him if it means we will be persecuted?

We are called to die (Matthew 10:38). Please do not misunderstand. Bearing a cross has little to do with dealing with hardships like illness and lost income. It is all about death. To bear a cross was to carry the instrument of your own death. Jesus calls us to die to self so that we might live for Him (cf. Galatians 2:20).

We often say, "Well, that is just my cross to bear." The truth is we have all been called to bear a cross. We are to lose our lives in Him because He is our life (Colossians 3:4).

Today, I will...seek to live a life worthy of the calling to which I have been called (Ephesians 4:1). I will die to self to live for God and neighbor (Matthew 22:37-39).

Week Three
Matthew 11-15

Charles Abernathy

Monday
The Perfect Night's Rest

Today's Scripture Matthew 11:28-30

Most of us have seen the ads for "MyPillow"—the pillow that can provide the best night of sleep ever. Mike Lindell, the inventor and CEO of MyPillow said, "My passion has always been to help people. What a blessing it has been to see my dreams become a reality." Mike's dream was to create the perfect pillow for the experience of an amazing night of sleep. He did it. He created a pillow that wouldn't go flat, that would stay cool through the night, and allow for the perfect position for sleeping to achieve amazing rest. Doctors, chiropractors, and people from all walks of life believe they have experienced the best night of rest ever!

Consider this, when Mike Lindell's infomercial first aired on October 7, 2011, it became a huge success! The MyPillow company went from 10 employees to 500 in just a few short months. It turns out that people from all over the country are truly longing for the best night of rest. Mike has capitalized on the idea that a pillow can provide perfect rest.

Rest is something that people across the ages and across the globe have been longing for in this life. It's true! People have a lot to worry about. People worry about marriage, kids, financial stress, health, war, spiritual warfare, death, and loneliness. We desire rest from these worries.

Do you think that you can find the perfect rest in a pillow? No! Jesus and Jesus alone is the only One who can provide the perfect rest that we need. He is the only One who can heal the sin sick soul. He takes care of our most import need—SALVATION.

Today, I will...learn to trust Jesus with every aspect of my life to find rest for my soul. I will go to Him in prayer and lay down the burdens of my heart and read His word to hear what He has to say about the issues of life.

Tuesday
We're Part of the Family

Today's Scripture Matthew 12:49-50

Cheryl from Westchester commented in the New York Times (September 23, 2013) in an article titled WHEN THERE'S NO FAMILY — "The presumption is that everyone has someone available, someone most likely younger or in better health, and better able to carry out one's wishes or make decisions with your guidance." The reality is some are extremely lonely and have no one to help. Loneliness is certainly one of the biggest challenges in this life. It is so sad to be alone and with no family.

Consider for a moment what God said in the very beginning when He created Adam, "Then the Lord God said, "It is not good that the man should be alone; I will make him a helper fit for him" (Genesis 2:18). God does not want us to be alone in this life! God created the physical family and spiritual family (The Church) to keep us from experiencing one of the most dreaded experiences in life — LONELINESS.

One of the most beautiful verses found in God's Word is 1 John 3:1, *"See what kind of love the Father has given to us, that we should be called children of God."* We are family (Ephesians 4:14-19)! A family that looks out for those who truly need companionship (James 1:27).

The blood of Jesus Christ and our obedience to the will of God (1 Peter 1:17-21) secure our place in the family of God. The Family of God (The Church) is a place where we will never have to be lonely again. A place where we can enjoy fellowship, spiritual growth, and family life together. A place where we can join in a common purpose, mission, and ministry to help "all men" (Galatians 6:10).

God wants you to be a part of His family so that you can experience the greatest blessings this life and the one to come will have to offer.

Today, I will...encourage someone who feels lost and alone and include them in my family plans.

Wednesday
Uncomfortable

It is Sunday morning and the church house is packed. You have done your job, invited friends (and they came), and not only you but other disciples have done the same. Enthusiasm is at an all-time high and you can feel the excitement. Your commitment to Jesus is rock solid and you can't wait for your friends and other visitors to meet your spiritual family and listen to a message from the preacher.

As the preacher begins, things seem to switch to an uneasy feeling. His words become very awkward. You can literally cut the UNCOMFORTABLE feeling and tension among your friends and other visitors with a knife. It's not the normal positive lessons you have heard on topics like, "Your Faith Can Move Mountains" or "Love The Unlovable" that are so frequently shared. You pull the preacher aside and ask him what is going on because you brought guests and you expect him to preach a powerful and motivating sermon? His response is extremely embarrassing. He says and I quote, "I preached this sermon because I knew they wouldn't get it. They never do!"

That scenario seems unthinkable. However, that is exactly what happens in Matthew 13 when the Lord speaks to crowd by the sea. He shares a parable that is confusing and the crowd does not understand it. The disciples pull Him aside and ask what His lesson means? He tells the disciples that the crowd will not understand what He is teaching them. He doesn't seem surprised that the crowd is UNCOMFORTABLE.

The point of the parable is this, if you don't understand the Word of God then study until you understand it and then make sure the conclusion is consistent with the rest of the scriptures. If you don't have a desire to dig deeper and gain a heart of wisdom then you are going to be UNCOMFORTABLE and leave without understanding.

Today, I will...be determined to not only read God's Word daily, but also understand what God is saying to us.

Thursday

Are There Giants Among Us?

If you were reading the Old Testament, you would learn that there were giants on earth in those days (Genesis 6:4). More than likely, the most familiar giant is Goliath, the one that David killed prior to his kingly reign (1 Samuel 17). There are several other references about giants throughout the Old Testament.

When you read the New Testament, there isn't the slightest mention of giants. They just vanish from the pages of scripture. One would conclude that there weren't any giants in New Testament times and that there are not any now. That would certainly be a fair and reasonable conclusion!

I'm convinced that there are giants in New Testament times and today. I have known them, been blessed by them, and have walked with them, and it was equally exciting and impressive to be in their presence. Of course, I am talking about SPIRITUAL GIANTS.

There are SPIRITUAL GIANTS mentioned in the New Testament. For example, John The Baptist is a spiritual giant mentioned in Matthew 14:1-12. Jesus said of John, "Truly, I say to you, among those born of women there has arisen no one greater than John the Baptist. Yet the one who is least in the kingdom of heaven is greater than he" (Matthew 11:11).

This spiritual giant had a tremendous impact on the Lord. When Jesus learned about the death of John, it moved Him to be alone with God because a spiritual giant had fallen.

There are spiritual giants among us today that stand tall, are undeniably faithful, and committed to the Lord and His will. They walk among us, teaching, preaching, visiting, loving, and sharing their lives to make us better. There are moments when some of these giants pass from this life to the next and enjoy the reward from their labors.

We thank God daily for the blessing of these Giants among us!

Today I will...send a card of thanks to the spiritual giants who have had a tremendous impact on my faith.

Friday
I Give Up

Giving up is not normally in our vocabulary as Christians. The Corinthians were encouraged by Paul to stick with working effectively for the Lord (1 Corinthians 15:58). The message given over and over is don't give up on Christ because it will be detrimental to your soul!

I want you to consider giving up, but for a totally different reason and in doing so, it will be a blessing to your life as a Christian. Forfeiting your doctrinal beliefs and practices that are inconsistent with the Word of God will be a blessing to you personally and it will extend to those you influence as well. Remember, the words of Jesus, *"If you love me keep my commandments."* (John 14:15). Jesus must take precedent over any doctrine that is inconsistent with His will and word.

A great example of "giving up" is found in Acts 9 with the apostle Paul. He was sincere, zealous, and had a love for God but he was sincerely wrong. For Paul, giving up and fully surrendering to Jesus Christ was essential for him eternally. Paul would learn with patience, love, and respect to give up his will for the will of Christ and do everything within his power not to trip up anyone in their faith in Jesus. You see, we must let go of our will to be blessed by God and to be a greater blessing to others.

The Scribes and Pharisees were so interested in doing religion their own way that Jesus speaks out against their unwillingness to "give up" their will for His. He quotes Isaiah 29:13 in condemnation for their actions. This example of the Scribes and Pharisees should be a vivid reminder to always do those things that are well pleasing to Him.

Today, I will...evaluate my doctrine and practice to make sure they are consistent with the word of God and change when necessary.

Week Four
Matthew 16 – 20

Steve Baggett

Monday
I Will Build My Church

Today's Scripture Matthew 16:16-18

As chapter 16 begins, Matthew is in the process of recording a number of different reactions people had to Jesus. In 16:1-4 we read of the Pharisees and Sadducees testing Him because of their unbelief. In 16:5-12 we read of Jesus' instructions to His disciples not to be led astray by the Pharisees. In 16:13-20 we read about Jesus questioning His disciples regarding their conviction of His identity. Following Peter's response that, "You are the Christ, the Son of the living God" (16:16), Jesus made the statement, "… on this rock, I will build My church" (16:18).

A few thoughts for today regarding the church:
1.   The church will stand forever. Jesus said that even "the gates of hell shall not prevail against it" (Matthew 16:18). While nations are crumbling and individuals are opposing the will of God, Christians may take comfort in the assurance that the church will never be destroyed!

2.   The church is the home of the saved. Following the conversion of 3,000 to Jesus (Acts 2:38-41), Peter stated that "the Lord added to the church daily those who were being saved" (Acts 2:47 NKJV).

3.   The church is the family of God. Paul referred many times to the church as "brothers" (Philippians 1:12, Colossians 1:2, 1 Thessalonians 1:4). As a family, we enjoy fellowship with and receive encouragement from Jesus our Head and our brethren in Christ.

4.   The church is the body of Christ. Paul said that "Christ is the head of the church, His body" (Ephesians 5:23). Just as individual parts of our physical bodies are important, Christians are also important/valued as members of the body of Christ.

5.   Every member of the body of Christ has a function (1 Corinthians 12:12-31).

6.   God's plan is for the church to grow (Ephesians 4:11-16).

Today, I will…offer a prayer of thanksgiving for the church and resolve faithfully to serve as a vital functioning member of God's family.

Tuesday
Talking to the Lord

Today's Scripture Matthew 17:1-8

Imagine that you are one of only three individuals privileged to be taken by Jesus high on a mountain to witness His transfiguration! How amazing to observe the time when, "His face shone like the sun, and His clothes became white as light" (17:2). What a blessing to see Moses and Elijah and hear these two great servants "talking with Him" (17:3). Luke tells us that Moses and Elijah "spoke of His departure, which He was about to accomplish in Jerusalem" (Luke 17:31). Apparently, they appeared to Jesus to encourage Him as He approached the cross! Just as Moses and Elijah talked with Jesus, Christians today enjoy the wonderful blessing of being able to talk to the Lord.

A few thoughts for today on prayer: Children of God are invited to: "with confidence draw near to the throne of grace that we may receive mercy and find grace to help in time of need" (Hebrews 4:16); "pray without ceasing" (1 Thessalonians 5:17), and to "confess your sins to one another and pray for one another" (James 5:16).

Several years ago, Keith Parker relied on the acronym "ACTS" to create the following recipe for effective prayer:
   Adoration – Make a habit of beginning every prayer with words of adoration and praise to our holy and awesome God! Jesus began the model prayer by saying, "Our Father in heaven, hallowed be Your name" (Matthew 6:9).
   Confession – When we have focused on and proclaimed God's holiness, power, and majesty, we are overwhelmed with our personal unworthiness. Then we should spend time in prayer confessing to God the sins and struggles of life and our desperate need for His presence.
   Thanksgiving – Following the time of praise and confession, we should spend time thanking God for our wonderful blessings, making sure to "name them one by one."
   Supplication – We should conclude our prayer with supplications (requests) for self and for others.

Today, I will...set aside a time to talk to the Lord fervently!

Wednesday
Greatness Comes Through Serving

Today's Scripture Matthew 18:1-6

The belief that there is no such thing as a bad question has, through the years, provided an excellent vehicle for individuals to learn and grow. Whether it is the innocent "Why?" of a toddler or the more "in-depth query" of a university student, one very good way to learn is to ask questions. On several occasions Jesus' disciples asked questions of Him. Perhaps none was of greater significance than, "Who is the greatest in the kingdom of heaven?" (Matthew 18:1).

The disciples' incorrect understanding of the kingdom (thinking it would be physical rather than spiritual) no doubt led to shock when Jesus said, "Whoever humbles himself like this child is the greatest in the kingdom of heaven" (18:4). Humble oneself "like a child?" What could a child do in a great military kingdom like the one Jesus is going to build? They were so sadly mistaken about greatness! They had no idea that true spiritual greatness comes through serving. Sellars Crain wrote, "The disciples were wrangling for positions in the kingdom, feeling confident that they would be a leading part of it. Jesus warned them that if they persisted in their arrogance and self-centeredness, they would not even enter it at all" (*Truth for Today Commentary, Matthew 14-28*, p.127).

A few thoughts for today on serving: First, serving others is Christ-like (Phil. 2:5-9). Jesus served the multitude by teaching them, preaching to them, and healing them (Matthew 9:35-36); He served the apostles by washing their feet (John 13:1-20); and He served mankind by taking their sins to the cross (2 Corinthians 5:21). Second, serving others is the direct result of humbling oneself before God (James 4:10). Third, serving others opens doors for conversations about Jesus. Philemon served Paul while he was in prison, and thus Paul was given the opportunity to teach him about Jesus and baptize him into Christ (Philemon 1-16). Finally, serving others is a wonderful way to "be kind to one another" (Ephesians 4:32).

Today, I will...look for ways to serve others as did Jesus!

Thursday
What God Has Joined Together

Today's Scripture Matthew 19:1-9

"I, _____, take you, _____, to be my lawfully wedded _____, to have and to hold from this day forward, in sickness and in health, for richer or for poorer, for better or for worse, as long as we both shall live."

With these or similar words, men and women through the years have pledged their love and faithfulness in marriage. Marriage was instituted by God (Genesis 2:18-25) and sanctioned by Christ (Matthew 19:1-9).

In the conversation Jesus had with the Pharisees regarding marriage, He refused to enter into their ongoing debate concerning the schools of thought regarding divorce. Rather, He went back to the very beginning and said, "Have you not read that He who created them from the beginning made them male and female, and said, 'Therefore a man shall leave his father and his mother and hold fast to his wife, and the two shall become one flesh'? So, they are no longer two but one flesh. What therefore God has joined together, let no man separate" (19:4-6).

A few thoughts for today on marriage: First, a successful marriage requires commitment, love, faithfulness, patience, humility, trust, and forgiveness. Second, a successful marriage results in joy, happiness, peace, contentment, companionship, and growth (individually and as a couple). Third, a successful marriage is permanent. When Hollywood portrays marriage as old-fashioned and out-of-date, when couples are living together without the benefit of a godly commitment to one another, and when marriages are viewed by many as disposable, Christian couples must work hard to buck those trends. A life-long commitment to one's spouse is not only a nice benefit of marriage, but also a command of God. When Jesus said, "What therefore God has joined together, let no man separate," He set forth God's decree of permanence!

Today, I will...thank God for His infinitely wise plan for marriage, and, if married, I will honor God, my spouse, and my marriage.

Friday
They Followed Him!

Today's Scripture Matthew 20:29-34

While the sight of two blind men sitting together by the side of the road would be uncommon today, it was not an unusual occurrence in Jesus' day. Matthew records that just such an event occurred as Jesus was leaving Jericho. Learning that Jesus was coming by, the two men cried out, "Lord, have mercy on us, Son of David" (20:30)! Even though the crowd tried to quieten the two men, they continued their persistent cries. Hearing them, Jesus stopped and asked, "What do you want me to do for you?" (20:32). They answered by requesting that He give them the ability to see. "Jesus in pity touched their eyes, and immediately they recovered their sight and followed Him" (20:34).

The question "What do you want me to do for you?" is a powerful question regardless of the one asking. Whether from a spouse, parent, teacher, employer, employee, friend, or relative...being asked what another can do for you is a great blessing! Just prior to this interaction with these blind men Jesus said, *"Whoever would be great among you must be your servant, and whoever would be first among you must be your slave, even as the Son of Man came not to be served but to serve, and to give his life as a ransom for many."* (Matthew 20:26-28)

However, while learning the lesson of serving others, let us not be guilty of overlooking the response of those two men. The text says, "Immediately they recovered their sight and followed Him" (20:34). As an expression of their thankfulness for the gift they received, they followed, i.e., went with, Jesus!

A few thoughts for today on following Jesus: Following Jesus means doing the will of His Father who is in heaven (Matthew 7:21). Following Jesus is the way to the Father (John 14:6). Following Jesus provides the opportunity to bring others to Him (John 1:40-42).

Today, I will...with a heart filled with thanks, strive to follow Jesus, obey His will, and look for opportunities to bring someone else to Him.

Week Five
Matthew 21-25

Keith Olbricht

Monday
The Lord Needs Them

As you read Matthew 21, there is a lot going on. Jesus was on His way into Jerusalem for His triumphal entry. When He got there, He cleansed the temple of the money changers and vendors. The next morning He cursed the fig tree, and then found Himself in a tense confrontation with the chief priests and elders. He followed that confrontation with two parables, both of which were designed to condemn the leaders of the people. All of these events had a direct impact on His being crucified on the cross of Calvary.

But in the midst of this active, dramatic chapter we find a wonderful occurrence. As Jesus prepared to enter Jerusalem He instructed His disciples to go get a donkey and colt, and if anyone asked what they were doing they were to answer, "The Lord needs them" (Matthew 21:3). The implication was there would be no argument to that answer, for knowing the Lord had need would be sufficient.

Is there a lot going on in your life? For most people, there usually is. There is church and work. There are ball games, birthday parties, travel, and a host of other things which constantly brings activity...and sometimes tension, confrontations, and drama. Those are times you find yourself juggling and struggling, trying to keep all the balls in the air and trying to satisfy the plethora of obligations which life has brought upon you. It takes a lot of time, energy, and resources to keep you and your family going.

No matter how busy you get though, there will be times when you have something that the Lord has need of. It may be your time, your house, your car, or just your attention. You may need to "rejoice with those who rejoice, and weep with those who weep" (Romans 12:15). You may need to "go...and proclaim the gospel" (Mark 16:15). You may need to lift up fallen hands or strengthen weak knees (Hebrews 12:12). When that time comes, will the fact that the Lord has need of you be sufficient?

Today I will...open my eyes to the needs of the Lord and will joyfully supply what is required, knowing the sufficiency of His grace in my life (2 Corinthians 12:9).

Tuesday
Authorized Personnel Only

Today's Scripture Matthew 22

You can go into almost any store, restaurant, airport, or public facility and see this sign: Authorized Personnel Only. Behind that door may be something dangerous like an electrical panel, or it may be something as simple as a break room for employees. Regardless, almost every place has some place to which everyone should not have access. You may have had occasion to have passed into such areas, maybe when delivering something or to talk to someone specific. Even in such instances where technically you were authorized to be there, you probably still had the feeling that you really did not belong.

Jesus gave a parable to the chief priests and Pharisees in Matthew 22. In this parable He described a king who gave a wedding feast for the prince. The guests who were invited to the wedding not only chose not to come, but utterly rejected the invitations. Therefore, the king sent out into the streets and invited strangers to come in to celebrate the marriage of his son. These were people who otherwise would not have belonged there—except for the invitation extended by the king. As the king went among the guests he spotted one who was there, yet without the proper attire. Jesus did not specify how the man got there, whether he entered mistakenly, whether someone snuck him in, or whether he brazenly waltzed right in. Regardless, he was somewhere he was not authorized to be.

Think about this. If you are in the Lord's kingdom, the church, you do not really belong. The church is where the saints are, the holy ones of God (1 Corinthians 1:2). No one of their own merit, wealth, health, strength, beauty, wit or charm is worthy, for none of those things can overcome the stain of sinfulness that all wear. Except for the Lord's invitation, none would be authorized to enter! And no one will be allowed to enter or remain without authorization.

Today I will live...worthy of the invitation I have received into the kingdom of God in my dress, my speech, my manners, and my attitude, and I will praise the King of Kings, His Son, and His bride, the church.

Wednesday
Woe. Whoa.

You know the people who are so over-the-top competitive that no one wants to play anything with them? You know the ones. Every family, church, youth group, and workplace has them. The ones who are never wrong, have an excuse for every perceived failure, and have never, ever admitted a mistake or a loss. Sure, you know them (Or maybe you are one of them?). They are great people to be around until that moment when the competition gene kicks in; but if you ever best them at anything, you better watch out. Please don't misunderstand. No one likes to lose, no one likes to be wrong, and no one likes their failures displayed to the public, but some simply do not know how to lose gracefully.

Matthew 23 is a hard chapter because Jesus shreds the scribes and Pharisees. He pronounced seven woes upon them for their behavior and their attitudes, and He did so publicly and forcefully. While it wasn't exactly a situation where there was a winner and a loser, the scribes and Pharisees were humiliated by Jesus' righteous allegations. They were not going to take it lightly; as a matter of fact, this event added fuel to the fire which led to them putting Jesus to death. It can be hard to read these woes against the attitudes and actions of the Jewish leaders because you know where this is going.

But what really makes Matthew 23 a hard chapter is when you look at those woes and compare them to your own life. Having one's hypocrisy pointed out in glaring fashion is hard to take. A careful, contextual look at Matthew 23 is likely going to step on at least one toe, and maybe an entire foot. How will you respond? Will you lash out, make excuses to the Lord for your failures, or perhaps even refuse to admit defeat? Or can you gracefully accept the potential chastening of the words of Jesus?

Today I will...not be a hypocrite, but will serve the Lord without excuse and without argument, putting His interests before my own.

This Land Is Your Land?

Chances are the day will come when the United States of America ceases to exist. That is not a prophecy, or a statement of doom and gloom, but a simple acknowledgment of the significance of history. To think of the dissolution of one's homeland from an academic and historical viewpoint is one thing, but to witness its destruction would be something else entirely. What if you knew the details of its pending end? What if you had instructions for what to do when it happened to protect yourself and your family? Without doubt you would be ready.

Much of Matthew 24 deals with the prophecy Jesus gave of the destruction of the city of Jerusalem (verses 1–35). He told His disciples in detail what was going to happen and gave them the signs of when it would occur. To have heard those words must have been heartbreaking to the faithful! The city they loved and the temple they adored was going to be horrifically razed with much loss of property and life. Yet thanks to the words of Jesus they would be prepared. Emotional trauma aside, they were going to be all right. Despite the tremendous bloodshed, history reports that not a single Christian lost their life in A.D. 70 when the city was leveled by Titus because they had heeded the words of Jesus and fled to safety.

What if Jesus told you that not only will your homeland would be destroyed, but the entire planet you live on will meet an end? Much like the destruction of Jerusalem, all that has been accomplished in all its existence will be lost, and no life will be spared. Its destruction will be total and complete, burnt up and dissolved, never to be resurrected, rebuilt, or restored (2 Peter 3:10).

Today I will…appreciate the eternal life I have been given in Jesus that will transcend the life I now know, and will give heed to the warnings He has given.

Friday
I Want to Be Ready!

Today's Scripture Matthew 25

If you have ever been on the hosting end of a large function, such as a benefit dinner, a wedding, or even a large birthday party, you know how much preparation goes into such an event. Weeks, perhaps even months, of planning, purchasing, arranging, decorating, and stressing. It feels like everything will never be ready, then when the time comes, it is all over in a flash. You enjoy the satisfaction of the moment, but part of you wonders where the time went, and what might have been if you had made better use of it.

In Matthew 25, Jesus gives a parable encouraging His disciples to be watchful, ready, and prepared, another parable depicting faithfulness, productivity, (and readiness), and finally a judgment scene. In each of the narratives there were those who were ready and those who were not. You feel the joy of those who were accepted and praised if you know the satisfaction of having done a job well; you feel the pain of those who were kept out and condemned if you have ever experienced the disappointment of having come up short. And if you know those joys and pains, you know with certainty the need for preparation.

As you read this chapter, you undoubtedly are telling yourself, I want to be ready! I want to be able to know I have used my time wisely in preparing for the greatest event the world will ever know. I don't want to be left standing there scratching my head wondering where I went wrong. I don't want to be arguing with the Great Judge of All saying, "But I did," only to hear Him say, "No, you didn't." I want to hear Him say, "Come, inherit the kingdom" (verse 34).

What will make the difference in your eternity? An attitude of "that ought to be good enough" may be sufficient for a birthday party, but what do you need to make your entrance into eternity "richly provided" (2 Peter 1:11)?

Today I will...make preparation by using the blessing of time and resources my Lord has provided to accomplish His will. I will tell myself, "I want to be ready!" and then I will make it so.

Week Six
Matthew 26–28
Mark 1–2

Jeff & Dale Jenkins

Everywhere the Gospel Is Proclaimed

Today's Scripture Matthew 26

Have you ever felt like when you get to Matthew 26 that the Gospel writer speeds up. For 25 chapters you have Jesus doing the impossible; healing, astounding listeners, raising the dead, feeding the hungry, promising a new Kingdom. Then in three chapters the world changes like at no other time. He will be betrayed, tried, and crucified, buried, risen, and make appearances in multiple places, be glorified, ascend and promise his return and it's all recorded in three amazing chapters.

Those are some heady events but for a brief moment here in Matthew 26 before the mayhem proceeds everything seems to slow down and we are reminded of why Jesus is here, who Jesus is, and what Jesus is doing. It was a moment that so impressed the Lord that He indicated that everywhere the Gospel is proclaimed, this story would be a part of it.

"Now when Jesus was at Bethany...a woman came up to him with an alabaster flask of very expensive ointment, and she poured it on his head as he reclined at table. And when the disciples saw it, they were indignant, saying, 'Why this waste? For this could have been sold for a large sum and given to the poor.' But Jesus, aware of this, said to them, "Why do you trouble the woman? For she has done a beautiful thing to me. For you always have the poor with you, but you will not always have me. In pouring this ointment on my body, she has done it to prepare me for burial. Truly, I say to you, wherever this gospel is proclaimed in the whole world, what she has done will also be told in memory of her.'" (Matthew 26:6-13)

Wow!

Today I will...remember that the things I say and do, big and little, do in fact matter to the Lord.

Tuesday
Don't Quit in the Fourth Quarter

Today's Scripture Matthew 27:3-5

Where do you begin if you want to write something from this chapter?

Pick a sentence, any sentence, volumes have been written on it already. Emotions spill forth from each word.

"Then when Judas, his betrayer, saw that Jesus was condemned, he changed his mind and brought back the thirty pieces of silver to the chief priests and the elders, saying, 'I have sinned by betraying innocent blood.' They said, 'What is that to us? See to it yourself.' And throwing down the pieces of silver into the temple, he departed, and he went and hanged himself" (Matthew 27:3-5).

With all that's going on around The Savior, some might wonder why I would choose to write our thought about "this man." Take your mind back before the betrayal for a moment. Judas was part of the most exclusive club of all time, hand-picked by the Lord, had a front-row pass to the most amazing teachings of all time, and got back-stage passes to see the Son of God do the impossible day in and day out for three years. He became a significant leader among this small band of the ultimate insiders—the treasurer. I imagine if we did not know what we know, it might be hard for us to say there was a more significant apostle.

There's the strongest warning for any of us who would say "not I"—He said it too (26:35). Any of us can be drawn away (James 1:14-15; Galatians 6:2). Beware, a life-well lived can go off track even at the end. If you still have life you still have something to give to God and to encourage others. Don't quit in the fourth quarter of life.

Today I will...evaluate the influences I am allowing into my life and the current direction of my life.

Wednesday
Last Words

Today's Scripture Matthew 28:18-20

They are forever burned on our hearts and in our minds. We hang on them with every fiber of our being. They might have been the last words spoken by our loved one before they passed away. They might be the last words spoken by a child before they leave for college. Last words are very meaningful to us.

Matthew was there. He heard those last words that came from the lips of our Savior. *"And Jesus came and said to them, 'All authority in heaven and on earth has been given to me. Go therefore and make disciples of all nations, baptizing them in the name of the Father and of the Son and of the Holy Spirit, teaching them to observe all that I have commanded you. And behold, I am with you always, to the end of the age.'" (Matthew 28:18-20)*

While these words were spoken directly to the disciples in the first century, they have application to disciples in every age. The Savior's last words contain a command and a promise.

The command is that we should tell everyone we know, everyone we see, the Good News about Jesus. The commission that has been given to us from our Lord is to make known His Name to all the nations. Jesus doesn't tell us how to go, He just tells us to go.

The promise is that He will be with us, as we do His work. He doesn't promise success in everything we do. He doesn't promise that it will be easy. He doesn't promise that there will not be opposition. He just promises us that He will be with us.

What a commission. What a promise. What a Savior!

Today I will...reach out to someone and share the greatest news ever known to man, and I will rest in the knowledge that my Lord is with me every step of the way.

Thursday
Follow Me

Today we begin our reading of Mark's account of the Good News. Mark's is the shortest of the accounts. Luke's has nearly twice the number of words. A good reader can read Mark aloud in about an hour.

The Gospel at full speed. There's not a lot of commentary, but there's certainly plenty of what Jesus did that reveals both the passion and compassion of the Lamb of God! Mark launches like a jet. For instance, Mark records Jesus healing Peter's mother-in-law within the first 15 verses. It's 215 verses before Mathew gives his account.

"Passing alongside the Sea of Galilee, he saw Simon and Andrew the brother of Simon casting a net into the sea, for they were fishermen. And Jesus said to them, 'Follow me, and I will make you become fishers of men.' And immediately they left their nets and followed him. And going on a little farther, he saw James the son of Zebedee and John his brother, who were in their boat mending the nets. And immediately he called them, and they left their father Zebedee in the boat with the hired servants and followed him." (Mark 1:16-20)

When following Jesus there are always things to be left behind. Sometimes those things are cherished. For Simon (Peter) and Andrew is was a profession, income, a potentially promising prosperity. For James and John it was family and servants. A few thoughts: First, sometimes those things we leave, we get back. That was the case with James and John who it appears had several family members who also followed Jesus. Second, the trade-off is always worth it. Peter and Andrew will face great days like Pentecost and challenging days like the crucifixion, but there is never an indication they regretted following the Lord. Finally, anything we love more than the Lord will get between us and Him. We must be willing to give up anything that would keep us from Him.

Today I will...consider what I am tempted to put before the Lord.

Friday
Invited to Follow Him

Today's Scripture Mark 2:13-17

Being the recipient of an invitation can produce emotions ranging from complete dejection to delirious excitement. An invitation to appear in court or an invite to meet with an IRS Agent might cause fear or trepidation. An invitation to wedding or to a big event can produce feelings of great joy.

For those who first heard the words, "Follow me," from Jesus, they must have been over the moon with excitement. After all, many of them had heard Him teach, they had witnessed miracles that he performed, and they had seen His great compassion in dealing with the hurting. Perhaps, they were shocked, surprised that One such as this Man would invite someone like them to be a part of His inner crowd.

"Follow Me." What does it mean? What is involved in following the Savior of the world? It means we will learn. "Follow Me, and I will make you fishers of men." It requires that deny ourselves. *"If anyone would come after Me, let him deny himself and take up his cross daily and follow Me."* (Luke 9:23)

It could result in our having to change or end some earthly relationships. *"If anyone comes to me and does not hate his own father and mother and wife and children and brothers and sisters, yes, and even his own life, he cannot be my disciple."* (Luke 14:26)

Following Jesus means we will put Him and His Kingdom first (Matthew 6:33). It means we will love Him with all that we are and all that we have (Matthew 22:37). Following the Savior will bring about loving obedience (John 14:15).

The best news of all: This invitation was not just for people who were contemporaries of Jesus. It is an invitation open to all men of every age. And when we accept this greatest of all invitations our lives will never be the same!

Today I will...Express my gratitude to the Lord for His wonderful invitation and I will share this invitation with everyone I possibly can.

Week Seven
Mark 3-7

Travis Bookout

Monday
To Do Good or Harm?

Today's Scripture Mark 3:1-6

Mark 3 continues a series of conflicts which began in chapter 2. The scene is set in a synagogue on the Sabbath where Jesus encounters a man with a withered hand. He is being watched closely, not to see His compassion or His great power from on High, but to see if He will break the Sabbath (3:2). In a dramatic showdown Jesus calls the man forward. After previously answering four accusatory questions hurled against Him and His disciples (2:7, 16, 18, 24), He will now ask the question: "Is it lawful on the Sabbath to do good or to do harm, to save life or to kill?"

This might seem like a strange question, since nobody advocated harming or killing the man, but it actually denotes an important principle: Neglecting those who are suffering equates to harming those who are suffering. You are either helping or harming, and ignoring the less fortunate does not help.

The non-canonical 1 Maccabees tells of Greek soldiers who attacked a group of Jews, but being the Sabbath the Jews refused to fight back. This resulted in the death of 1000 Jewish men, women, and children. In response, the Jews decided to fight and kill even on the Sabbath to protect themselves and their Law (1 Maccabees 2:29-48). At the time of Jesus, killing on the Sabbath was acceptable, if the need arose.

What if the need arose to help or to heal? Jesus raises this question and they ignore it. In reality this should not be a difficult question. Sometimes the heart of man can grow so hard (3:5) that we no longer feel compassion. It can grow so hard that we ignore the intrinsic value of a fellow person equally created in God's image, so we can focus on other issues. They put a man-made Sabbath regulation over the needs of a human being. In frustration, Jesus heals the man, which inevitably leads to a plot against His life (3:6; cf. Mark 12:13-17).

Today, I will...resist apathy and actively help another person.

Tuesday
Good Soil

Mark four introduces us to Jesus' parables and begins with a peculiar description of the setting; teaching the massive crowds Jesus enters a boat to speak, but the crowds remain "on the land" to listen (4:1). The word "land" is the same Greek word as "ground," "earth," or "soil" and is noteworthy because it will be repeated throughout this chapter. Jesus gives three parables that deal with "seed" falling "on the soil" (4:8, 20, 26, 31). That the crowds are standing "on the soil" (the exact same phrase in Greek) places them directly into the application of Jesus' parables. When Jesus delivers His Word to those standing on the soil, it is the actualization of the sower scattering seed on the soil.

Throughout this chapter, Jesus periodically explains why He teaches in parables. At this point in Jesus' ministry the parables are mysterious, hidden, secretive, and the explanations are private (4:11, 22, 33). Their purpose is not yet to bring about clear understanding or mass repentance (4:12), but to call honest listeners; to find good soil. They will not be hidden forever, for "nothing is hidden, except to be revealed" (4:21). Jesus privately explains the meaning of the parables to His disciples (Mark 4:33-34), but the time will come when they will publicly reveal these mysteries of the kingdom.

This is why it is imperative to be a good listener and to receive sincerely the Word of God. Those standing "on the soil" (4:1) must ensure that they are standing on the figurative "good soil." When the Word is received on the good soil, it produces great things (4:20). We don't always know how, as is the point of the second parable (4:26-29), but produce it will. In fact, it produces far greater things than one might expect at first glance, like the parable of the mustard seed (4:30-34). But it must be received openly and honestly, on good soil.

Today, I will...listen with honesty and sincerity to the Word of Jesus, I will receive it like good soil.

39

Wednesday
Faith and Healing

Today's Scripture Mark 5:21-43

One of Mark's most interesting writing techniques is to tell a story within a story, a narrative "sandwich." Mark often begins a story, breaks into a seemingly unrelated story, then finishes the original story. Upon reflection, connections between the two stories will begin to materialize (see Mark 3:20-35; 4:1-25; Mark 11:12-21). Mark 5:21-43 is one of these sandwiches.

How do these stories connect?

-Both females are nameless and known as "daughter" (Mark 5:23, 34).
-Both stories have one falling before Jesus (Mark 5:22, 33).
-Both stories have Jesus being misunderstood (Mark 5:31, 40).
-Both stories have a mixture of fear and faith (Mark 5:33-34, 36).
-Both healings happen "immediately" (Mark 5:29, 42).
-Both stories mention "12 years" (Mark 5:25, 42).
-Both stories have a problem only Jesus can solve.

The two interrelated stores begin with a man in desperate need falling down before Jesus. His little daughter is hopelessly ill and he begs Jesus to come and heal her. He agrees.

Along the way, they press through the crowds and of the many hands touching Jesus, one belongs to a woman in need. She's had a twelve year incurable flow of blood, making her unclean. She is excluded from the temple and ordinary Israelite life (Leviticus 15:19-30). Rather than ask Jesus for help, she believes that if she simply touches Him as He passes, she will be healed. She was correct. As Jesus speaks to her and commends her faith, the first story continues.

The girl died while Jesus was healing the woman. Rather than give up, Jesus goes to the house anyway. He finds the lifeless girl and raises her back to life. By the way, she was twelve years old, as old as the woman's flow of blood.

Deep faith saturates these stories, driving those in need to fall before Jesus. A desperate woman and a desperate father are comforted by Him. In times of desperation, throwing yourself in faith before Jesus is always the best solution.

Today, I will...fall before Jesus with the problems only He can solve.

Thursday
The Shepherd

When reading any book of the Bible, it is important to see how the stories shape and build upon one another. In Mark 4:35-41, Jesus calms a storm on the Sea of Galilee and His disciples' ask, "Who then is this, that even the wind and the sea obey Him?" While the answer is not given, the Psalms teach this to be a divine act accomplished only by the LORD (Psalm 65:7; 89:9; 107:23-29). Jesus is the LORD who calms the seas.

Jumping to Mark 6:33-44, Jesus stands on the sea shore watching large crowds of followers. He feels compassion "because they were like sheep without a shepherd" (6:34). With only five loaves and two fish, Jesus commands them to sit "on the green grass" before miraculously preparing a meal that satisfies 5,000 men.

Think for a moment about a Shepherd on a sea shore telling His sheep to sit down on the "green" grass while he prepares a meal for them. This story offers a subtle picture of Psalm 23 with Jesus as the shepherding LORD.

Immediately following this, the disciples get back on a boat in the Sea of Galilee. Again a storm arises, but this time they are alone. Jesus is not in the boat. Instead He walks out to them on the water. They become terrified and mistake Him for a ghost (6:49), yet Jesus says, "Take heart; it is I. Do not be afraid" (6:50). Entering the boat, He calms the wind and sea (a second time), but the disciples are "utterly astounded, for they did not understand about the loaves, but their hearts were hardened" (6:52).

Their hardened hearts caused them to miss Jesus' true identity. They forgot to trust. There was a message in the loaves (see Mark 8:1-9) that they should have been learning (Mark 8:14-21). They should have learned that Jesus was their providing Shepherd and LORD. Instead, they feared because they didn't recognize the LORD was with them (Psalm 23:4).

Today, I will...take comfort and trust in Jesus as my LORD and Shepherd.

Friday
The Heart of Man

Today's Scripture Mark 7:14-23

To Jesus, purity is not a matter of diet, but heart (Mark 7:14-23). Jesus realized that since food never enters the heart, it is irrelevant to the heart's purity. "Thus he declared all foods clean" (Mark 7:19). This was a revolutionary idea.

To many Jews, food laws were literally a matter of life or death. Daniel was determined to die rather than defile himself with the king's food (Daniel 1:8). 1 Maccabees tells of the persecutions Jews faced for resisting Greek influences: "Many in Israel stood firm and were resolved in their hearts not to eat unclean food. They chose to die rather than to be defiled by food or to profane the holy covenant; and they did die" (1 Maccabees 1:62-63). These martyrs became heroes to Jesus contemporaries. To say that food regulations were unnecessary was radical and offensive.

This may be why His disciples didn't understand His parable (Mark 7:17-18): "There is nothing outside a person that by going into him can defile him, but the things that come out of a person are what defile him" (Mark 7:15). The early church struggled with this teaching also. Peter refused it for years! (Acts 10:9-16).

Jesus' words were difficult, but vital. To miss them is to miss the kingdom (Romans 14:17). He had just rebuked the Pharisees, quoting, "This people honors me with their lips, but their heart is far from me" (Mark 7:6; Isaiah 29:13). You can have clean hands, reverent words, a perfect diet, but a distant heart. Jesus needed that to change. His kingdom needs sincerity over ceremony.

This makes things hard. It's easier to avoid certain foods than to live a pure life. But Jesus demands complete purity, from the inside out. He requires purity in everything you think, say, or do (Mark 7:20-23). And the heart determines your response to Jesus (Mark 2:6-8; 3:5; 6:52; 7:6; 8:17; 11:23; 12:30). The heart determines your actions. The heart determines your purity.

Today, I will...meditate on the spiritual condition of my heart and make whatever changes are necessary.

Week Eight
Mark 8–12

Chris McCurley

Monday
What Has Following Jesus Cost You?

Today's Scripture Mark 8:34-37

And calling the crowd to Him with his disciples, he said to them, "If anyone would come after Me, let him deny himself and take up his cross and follow Me. For whoever would save his life will lose it, but whoever loses his life for My sake and the gospel's will save it. For what does it profit a man to gain the whole world and forfeit his soul? For what can a man give in return for his soul?" (Mark 8:34-37)

Discipleship is costly, and Jesus was honest enough to tell prospective disciples what following Him would truly mean. The Christian life is not some magical elixir that automatically cures all of life's ills. Following Jesus does not guarantee a life of comfort and convenience. In fact, in the first-century, it all but guaranteed persecution; perhaps even death.

As modern-day followers of Jesus, we may not face physical abuse or execution; however, there is still a cost involved. The primary prerequisite to being a true follower is a denial of self. We are naturally "lovers of self." To deny oneself is a concept that is completely foreign to many folks, but lovers of self cannot be followers of Jesus. One cannot faithfully follow Christ when their first allegiance is to themselves. Discipleship is a full-on commitment. This is no casual relationship. Christianity demands that we be done with ourselves altogether.

There are many people in this world who believe in Jesus, who admire Jesus, who want to follow Jesus, but do not want to make any changes. They will follow as long as following does not require too much of them. The reality that all prospective disciples must face is this: following Jesus will disrupt your life! It will cost you something.

What have you sacrificed to follow Jesus? If the answer is, "Nothing," then are you truly following? Jesus is not asking to be a priority in your life. He is not even asking to be top priority in your life. He is asking to be your life.

Today, I will...be more intentional about discipleship by considering ways in which I can serve Him by serving others.

Tuesday
Help My Unbelief!

And they brought the boy to Him. And when the spirit saw Him, immediately it convulsed the boy, and he fell on the ground and rolled about, foaming at the mouth. And Jesus asked his father, "How long has this been happening to him?" And he said, "From childhood. And it has often cast him into fire and into water, to destroy him. But if You can do anything, have compassion on us and help us." And Jesus said to him, "'If You can!' All things are possible for one who believes." Immediately the father of the child cried out and said, "I believe; help my unbelief!" (Mark 9:20-24)

We may find our own sentiments in the words of this father. Many of us can recite the same statement and feel it with every fiber of our being. Implied within these words is a heart-felt plea: "My faith is somewhat lacking, but please do not hold that against my son." Notice that Jesus does not rebuke the man for his honesty. He heals the father's son, and strengthens his faith in the process.

Doubt can be a destructive device of the devil. There is a fictional story about Satan and how he was selling all his tools of deception. One of his demons asked him, "How much for this wedge of doubt?" To which the devil replied, "Oh, that's not for sale. With doubt, I can get back into business at any time." Doubt can be very destructive to our faith: however, it must be understood that doubt is not the opposite of faith. Unbelief is the opposite of faith. Doubt does not mean denial.

Faith is not a leap in the dark. The Bible presents the story of Jesus. The divine narrative is available for us to read and bear witness to. The evidence is astounding and overwhelming. It is up to us to do something with it. At its taproot, faith is a will to believe. We choose faith by choosing to accept the divine record. And, we continue to choose faith by living in a godly direction, seeking to carry out His will.

Today, I will...strengthen my faith by filling my thoughts with truth; studying the Biblical evidence to affirm what I believe.

Wednesday
Who or What Has Your Heart?

Today's Scripture Mark 10:23-25

And Jesus looked around and said to His disciples, "How difficult it will be for those who have wealth to enter the kingdom of God!" And the disciples were amazed at His words. But Jesus said to them again, "Children, how difficult it is to enter the kingdom of God! It is easier for a camel to go through the eye of a needle than for a rich person to enter the kingdom of God." (Mark 10:23-25)

These words come on the heels of Jesus' discourse with a rich, young ruler who was unwilling to trade his stuff for salvation. A love for money causes people to do some strange things. It leads to greediness and covetousness. It can cause one to lie, cheat, and steal. We all need a certain amount of money to get by in life but, all too often, money becomes an easy god for people. It becomes a substitute for faith. Our world is full of individuals who are bowing down to the almighty dollar rather than the Almighty God.

Perhaps the greatest threat a love of money poses is a lack of neediness. A love for money can shield us from our greatest need. Our possessions possess us and we find our security in the earthly rather than the eternal. This is why it is impossible for the rich man to go to heaven. He does not see himself as needy. A love of money, and the things it can buy, has dethroned God in his heart.

In contrast to the rich, young ruler is a man by the name of Zaccheus (Luke 19:1-10). This "wee little man" was a real-life mission impossible story. He entered the kingdom of God by trusting in Jesus and letting go of his riches. The difference between Zaccheus and the rich, young ruler was the heart. Zaccheus recognized his real need, while the rich, young ruler did not.

Stewardship is a lordship issue. Who or what has your heart? Your money and your stuff, or the One who blessed you with your money and your stuff? Keep in mind that money is a great servant, but it is a terrible master.

Today, I will...examine my heart along with my spending habits. I will consider how much I give versus how much I keep for myself.

Thursday
Where Are You at the Parade?

Today's Scripture Mark 11:1-11

Who does not love a parade? Parades are a time of celebration. Bands play, confetti and streamers are thrown, girls toss batons, and celebrities ride in convertible cars. Parades are a time of great excitement. In Mark 11:1-10, we read about a parade being held for Jesus. Hordes of people were present. "Many spread their cloaks on the road, and others spread leafy branches that they had cut from the fields (v. 8)." With throngs of people leading and following Jesus, our Lord enters Jerusalem to shouts of, "Hosanna! Blessed is He who comes in the name of the Lord! Blessed is the coming kingdom of our father David! Hosanna in the highest!" (11:9-10)

Picture the scene. People crowding the streets, climbing trees, just to catch a glimpse of the Messiah. Children sitting on their father's shoulders. The shouts of "Hosanna!" ringing in the distance, but growing louder as the parade inched closer and closer. What the people saw that day was the savior of the world riding on the back of a donkey. How appropriate that the humble Son of God who came into this world with nowhere to lay his head but in a feed trough was now making his way to the cross, not on a massive white stallion, but on a little beast of burden.

The on-lookers were a diverse group. There were those who were curious, those who were contemptuous, and those who were captivated. Dotted among the throng were those who hoped for a brighter tomorrow. They were the poor and outcast. Some, no doubt, had been healed by Jesus. Some had felt his warmth and compassion. Society wanted nothing to do with them, but they found a friend in Jesus. They led the way. They shouted the loudest. They rolled out the red carpet, so to speak, as they threw down their cloaks. To them, Jesus was one of them.

Where are you at the parade? Are you a curious on-looker? Are you a captivated observer? Hopefully, you are not a contemptuous spectator. Are you leading the procession? May we all be out in front shouting "Hosanna, Blessed is he who comes in the name of the Lord!" And may we all be following his lead daily.

Today, I will...be more deliberate to show and tell what Jesus has done for me.

Friday
A Top-Button Lifestyle

Guys who wear button-up shirts know the struggle that comes with being in a hurry and trying to line all the buttons up and getting them pushed through the proper slot. On more than one occasion, I have worked my way down from top to bottom, pushing each button through the button hole, only to reach the end and discover that the buttons were misaligned. I had slipped the top button through the wrong slot and, well, you can guess what happened.

If you get the top button right, every other button falls into place. What is true in a fashion sense, is even truer in a spiritual sense. If we place God in the proper place in our lives, everything else falls into place. We might call this a "top button lifestyle." You get God right; you get everything right. This does not mean, of course, that your life will be one endless episode of colossal bliss. However, even the misalignments in life are easier to bear with God on your side.

In Mark 12:28, a scribe asks Jesus, *"Which commandment is the most important of all?"*

Jesus responds by stating, *"The most important is, 'Hear, O Israel: The Lord our God, the Lord is one. And you shall love the Lord your God with all your heart and with all your soul and with all your mind and with all your strength.'"* (Mark 12:29-30)

Without further prompting, Jesus continues, *"The second is this: 'You shall love your neighbor as yourself.' There is no other commandment greater than these."* (Mark 12:31)

This is the essence of Christianity—love God with all your being, and love your neighbor as yourself. These two commandments should be the core of our existence. They are the top two buttons. When we fit them in the proper slots, everything else aligns appropriately. If a devotion to God comes first, loving our neighbor will naturally follow. The other buttons like: family, friends, work, etc., will fall into the proper order as well.

Put God in His place. Put others in their place. Make loving God and loving others top priority!

Today, I will...seek one person that I can serve. I will show Christ to them by helping them in some way.

Week Nine

Mark 13–16
Luke 1

Brian McAlister

Fig Trees and Final Days

Today's Scripture Mark 13:28-37

The compendium of "end of the world predictions" seems to regularly garner a new installment. As recently as September 23, 2017, the world was to have been met with a "sign" of destruction if not destruction itself. If it's possible to find any nobility in these predictions, it may be housed in the thought that these fallible prognosticators believe in the end of the world, and the need for warning. Sadly, their certainties are wrapped in concepts and not the confidence of scripture.

Mark's 13th chapter seems to zero in on the conversation surrounding the predicted destruction of Jerusalem, the signs of the return of the Son of God, and man's inability to predict with certainty the day and hour of the latter. Concerning the desolation of Jerusalem, the Lord wanted to be certain that others could see and know the signs of these events, and be ready. By illustration, a fig tree is used to make a point (mind you, the is not the first time our Lord used a fig tree, see Mark 11:12-14, 20-26). Just as the leaves of a fig tree point to the coming of summer, so too would "these things" point to the need for a generation to make ready, a tribulation.

His transition is clear from the "signs of summer" to the "single day" of the Lord's return: no one knows (Mark 13:32), but the Father only. While we confirm this truth, "no man knows," Christians should conform their lives to the anticipation of the Lord's return. Our words, actions, and lives may be the only signs others see in order to ready themselves for the Lord's return. Christians should make every insistence that they choose to live in holy anticipation for their Master's return. Long after the empty cry of "wolf" has echoed through the air, the righteous conviction of the Christian life lived in authenticity will still be heard.

Today, I will...examine my life to live in authentic anticipation of the Lord's return.

Tuesday
How Much Did It Cost You?

Today's Scripture Mark 14:3-9

There was a woman who came to Jesus just before He would be betrayed and taken unlawfully in the night by Roman soldiers to Jewish authorities. Her purpose in coming was to do nothing more than take a flask of "very costly oil" and pour it on the head of Jesus. She was criticized for what she did by those who witnessed her actions. Yet our Lord's eyes saw the "lovely" when He said, "Let her alone...she has done what she could" (Mark 14:8). There were plenty who saw this woman for what she wasn't; what she couldn't, and what she didn't do. But it was Jesus who saw through everything she wasn't and what she was in that moment: willing.

The Lord is still waiting for some today to stand and do what they are able to do. Here's a hint, He won't wait forever. This woman wanted to serve Jesus; she had no other motive than to be near Him and do for Him what she could. You and I need to open our eyes to what is around us to see through the clutter of criticism, and create opportunity to serve our friends and neighbors. Through the life of this one woman, she saved and planned, prepared and purposed this one moment in her life for the distinct pleasure of serving her Lord.

How often do we miss the point? How often do we comment on what was overlooked, left out, or forgotten in light of what was seen, included, and remembered? How often do we tell others what was not done, not said, not offered instead of what was supported, was spoken, and was supplied? How often do our eyes, our minds, fail to find the lovely in light of what we think is all there is to see—the negative?

Today, I will...Pray about how I serve the Lord and plan to devote more of what He has given me back to Him.

Wednesday
When the End Comes

Today's Scripture Mark 15

Cyrene was a port city, accustomed to receiving the merchants and traders from around and beyond the Mediterranean. The trading ships would carry with them not only merchandise, but messages from around their routes of travel. As word began to spread of the mighty works being done by some villager from the region of Galilee, many from the Jewish Community of the Greek colony would be particularly intrigued. Then one day the port was filled with the news that by a spoken word of this one they called Jesus, a man who once occupied a grave, came to life. Look among the crowd at the port of Cyrene, and you'll see the face of Simon.

The gospels mention the life of Simon of Cyrene as almost a footnote, but his place in the story of Jesus Christ is our place in the Master's Story. Matthew says Simon was found (Matthew 27:32); Mark notes he was a father (Mark 15:21), and Luke implies he was forced (Luke 23:26). All three point to the form of his involvement as though it could have been us standing there watching. Simon served as an unsuspecting spectator in the story of Jesus, looking upon His life as a face in the crowd, not believing he is directly involved in the events he is witnessing. Little did he know, he would look upon the lamb who takes away the sins of the world and never be the same.

For many of us, all of us really, we fail to see our part in the story of Jesus. We believe we can stand on the sideline and watch as He passes by but we do not not have to be directly impacted by His life. We foolishly believe whatever He has done by His work of the cross, He has done for another, not for us. But Simon was compelled, he was drawn into the life and journey of Jesus. Will you be equally compelled?

Today, I will...See the journey of my Lord to Golgotha was made for my sake, not His.

Thursday

No Crucifixion, No Resurrection

Today's Scripture Mark 16

Mark's last word of his writing is as powerful as his first. He has through his "immediate" writing shown a sense of urgency in learning of and following the life of Jesus. In this closing installment Mark points the reader to the resurrection, the announcement of the resurrection, the preaching of the resurrection, and the miracles which accompanied the preaching of the resurrection. Each message, each point, is critical, and with such brevity of words Mark reveals the voluminous emphasis each one deserves in the life of the follow of the Savior.

Mark employs subtlety in a most effective manner. There's the dread and agony of coming to this gravesite when you read the words, "Who will roll away the stone for us from the entrance of the tomb?" (Mark 16:4). You hear the hopelessness in the followers of Jesus when the few words are recorded, "they did not believe them" (Mark 16:13). There's also the emphasis placed in sending out the message of the resurrection and the power of transformation which comes through yielding to the Savior of all. It takes only a few words, "Whoever believes and is baptized will be saved" (Mark 16:16).

Yet through the subtlety, there is the message of who this is done for and to whom all of this applies. When the young messenger of Mark 16:5 declares the Lord has risen from the dead, he then sends them to tell others, but not before he delivered a message to one follower in particular, Peter. "But go, tell his disciples and Peter" is enough of an indicator to show the depth of the Lord's love, and even in this message is contained the whole image of the gospel and the resurrection, the Lord came for all, for every heart, and the message is for each and every heart, especially the broken ones.

Today, I will...Remember in prayer my Savior's sacrifice and His unyielding love shown to me when He forgave my sins.

Friday
Assurance of the Things We Believe

Today's Scripture Luke 1:1-14

So much of life, whether you are a person of faith or not, can be spent searching for answers to why things are the way they are. No doubt you've experienced that in your own life. You have searched for answers to why things happened the way they happen. Sometimes you are able to see the answers clearly, while other times, many times, we fail to see the reason or the purpose behind why things in our lives occur. What do you do when you struggle with searching for an answer or trying to understand a way or a moment that does not make sense to you?

Believe it or not, doubt is a part of every believers' life. Doubt does not always convey a sense of defeat; sometimes we doubt because we want to be definitive in our commitment and in our conscience. We want to believe in and know the one we call Jesus really is the one, and there is reason to call Him Lord, Master, Savior, and Christ. What will you do when your faith doubts? Will you become an atheist? Atheists believe in aliens...good luck with that. Will you walk through life driven by doubt, or will all your doubts to be dissolved by the image, insight, and indisputable truth of Jesus Christ?

Unlike John, Luke provides no prologue of the Deity incarnate he would write about. However, Luke's prologue is one of discovery. Luke's intent is to "compile, deliver, and write" from the perspective of "eyewitnesses and ministers" a "narrative" providing an "orderly account" (Luke 1:1-4). No small part of this discovery would be for the goal of the head and heart to find a "certainty" for the searching soul and to find hope in the Son of Man who came to save all from their sins. Luke 1's account of Zechariah and Mary displays a great contrast between the power of doubt and the power of deity to overcome our doubts.

Today, I will...Commit once more to searching the scriptures daily to secure my faith in God's promises.

Week Ten
Luke 2-6

Joey Sparks

Monday
Peace to Men on Earth

Today's Scripture Luke 2:8-20

Luke 2 opens describing the humble birth of Jesus in Bethlehem. Beginning in 2:8, an angel tells the shepherds about Jesus including why His birth is significant: first, it is good news of great joy and it is for all people; second, verse 11 identifies Him as the Messiah (fulfilling the promise of being born in Bethlehem, the City of David, Micah 5:2), Savior, Christ, and Lord.

In 2:13-14, the angel is joined by heavenly host who praise God: "Glory" and "peace," "to God" and "to men," and "in the highest" and "on earth" are each parallel to one another, emphasizing the significance of the moment. This chorus invites all to see that the will of God is coming down to earth in the form of Jesus Christ.

The shepherds respond by saying, "Let us go see this thing that is happening." The heavenly messengers speak of Jesus in such a way that the shepherds can't help but investigate. But also notice when they describe the message, they attribute it to the Lord. Though an angel and angelic host were the specific messengers, they knew the message came from God.

When they tell the experience to Jesus' family, all who heard wondered and marveled at what the shepherds had said about Jesus. Mary even stored up these things in her heart. The shepherds then leave, and as they return glorify and praise God for all they had heard and seen, just as they'd been told. After seeing Jesus the shepherds have the same reaction as the angels—that of praise and worship.

The shepherds needed messengers from God to alert them about Jesus and the significance of His coming to earth. Today people need us to be messengers from God pointing them to Jesus, not just in the manger, but as Savior and Lord. Just as the shepherds were changed by what they saw and heard, lives will be changed when we alert them to "the good news of great joy for all the people."

Today, I will...speak of Jesus to someone else in a way that elicits wonder about why He came to earth.

Tuesday
The Fruit of Repentance

Today's Scripture Luke 3:1-22

When John preaches his baptism, he connects forgiveness of sins and repentance. These concepts are not only logically connected, they are prominent in Luke and Acts (see Luke 24:47, Acts 2:38, and Acts 5:31).

John preaches from Isaiah 40 in Luke 3:4-6. This quotation is also found in accounts by Matthew and Mark, except for Isaiah 40:5, "and all flesh shall see the salvation of God," which is unique to Luke. This continues a theme began in 1:14, 1:48, 1:79, and 2:31-32. Luke's gospel emphasizes the universal appeal of salvation through Jesus.

When John preaches to the crowds, he tells them to "bear fruits in keeping with repentance." He warns that God can easily raise up a physical generation on His own, but instead He desires a spiritual heritage of people who obey Him. Thus, they are to live in ways that prove their repentance. The consequences for the Jews who fail to repent are dire, as "every tree that does not bear good fruit is cut down and thrown into the fire" (3:9).

In response to this strong challenge, the crowds ask three times, "What shall we do?" (cf. Acts 2:37). John tells the rich to share with the needy, emphasizing compassion for the poor. He tells tax collectors to conduct themselves with ethical behavior. They are not told to quit their jobs, but instead to be honest. He tells soldiers not to take advantage of others through their strength or position, but instead to be content with their wages. Again, they are not told to resign, but to be responsible and concerned for others while serving in this capacity.

Hearts that are open and receptive to the news of Jesus are hearts that are willing to repent. Repentance demands a complete change from sinful living. This change is clearly seen in how we treat others (1 John 4:20-21).

Today, I will...list three ways my interactions with others today will "bear fruit in keeping with repentance."

Wednesday
Fulfilled In Your Hearing

Following His wilderness temptations, Jesus' earthly ministry begins in Galilee and Nazareth, His hometown. In the synagogue on the Sabbath, Jesus stands up and reads from Isaiah 61. The moment is significant as it shows the role of the Messiah to help and redeem those most in need.

Jesus reads that the Spirit of the Lord is upon the Lord's servant to proclaim good news to the poor, the captives, the blind, and the oppressed. After reading the text, the crowd's eyes focus on Jesus, and He tells them, "Today this scripture has been fulfilled in your hearing."

From the beginning of his ministry, Jesus shows He is not only a Savior, but He is the Messiah sent from God. He fulfills the Old Testamane promises of deliverance.

But even though they knew the Old Testament Scriptures and prophecies about the Messiah, they still reject Jesus' claim that he was the Messiah. Even though they all needed a Savior, they rejected Jesus' anointing as the one who would bring them deliverance. Their rejection is swift and intense, as they attempt to throw Him off a cliff to his death.

If we are not careful and humble before Scripture, we can miss truth just as those in Nazareth did. They allowed their familiarity with the childhood Jesus to stand in the way. Any number of factors today can keep us from seeing the truth God wants us to know about his Son. Long-held or popular doctrines can keep us from learning directly from God. Family allegiances can keep us from submitting to clear texts. The emotions of what we desire can keep us from accepting truth. Our complacency with knowing the text without knowing the author of the text can keep us from enjoying the riches of the text.

Today, I will...read Isaiah 61 in its entirety and note what other elements are fulfilled in the life and teaching of Jesus and in the rest of the New Testament.

Thursday
Jesus Eats with Sinners

Today's Scripture Luke 5:1-11, 27-32

In Luke 5, Jesus gives the disciples a miraculous catch of fish. In response to their astonishment, Jesus tells them, "From now on you will be catching men."

Luke 5:12-32 outlines the kinds of men they will be catching. As in the text of Isaiah 61:1-2 that Jesus reads in 4:18-19, these are people who are easily pushed to the margins of society because they are often hardest to love.

First Jesus cleanses a leper (5:12-14), who represents the unclean and oft-separated from society. Then He heals a paralytic when the man's friends let him down through the roof. Paralytics were limited in their abilities, and they were often a physical or financial burden on those who cared for them. Next Jesus calls Levi—better known as Matthew—to follow him. Matthew leaves everything in order to follow Jesus. Tax collectors were often despised because of their loyalty to the Romans and their unethical practices.

The following scene in Matthew's house gives insight into Jesus' mission to reach sinners. When the Pharisees see Jesus eating with Matthew and other tax collectors, they ask why He eats and drinks with sinners. Jesus answers, "Those who are well have no need of a physician, but those who are sick. I have not come to call the righteous but sinners to repentance" (5:31-32). Matthew and Mark relay this same exchange in their gospel accounts, but Luke's specifically includes what He calls sinners to do: repent.

Not only did Jesus come to serve those who are marginalized, but He provides a new way of living for all sinners (cf. Luke 19:10). Jesus' emphasis on loving those most in need and the Pharisees' accusation in 5:30 later become the framework for the series of parables in Luke 14 and 15. Indeed, the Pharisees were correct, Jesus does receive sinners.

> *Sing it o'er and over again; Christ receiveth sinful men;*
> *Make the message clear and plain: Christ receiveth sinful men.*

Today, I will...identify an overlooked and under-served group of people in my community and spend time praying about how to reach them with the love of Jesus.

Friday
Sons of the Most High

Today's Scripture Luke 6:20-36

Luke 6 contains Jesus Sermon on the Plain (6:17-49), which bears many similarities to Jesus Sermon on the Mount in Matthew 5-7. The beatitudes section which opens the sermon (6:20-23) is shorter in Luke and contains four beatitudes, as opposed to Matthew's nine. Four woes follow in Luke 6:24-26, each reflecting the opposite of the four beatitudes. There is a decidedly spiritual emphasis in these beatitudes and woes. Those who find their satisfaction from any source other than the Lord will be rejected by the Lord. The contrast between the beatitudes and woes reveals a clear role reversal in the kingdom. Those whom the world blesses are not the same as those God blesses.

Luke 6:27-36 contains a significant application of this reversal. Jesus tells His disciples, *"Love your enemies, do good to those who hate you, bless those who curse you, pray for those who abuse you."*

Jesus then explains why this is so significant. Even sinners love those who will return their love. God's people will love their enemies because they choose to live like God. We love our enemies because God loves his enemies.

It is worth remembering that God's kindness, mercy, and love toward us as His enemies is active in our best interests. Consider God's kindness and love toward us in Titus 3:1-5, which says, *"But when the goodness and loving kindness of God our Savior appeared, he saved us."* Additionally, Romans 5:8 says, *"But God shows His love for us in that while we were still sinners, Christ died for us."* In order to love our enemies, we act in their best interests, not merely share positive feelings about them.

This charge is difficult: the greatest test of loving like God is to love those who hurt us and choose not to return our love.

Today, I will...by name, pray for my enemies and those whom it's hardest to love; I will ask God for patience, wisdom, and compassion to show them His love.

Week Eleven
Luke 7-11

Chuck Monan

Monday
Shall We Look for Another?

John was chosen before birth to prepare the way for the Messiah. His mission as the forerunner would make him great before the Lord (Luke 1:15).

But even those great before the Lord struggle with doubt.

Languishing in Herod's prison, John knew his life was in peril. Wondering what he had spent his life pursuing, he sent messengers to Jesus for reassurance: "Are you the one who is to come, or shall we look for another?" (Luke 7:20). Jesus didn't rebuke John for a lack of faith, but sent word back of the miraculous things happening (7:22–23). In fact, John's question is book-ended in Luke 7 by the mighty deeds of God being done by Jesus, from the treating of the centurion's servant, to the raising from the dead of a widow's son, to the forgiveness of a sinful woman – proof of Jesus' divinity.

The faith of a pagan centurion is remarkable. He doesn't even think it necessary for Jesus to come to his house, but "say the word, and let my servant be healed" (Luke7:7). John, by contrast, is worn down and demoralized by being rewarded for his faithfulness with imprisonment and death. Was it all in vain?

Life cannot be tied up in a nice, neat package of cause and effect, as Job's friends believed. Frequently life is unfair, and can seem pointless. But faith is the light that cuts through the darkness. "Everyone who lives and believes in Me shall never die. Do you believe this?" (John 11:26).

Do you?

Only God's power can accomplish the impossible. Only God's Son can change our lives in an instant. And only through faith in Jesus as the Christ can the battle of life be won.

It is not a sin to doubt. It is a sin to quit. "Blessed is the one who is not offended by Me" (Luke 7:23).

Today, I will...believe even when I struggle with doubt.

Tuesday
Jesus Is Lord

Today's Scripture Luke 8:1-56

If you were a Christian living in the first century you would face the pressure in many parts of the Roman Empire of the Cult of Emperor Worship. Rome allowed its conquered subjects to retain their own religions, provided they pledged allegiance to the emperor by confessing "Caesar is Lord." After all, Rome's domination of the ancient world was the kind of thing only gods could do. Worshiping the emperor and acknowledging his power would help unify the empire.

Christians who believed that Jesus is Lord refused to bend the knee. The Gospels bear witness to the incomparable *kyrios*, Jesus of Nazareth. The eighth chapter of Luke offers a treasure trove of evidence pointing to the authority and power of Lord Jesus:

Jesus is Lord with the power to cure infirmities: some of those belonging to Jesus' entourage were healed of various ailments (8:1-3).

Jesus is Lord with the power to grow faith: the parable of the sower reminds that the fertile soil of a sincere heart produces life where before there had been nothing (8:4-15).

Jesus is Lord with the power to expose secrets and hypocrisy: "Nothing is hidden that will not be made manifest, nor is anything secret that will not be known and come to light" (8:17).

Jesus is Lord with the power to lift up or lay low: "Take care then how you hear, for to the one who has, more will be given, and from the one who has not, even what he thinks that he has will be taken away" (8:18).

Jesus is Lord with the power to create relationships: as precious as family ties are, even more special is the family Christ gives to all who hear the word of God and do it (8:19-21).

Jesus is Lord with the power to calm the storm: "Who then is this, that He commands even winds and water, and they obey Him?" (8:22-25).

Jesus is Lord with the power to cast out demons: the very real spiritual forces of evil cannot stand against God's Son (8:26-39).

Jesus is Lord with the power over life and death: the one who created life, and laid down his life only to take it back up, will be with us until he puts his last enemy under his feet (8:40-56).

Today, I will...trust in Jesus as Lord.

Wednesday
What Does It Profit a Man?

Today's Scripture Luke 9:1-62

Why are we here? What is the purpose of life? Where are we going? These questions have always haunted the thoughtful, introspective person. As more people today ignore them and live for the moment, the words of Jesus call a lost world to think on them: "If anyone would come after Me, let him deny himself and take up his cross daily and follow Me. For whoever would save his life will lose it, but whoever loses his life for My sake will save it. For what does it profit a man if he gains the whole world and loses or forfeits himself?" (Luke 9: 23-25)

Luke 9 provides a glimpse at how His contemporaries responded to Jesus and His profound words on the meaning of life:

*The twelve apostles devoted themselves to Jesus' mission of proclaiming the kingdom of God (9:1-6).

*Herod was perplexed by Jesus, thinking He was John the Baptist raised from the dead (9:7-9).

*The five thousand were searching for the bread of life, but were satisfied with physical bread (9:10-17).

*Peter confessed that Jesus is the Christ of God (9:18-20).

*Peter, James, and John saw Jesus transfigured, an experience that would steel them to face the suffering yet in the future (9:28-36).

*A boy with an unclean spirit was healed by God's power (9:37-43).

*The disciples let pride and ego take over their agenda (9:46-50).

*Samaritan rejection fueled the desire for retribution, but the way to Jesus is forgiveness (9:51-56).

*Those whose commitment to Jesus is shallow or halfhearted will not last (9:57-62).

It is easy to fill our lives with trivial pursuits. But the wise man or woman remembers that even if we gain the whole world, if we lose our eternal soul, it is all for nothing. "No one who puts his hand to the plow and looks back is fit for the kingdom of God" (9:62).

Today, I will...live my life remembering that eternity looms before me.

Great Opportunity Means Great Responsibility

Today's Scripture Luke 10:1–41

The founding document of America declares "All men are created equal…" But this refers to all of us being God's creation. In terms of talents and abilities, inequality is a reality. So, too, are opportunities. One politician disparaged a rival by saying he "was born on third base and woke up and thought he'd hit a triple."

Jesus recognizes that some are put in more privileged, advantageous positions than others. With such opportunities come great responsibility: *"Everyone to whom much is given, of him much will be required, and to him from whom then entrusted much, they will demand the more."* (Luke 12:48)

Chapter 10 of Luke's gospel illustrates the varied opportunities people have in encountering Jesus – and the respective responsibilities that go with them.

The seventy-two sent out by Jesus to proclaim the kingdom of God were given specific instruction for their work. As in Luke 9:5, Jesus repeats the charge to shake the dust off your feet against the town that rejects God's message and messengers.

Even more pronounced are the woes for Chorazin, Bethsaida, and Capernaum. These towns heard the message and witnessed the miracles of Jesus firsthand – and still rejected Him. An even harsher judgment than that of Tyre and Sidon awaited them.

Though the opportunities people have to know Jesus vary, all of us still will answer for how we respond. Martha chose household activities over drinking in the living water of Jesus' teaching, while Mary chose the good portion (10:38–42). A despised foreigner went to great trouble and expense to be a good neighbor to a stranger who, had circumstances been reversed, wouldn't have given him the time of day. The words of Jesus to "Go, and do likewise" have great implications for how we live our lives.

Today, I will…use the opportunities God has given me to love Him and be a blessing to others.

Friday
Don't Believe the Truth

Today's Scripture Luke 11:1–54

"Whoever is not with Me is against Me, and whoever does not gather with Me scatters." (Luke 11:23)

As opposition grew during Jesus' ministry, some of the first casualties were fact, logic and common sense. So obstinate were the enemies of Jesus that they would blindly follow any explanation for His miracles except acknowledging that He was empowered by the Father.

When Jesus cast a demon out of a mute man, enabling him to speak, the naysayers had a ready-made answer for this remarkable event: "He casts out demons by Beelzebul, the prince of demons" (11:15). Common sense dictated that Satan would have no interest in fighting against his own interests, because a house divided against itself cannot stand (11:17).

But there was something far more sinister at work here.

The Pharisees and lawyers were not concerned with bringing people closer to God through devotion and obedience. Jesus charged them with loading "people with burdens hard to bear, and you yourselves do not touch the burdens with one of your fingers" (11:46). Their concern was to impress others with their outward piety even as their hearts were corrupt and far from God (11:37–41).

Without love or truth as motivation, protecting their reputation and preserving their status was paramount to the Pharisees. For this reason, it mattered not what Jesus did or said — He was a threat to the established order (John 11:50). This unclean spirit was affecting the entire nation, corrupting the entire entity of Judaism from the top down (Luke 11:24–26). For this reason, no sign would be given: *"This generation is an evil generation. It seeks for a sign, but no sign will be given to it but the sign of Jonah. For as Jonah became a sign to the people of Nineveh, so will the Son of Man to this generation."* (Luke 11:29–30)

The Jewish leaders refused to believe in Jesus because they did not want to lose their authority, influence and privilege. They looked the Truth in the face...and chose not to believe it.

Today, I will...follow the One who is the Way, the Truth, and the Life.

Week Twelve
Luke 12–16

David Salisbury

Monday
Live Generously

Today's Scripture Luke 12

I've worn glasses since I was in elementary school. Way back then I just needed them to see things far away. But I still remember what it felt like to put on my glasses and see things I hadn't been able to see before. I could see leaves on trees instead of just green fuzz. It was amazing!

A regular theme in scripture is that our devotion to God will open our eyes to things we failed to notice before. In Luke 12, we meet a man whose only identifying trait is that he is rich. He has a lot of money and a lot of land. By the end of the story, he has a lot of crops, too. He reminds us that people can be rich in many different ways.

As we read we find that the man is blind to the source of his blessings. He takes in a great harvest and takes all the credit for it. He couldn't see the Lord's hand in his blessings. But he's also blind to other people. When he brings in a bumper crop, he only thinks about himself. In just three sentences, the rich fool uses the words "I" or "me" twelve times! Finally, he is blind towards eternity. He never once thinks about the end of his life (which turns out to be a LOT closer than he thought!) or where he will spend eternity. Jesus warns us all, *"Take care, and be on your guard against all covetousness, for one's life does not consist in the abundance of his possessions."* (Luke 12:15)

Today, I will...resolve to live generously. Open your eyes! Whatever blessings God has placed in your life, share them. If it is money, give some of it away. If it is time, devote it to the Lord's work and spending time with others. If it is a talent, use it for the glory of God. When you are blessed, live generously.

Tuesday
Think Globally and Act Locally

Today's Scripture Luke 13

It seems that those in politics believes they are right and their opposition is wrong. More and more we have seen political leaders run afoul of the law or offend our moral conscience. It's hard to vote for someone if you don't believe he or she is a "good" candidate. Many people are hoping religion and the church can save our country.

I'm concerned about our nation and the direction we seem to be headed. Our culture seems determined to dive deeper into the sewer morally rather than try to improve. But I'm not sure the solution will come from the ballot box. If you could pass a law that required everyone to be "good," you still wouldn't change hearts.

In Luke 13 Jesus says the kingdom of God is like a mustard seed or a handful of leaven in a large lump of dough. It works from the inside out. It starts small and grows into something great. Some of the greatest spiritual giants in the church have come from some of the most humble beginnings. Who will be the next great gospel preacher? Who will bring a revival to the people of our land? Who is the next great author who can write books that help us understand the Bible and encourage us to live godly lives? Who will write the great hymns of tomorrow? Who will be the mustard seeds of the church? They might be reading this book. Or their parents might. Or their aunt or uncle, or a friend who will lead them to Christ, may be reading these words. What can God do through you to make a difference?

Today, I will...resolve to "think globally and act locally" in regard to the church. I will pray for the kingdom of God to grow worldwide and I will look for one person I know that I can reach with the gospel. I will look for ways to let the gospel change my heart, too.

Wednesday
Keep the Invitation

As kids we had lots of rules about meals at the table. We didn't eat until everyone was at the table and we had prayed for our meal. Jesus liked to use meal times as teaching times. Whether it was the wedding in Cana or the last supper, Jesus didn't let those moments at the table pass by.

In Luke 14, Jesus uses a meal at the home of a Pharisee as a teaching opportunity. After reminding them to be humble, Jesus talks about what it means to accept an invitation (vs 15-24). In His story, a group of people accepts an invitation to a meal. In their day, you would send out invitations in advance and folks would RSVP that they would come. Then, on the day of the feast, you would send a servant to call people when the food was ready. In this story, when the food is ready, the guests begin to make excuses. Suddenly they don't want to come, even though they accepted the invitation. It would be as if you invited several friends to your home. They got there just as you were finishing up the preparations for the meal. While they sit and fellowship, you pull the main course out of the oven and bring it to the table. Suddenly your guests begin to make excuses for why they have to leave. One needs to finish his taxes, even though it is June. Another suddenly remembers a doctor appointment even though it is 6:00 in the evening. It becomes clear that they don't want to eat what you are serving. Jesus says that God told Israel what they were signing up for and Israel accepted the invitation, but now they want to back out so God will invite others.

Today, I will...remember that accepting God's invitation means accepting all the terms of His invitation. I will refuse to make excuses for not doing what the Lord expects me to do.

Thursday
God Loves Sinners and Expects Us To

Today's Scripture Luke 15

The parable of the Prodigal Son is one of the most well known stories Jesus told. In Luke 15 it is the third in a three part series of stories. First, Jesus tells about a shepherd who lost one of his 100 sheep. He searches for it diligently and rejoices when he can reunite it with the rest of the flock. Then Jesus tells about a woman who has a special collection of ten coins. When one of them is lost she cleans her house top to bottom and celebrates when she finds the lost coin. In both of these parables, Jesus tells us the meaning. "Just so, I tell you, there will be more joy in heaven over one sinner who repents than over ninety-nine righteous persons who need no repentance" (Luke 15:7). God wants sinners to be saved. Everyone has a place among the people of God and you are missed if you are outside of God.

Then Jesus tells the story of the Prodigal Son. As He tells the story of the son who is lost and then found, the point that God loves sinners is reinforced in a beautiful way. The sheep just wandered off and the coin fell through the cracks and got overlooked. The son openly rebelled but then he repented. In each instance, sinners find some comfort that God wants them to come home. However you may come to find yourself outside the church, God wants you to return and be restored to your place among His people.

But just as all the religious folks are patting themselves on the back for never leaving in the first place, Jesus tells about the older brother who never strayed from home but never understood the father's love, either. Instead, he got angry when his younger brother was restored to the family. And suddenly we see that God loves sinners and He expects us to love them, too.

Today, I will...pray for the lost. I will pray that they come home and resolve to do all I can to make my church a safe place for sinners to be restored.

Listen to the Truth We Already Have

Today's Scripture Luke 16

The piercing alert of a smoke detector is designed to wake up and snap us to our senses. No one makes a soothing smoke detector. And truthfully, no wants a smoke detector that is calming. That's not the job of a smoke detector.

Luke 16 is a smoke detector in the New Testament. It wakes us up to the reality of God's punishment and calls us to come to our senses before we are lost. In the latter half of the chapter Jesus tells the story of two individuals. Lazarus is a poor beggar and he sits outside the gates of a rich man. Both men die and enter eternity. Lazarus finds himself in a place of joy and peace. The rich man, on the other hand, is in a place of torment and agony. The rich man's wealth didn't keep him out of hell, and Lazarus's poverty didn't prevent him from being with the Lord. God cares about more than just our bank account. We also learn from Jesus that after we die, our destination is sealed. People cannot cross from heaven to hell or from hell to heaven. The rich man realizes that it is too late for him but begs that a warning could be sent to his brothers who are still alive. He is told that words of the Scriptures are sufficient to tell us all we need to know to be properly prepared for eternity.

We don't need a new person to tell us old news, we need to listen to the truth we already have!

Today, I will...remember that Hell is real and real people will really go there. I will resolve to live a godly life and tell lost people about the gospel. I will pick 5 people I know who are lost and pray for them. I will look for an opportunity in the next week to invite them to church or Bible study.

Week Thirteen
Luke 17–21

Mike Moss

Jesus Heals

Today's Scripture Luke 17:11-19

"On the way to Jerusalem he entered a village, He was met by ten lepers, who stood at a distance and lifted up their voices, saying, 'Jesus, Master, have mercy on us.' When He saw them He said to them, 'Go and show yourselves to the priests.' And as they went they were cleansed. Then one of them, when he saw that he was healed, turned back, praising God with a loud voice; and he fell on his face at Jesus' feet, giving Him thanks. Now he was a Samaritan. Then Jesus answered, 'Were not ten cleansed? Where are the nine? Was no one found to return and give praise to God except this foreigner?' And He said to him, 'Rise and go your way; your faith has made you well.'" (Luke 17:11-19)

Today we use leprosy to describe Hanson's disease. In biblical times, it was used of any skin disease, even a severe case of acne. Even a house could have leprosy.

Lepers had to live apart from the community, even their families (cf. Leviticus 13:38-46; Numbers 5:2-4). They were spiritually unclean. As they approached, they were required to proclaim "unclean, unclean." No one ever touched them. They formed a community of their own. As lepers, it made little difference whether one was a Jew or a Samaritan.

Seeing Jesus, they stood at a distance as required by the Law. They addressed Jesus as "Lord," begging Him "Have mercy on us."

After healing them Jesus said, "Go show yourselves to the priests." Priests were the community health agents. As they went their way, they were cleansed.

One returned to thank Jesus, a Samaritan. Luke's readers might remember the Good Samaritan and the Gentile mission.

Jesus asks "Where are the nine? Does only this foreigner praise God?" Jesus will say to him, "Your faith has made you well"—literally "saved you."

There are two kinds of healings in this story—from leprosy and from sin.

Today, I will...thank God for what He has done for me in Jesus.

Tuesday

Two Men Prayed, Only One Is Honored

Today's Scripture Luke 18:9-14

He also told this parable to some who trusted in themselves that they were righteous, and treated others with contempt: "Two men went up into the temple to pray, one a Pharisee and the other a tax collector.

After a parable about the need to pray when we get discouraged at the delay of the second coming, Jesus notices some people who were confident of their own righteousness. He then tells a parable well known by any student of the Bible.

Luke does not identify the "some," but in 16:14-15 Jesus identifies the Pharisees as those who "justify yourselves in the eyes of men."

The parable begins with two men who went up to the temple to pray. The first man was a Pharisee. The phrase "he stood by himself" may well be misplaced in the ESV. The NASB translates the verse as "The Pharisee stood and was praying this to himself." The NIV Readers Version translates it "[He] stood up and prayed about himself." He offers no petition, not thinking he needed God.

The Pharisee begins "I am not like other men," not like robbers, evil doers, adulterers and most of all not like this tax collector. Praying out loud, the Pharisee would have been heard by the tax collector.

The Pharisee fasted twice a week, required by the Law only on the Day of Atonement. Good Jews fasted on Monday and Thursday. He gave a tenth of all he got, required of only the major crops. He was convinced he did more than God required of him.

"Tax collector" was often used in combination with "sinners," and even "prostitutes." The tax collector stood at a distance, seeing himself as unworthy in need of the grace of God. Not even to look up to heaven, he beat his breast, a sign of contrition.

Jesus concludes that "this man (the tax collector) rather than the other (the Pharisee)" went home justified, a reversal: the honored is shamed; the shamed is honored.

Today, I will...recognize that I have no room to boasting and that I need God's grace.

Wednesday
Zacchaeus, A Son of Abraham

"He entered Jericho and was passing through...Zacchaeus...was a chief tax collector and was rich. And he was seeking to see who Jesus was, but on account of the crowd he could not, because he was small in stature. So he ran on ahead and climbed up into a sycamore tree to see Him...And when Jesus came to the place, He looked up and said to him, "Zacchaeus, hurry and come down, for I must stay at your house today." So he hurried and came down and received Him joyfully. And when they saw it, they all grumbled, "He has gone in to be the guest of a man who is a sinner." And Zacchaeus...said..."Behold, Lord, the half of my goods I give to the poor. And if I have defrauded anyone of anything, I restore it fourfold." And Jesus said to him, "Today salvation has come to this house, since he also is a son of Abraham. For the Son of Man came to seek and to save the lost." (Luke 19:1–10)

Passing through Jericho, Jesus met Zacchaeus, a wealthy "chief tax collector." As a tax collector in the Jewish world, he was an outsider, unimportant, hated.

Being small in stature, unable to see Jesus, Zacchaeus runs ahead of the crowd and climbs a sycamore tree, an undignified action for a prominent man.

Jesus said, "Zacchaeus, hurry down, today, I must stay at your home." Amazingly Jesus knew his name. The word "must" indicates a sense of the divine plan. The crowd began to grumble, not pleased with Jesus' action. Zacchaeus came down indicating his repentance, "I give half of what I have to the poor. If I have cheated anyone, I will give back four times as much."

Jesus said to him, "Today salvation has come to this house, this son of Abraham." Zacchaeus had demonstrated the faith of Abraham. Zacchaeus was sought. And was now saved.

Today, I will...put my faith into action.

Thursday
He Is the God of the Living

Today's Scripture Luke 20:27-40

Luke 20:27...some Sadducees, those who deny that there is a resurrection... asked Him a question, saying, *"Teacher, Moses wrote for us that if a man's brother dies, having a wife but no children, the man must take the widow and raise up offspring for his brother. Now there were seven brothers. The first took a wife, and died without children. And the second and the third took her, and likewise all seven left no children and died. Afterward the woman also died. In the resurrection, therefore, whose wife will the woman be?"* (Luke 20:28-33)

After the Pharisees attempt to catch Him on taxes, the Sadducees also came to trap Jesus. From generally high priestly families, they saw themselves as guardians of "true religion." They accepted only the Pentateuch, and didn't believe in angels, demons, or the resurrection. They planned to get Jesus and make the Pharisees look bad probably seeing Him as a Pharisee.

Their question regarded levirate marriage. Seven brothers each in turn dies without an heir. Finally, the woman dies, having been married to all seven. At the time of the resurrection whose wife would she be? Polygamy they could imagine but never polyandry. They assumed their question proved that there could not be a resurrection.

Jesus notes their flaw—equating this age and the age to come. The need for companionship supplied by marriage in this age would be filled by God himself and believers in the next. People will no longer die, and like angels they will be asexual beings.

Jesus indicates proof of the resurrection in the story about Moses in the burning bush episode, a portion of the OT the Sadducees would accept. Moses calls God "the God of Abraham, God of Isaac, God of Jacob." Only living people can have a God. Moses did not say not "He was the God of..." but "He is the God of..."

Jesus' surpassing knowledge and wisdom drives His opponents again to silence.

Today, I will...appreciate the resurrection of Jesus and the promise of my resurrection.

Friday
She Gave All She Had

"Jesus looked up and saw the rich putting their gifts into the offering box, and He saw a poor widow put in two small copper coins. And He said, "Truly, I tell you, this poor widow has put in more than all of them. For they all contributed out of their abundance, but she out of her poverty put in all she had to live on." (Luke 21:1-4)

The reference to widows in 20:46 provides the natural link to this story. The widow was rich toward God, but poor in man's view.

The story takes place at the temple treasury in the Court of the Women. In the Court there were thirteen trumpet-shaped vessels where worshipers would place their contributions. The rich who could afford larger sums would make a big show of their contribution.

A poor widow places two small copper coins, literally two lepta. Our English translations will typically call these coins "two mites." A lepta was one one-hundred-and-twenty-eighth of a denarius, the smallest coin in the Greco-Roman world. A denarius was minimum wage for a day's work. Despite the fact that many translations or commentaries will suggest that each coin is a cent, the smallest coin for us—a penny, it would be more like fifty cents in terms of spending money today. The widow puts in her last dollar, all of her bios, life or better livelihood.

Jesus says she has given more than all the others. She gave all that she had. She trusted God to provide for her.

The measure of a gift is not how big it is, but how much one has left. A gift is measured by the spirit with which it is given; giving is commensurate with means.

The story is consistent with a theme that runs throughout Luke's gospel, the great reversal, like the parable of the beggar, Lazarus, and the rich man. The one with almost nothing offers the most and is received. Those who offer the most are rejected.

Today, I will...appreciate what God has given me in Jesus and will share my blessings with others.

Week Fourteen
Luke 22-24
John 1-2

Doug Burleson

Monday
Confess Me

Luke 22 begins with Judas taking money to betray Jesus, while Peter and John helped prepare the Passover where Jesus instituted the Lord's Supper (vv. 1–23). Satan was at work, but Jesus' followers were continuing to serve Him too. Yet, at Passover a fight broke out over which of the apostles was most important (vv. 24–38). In the midst of that argument, Jesus warned Peter that Satan would tempt him and would be successful before the rooster crowed, but that Peter "once you have turned again" would need to strengthen his brothers (vv. 31–34)

Peter was among the sleepy disciples who accompanied Jesus to the Garden (vv. 39–46) and, shortly after Judas betrayed Jesus with a kiss (vv. 47–53), found himself being accused of having been associated with Jesus (vv. 54–62). After having already denied being with Jesus twice, another person accused Peter of being with Jesus and insisted that his claim was true.

"But Peter said, 'Man, I do not know what you are talking about.' And immediately, while he was still speaking, the rooster crowed. And the Lord turned and looked at Peter." (Luke 22:60–61a)

When following Jesus one has to decide to confess Him even when the way is tough. Even when others bring accusations against us. Even when it might cost us everything.

A few thoughts: We will all occasionally fail. Yet, we serve a God who is willing to forgive. Jesus knew Peter was going to fail, but He loved him anyway. Peter's sin certainly grieved Him, but in redemption Peter found all the more reasons to confess Christ. When Jesus turned to look at Peter, I do not believe Jesus gave him a hateful look, but Jesus didn't look the other way either. Peter sank into the sea when he took his eyes off the Lord (cf. Matt. 14:22–33), but Jesus continued to look at Peter even after he vehemently denied any association.

Today, I will...commit to confessing Jesus on a daily basis even on the difficult days.

Tuesday
Forgive with Me

Since Luke 9:51 Jesus' face had been set towards Jerusalem. In Luke 23 Jesus' exodus to the city of David culminated at the cross. Jesus appeared before Pilate (vv. 1–5, 13–25) and Herod Antipas (vv. 6–12) and was led away to be crucified.

The Golgotha scene is loud, chaotic, and heartbreaking, yet illustrates perfectly the difference between human wisdom and God's wisdom. As crowds shout "crucify Him!," rulers struggle to rule wisely, a pilgrim to Jerusalem struggles to carry the cross of Jesus, women struggle with tears to understand why this was happening, Jesus speaks. Between two thieves the crucified Christ looked at the scene at Golgotha and spoke words of incredible grace and mercy.

"And Jesus said, 'Father, forgive them, for they know not what they do.' And they cast lots to divide His garments. And the people stood by, watching, but the rulers scoffed at Him, saying, 'He saved others; let him save Himself, if He is the Christ of God, His Chosen One!'" (Luke 23:34–35)

The Spirit through Luke doesn't miss an opportunity to make the contrast clear. Jesus spoke words of forgiveness while His earthly possessions were being gambled over, while worldly rulers continued to ridicule Him and foolishly challenge Him to do something He certainly could have chosen to do (cf. Matthew 26:53).

A few thoughts: First, we are not as smart and insightful as we think we are. The crowds like to share and draw conclusions that can quickly gain popularity and carry the day. Yet in contrast to the noise and slanderous assaults on character stands a forgiving God who continues to pursue a relationship with those made in His image. Listen to what Jesus says. Without pretense. Without someone asking for forgiveness first. Without malice or ill will, Jesus made God's "1 Timothy 2:4 desire" clear.

Today, I will...find comfort in following Christ rather than in the foolishness of the crowd.

Wednesday
Remember Me

Only Luke tells the story on what happened with Cleopas and his friend on the road to Emmaus. What an incredible day it had been! The "very day" (Luke 24:13) of Jesus' resurrection these friends were talking about Jesus when Jesus walked up to travel with them. As their eyes "were kept from recognizing Him" (v. 16) they shared how Jesus, the mighty prophet, had been crucified three days earlier despite their hopes that He was "the one to redeem Israel" (v. 21). Now His body was missing and they were more perplexed than ever.

Cleopas and his travelling companion were interrupted with a rebuke from their unknown guest. Jesus spoke of the necessity of His suffering and explained from "all the Scriptures" (v. 27) exactly what the Christ was to do. As the lesson ended the two men showed hospitality towards the stranger and invited Him to stay. Even though it was their invitation, Jesus quickly became host.

"When He was at table with them, He took the bread and blessed and broke it and gave it to them. And their eyes were opened, and they recognized Him. And He vanished from their sight." (Luke 24:30-31)

These two men were changed by this encounter. Once they recognized Jesus they returned that very hour to the eleven apostles to share their experience. There they encountered Jesus again and found even more blessings in Christ.

A few thoughts: Sometimes we think we have the story figured out. We have read it, studied it, proclaimed it in-and-out and might feel that there is nothing left to learn. But then we encounter Christ anew in the text and find ourselves with open eyes and hearts on fire, ready to share what we have been given with others. Let us not let the Gospel grow cold. Let us not let "the old, old story" get old.

Today, I will...remember what the risen Lord does as host and share that good news with as many people as possible.

Thursday
Respect Me

Today we read the first chapter in "the Gospel of belief." John's Gospel is equal to yet different from Matthew, Mark, and Luke. John begins by taking us back to the beginning—long before Christ was born in Bethlehem.

One needs to read the first sixteen chapters of Matthew, eight chapters of Mark, or nine chapters of Luke to hear one of the participants in the story confess that Jesus is Lord. In John it takes only a few words. In the first eighteen verses of John's Gospel one learns that Jesus is the Word, God, and the Light.

"In the beginning was the Word, and the Word was with God, and the Word was God. He was in the beginning with God. All things were made through Him, and without Him was not any thing made that has been made. In Him was life, and the life was the light of men. The light shines in the darkness, and the darkness has not overcome it." (John 1:1–5)

John begins by taking us back to the beginning. No story of Jesus' birth. No genealogy. Just the stark reality that Jesus is fully man and fully God. He is the Word made flesh. Jesus was not created, nor did He begin in Bethlehem. He has no beginning or end.

A few thoughts: In harmonizing the story of Jesus from the four inspired Gospel accounts we must not forget what John shares here. Jesus is divine. We must also not forget that our beginning is found in Him as well. Remembrance is not just an academic exercise however as we must continually seek to represent the light rather than the darkness. The darkness will never overcome the light of Christ, thus the darkness must not overcome those who walk in his light either.

Today, I will...consider how my origin and purpose are directly related to the Christ who has no beginning or end.

Friday
Serve Like Me

Two powerful events are described in John 2: Jesus turning the water to wine (vv. 1-2) and cleansing the Temple (vv. 13-25). Many commentators spend time describing the contextual or chronological issues in this chapter. Let us not miss what we learn about Jesus here.

In John 2 Jesus had to remind His mother that His hour had not yet come (v. 4) and the Jewish authorities about what the Temple really was for (v. 16). It seems that many had missed what Jesus' mission was primarily about. As Jesus' disciples were striving to understand Jesus' teaching, including the foreshadowing of his resurrection in 2:21-22, John reminds us of what Jesus knew.

"Now when He was in Jerusalem at the Passover feast, many believed in His name when they saw the signs that He was doing. But Jesus on His part did not entrust Himself to them, because He knew all people and needed no one to bear witness about man, for He Himself knew what was in man." (John 2:23-25)

Before Nicodemus would come to Jesus in the next verse (John 3:1), Jesus knew what was in him. Jesus knew the hearts of those He encountered and yet consistently sought to say and to show them God's intent for their lives.

A few thoughts: We do not know what is in the heart of a particular person. How much more difficult would it be to love and serve others if we could read their hearts? While there would be some encouraging moments, I would imagine our discouragement might increase as we saw hypocrisy, jealousy, and enmity in the hearts of people who we would otherwise respect. Jesus was wise to not fall prey to the whims of those around Him, but He did not allow the evil that was within many of the people He encountered to prevent Him from speaking the truth or showing them love.

Today, I will...consider the example of the Lord, who knew the hearts of people, in serving others as I seek to also help others.

Week Fifteen
John 3-7

Buddy Johnson

That He Gave

Today's Scripture John 3:16–17

I want to tell you a story about a man named William Dixon who lived in England. He was a widower who had lost his only son at a young age. One day he saw that his neighbor's house was on fire. Although the aged owner was quickly rescued, her orphaned grandson was trapped upstairs in the blaze. Dixon climbed an iron pipe on the side of the house to reach the boy. The pipe was hot and badly burned his hands as he climbed up and down and lowered the boy to safety.

Shortly after the fire, the grandmother died. The townspeople wondered who would care for the boy. Two volunteers appeared before the town council. One was a father who had lost his son and would like to adopt the orphan as his own. William Dixon was to speak next, but instead of saying anything he merely held up his scarred hands. When the vote was taken, the boy was given to him.

Do you understand just how much God loves you? When God sent his only Son Jesus to the cross, He was thinking about you. When Jesus let those Roman soldiers drive the nails into his hands, he was thinking of you. When he drew his last breath, he was thinking of you.

"For God so loved the world, that he gave his only Son, that whoever believes in him should not perish but have eternal life. For God did not send his Son into the world to condemn the world, but in order that the world might be saved through him." (John 3:16–17)

One day Satan will stand before the throne and demand your soul. God the Judge who sits on the throne will turn to Jesus and He will not need to speak. He will simply hold up His scarred hands.

Today, I will...thank God for His costly love.

Tuesday
The Head and the Heart

Today's Scripture John 4:23-24

In the book of Isaiah, the Israelites were just going through the motions in worship, and God was not pleased. Listen to God's words in Isaiah 29.13: *"These people honor me with their lips, but their hearts are far from me. They worship me in vain; their teachings are but rules taught by men"* (NIV84).

God wants us to pour our heart and soul into worship. He created us to be emotional beings. We are commanded in Scripture to "love the Lord your God will all your heart and with all your soul and with all your mind." Let's substitute the word worship for love in this verse: "You shall worship the Lord your God with all your heart and with all your soul and with all your mind." Do you do that? Do you pour out your heart in worship? Do you worship God from the depth of your soul? Do you stretch your mind as you try to grasp the deeper teachings of God?

Remember what Jesus told the Samaritan woman in John 4:23-24: *"But the hour is coming, and is now here, when the true worshipers will worship the Father in spirit and truth, for the Father is seeking such people to worship Him. God is spirit, and those who worship Him must worship in spirit and truth."*

How do you worship? Do you sing with great excitement? Do you shed tears of joy as you eat the Lord's Supper? Do you shout hallelujah when a sinner is baptized? You may be thinking, "We don't worship that way at our church." Well maybe you should. Maybe we all should.

We must grow in our understanding of what God wants in worship. Worship is a matter of both head and heart. God wants us to pour our hearts into worship… and He wants us to do so in a true and biblical way. When we find that balance, then we will experience true worship.

Today, I will…worship God in spirit and truth.

Wednesday
Do You Want to Be Healed?

Today's Scripture John 5:1-6

Imagine that you walk into your doctor's office and are sick with the flu. After asking several questions and diagnosing your sickness, the doctor asks you one more question: "Do you want to be healed?" That question would surprise us. Of course we want to be healed! What a silly question!

In John 5, Jesus asks that question...

"After this there was a feast of the Jews, and Jesus went up to Jerusalem. Now there is in Jerusalem by the Sheep Gate a pool, in Aramaic called Bethesda, which has five roofed colonnades. In these lay a multitude of invalids—blind, lame, and paralyzed. One man was there who had been an invalid for thirty-eight years. When Jesus saw him lying there and knew that he had already been there a long time, he said to him, 'Do you want to be healed?'" (John 5:1-6)

John noted that the man had been ill for 38 years. Perhaps He saw in this a picture of His own Jewish nation that had wandered in the wilderness for 38 years (Deuteronomy 2:14). Spiritually speaking, Israel was a nation of sinful people who desperately needed God's help. This man needed help too. You would think that the invalid would have responded with an enthusiastic, "Yes! I want to be healed!" But he didn't. Instead, he began to make excuses.

Sometimes we do the same. We walk into our "house of grace" (that is what Bethesda means) on Sunday mornings and we are sick with sin. Do we want to be healed? Or do we make excuses about our sins? You would think that we would cry out, "Yes! I want to be healed!" But Sunday after Sunday we don't. We hide our sin. We excuse our sin. We rationalize our sin. We justify our sin. But we don't confess our sin.

James 5.16 says, *"Therefore, confess your sins to one another and pray for one another, that you may be healed."*

Do you want to be healed? Say yes!

Today, I will...ask God for healing.

Thursday
Give Us This Bread Always

Can you name the only miracle story that is included in all four gospels? It is the feeding of the 5,000. It says something so important that every gospel writer included the miracle. But John gives us more-the miracle and the message.

When Jesus looked up and saw a large crowd coming toward Him, He said to Philip, "Where are we to buy bread, so that these people may eat?" (John 6:5). Philip was the natural person to ask where food might be found to feed them all; he grew up in Bethsaida. But Jesus already knew what He was going to do. So this is a test. It's a test for Philip. It's a test for the disciples. It's also a test for us.

Jesus feeds the 5,000 with five barley loaves and two fish. It's a miracle! But don't miss the message. Jesus is offering something better than fish and barley loaves. However, the crowd doesn't get it. They are following Jesus because their hunger has been satisfied. They were moved not by full hearts, but by full bellies. They had the experience but missed the meaning.

"Jesus then said to them, 'Truly, truly, I say to you, it was not Moses who gave you the bread from heaven, but my Father gives you the true bread from heaven. For the bread of God is he who comes down from heaven and gives life to the world.' They said to him, 'Sir, give us this bread always.' Jesus said to them, 'I am the bread of life; whoever comes to me shall not hunger, and whoever believes in me shall never thirst.'" (John 6:32-35)

In the end, this story isn't about Philip. It isn't about Andrew. It's about Jesus and what He gives. What He gives is not just bread or fish. In the end, He gives himself. And that is exactly what we need.

Today, I will...feast on the bread of life.

Friday
No Other Stream

In The Silver Chair (The Chronicles of Narnia), Jill desperately needs a drink. She comes up to the river, but a lion is there. The lion said, "If you are thirsty, you may drink." Jill is afraid. She wants to leave and look for another stream. "There is no other stream," said the lion. It was the hardest thing she ever had to do, but she knelt down and began scooping up water in her hand. It was the coldest, most refreshing water she had ever tasted. And she didn't need to drink much of it before it quenched her thirst all at once.

This story reminds me of Jesus' invitation to come and drink in John 7.

"On the last day of the feast, the great day, Jesus stood up and cried out, 'If anyone thirsts, let him come to me and drink. Whoever believes in me, as the Scripture has said, "Out of his heart will flow rivers of living water."' Now this He said about the Spirit, whom those who believed in Him were to receive." (John 7:37-39)

This living water, this rushing river, is the Holy Spirit—the Paraclete who brings comfort and strengthening aid. This is Aqua Viva—Living Water.

The Spirit is not just for you. God's intention for this living water of the Spirit is to flow out of us into the world because God wants everyone to experience this new life. We must allow God's Spirit to flow through us into the world. Otherwise, the church becomes a stagnant pool.

Jesus says, "My dear brothers and sisters, you are thirsty. Come to me and drink. Come to me and let me fill you with this living water. Be filled with the Spirit. Let the Spirit fill your life. Let the Spirit fill your church. Allow this Spirit to flow out of you into the world. Be a people through whom the Spirit is flowing."

There is no other stream.

Today, I will...come to Jesus and drink deeply of His Spirit.

Week Sixteen
John 8–12

Cecil May, Jr.

Monday
You Shall Know the Truth

Jesus famously said, *"You will know the truth and the truth will set you free"* (John 8:32). This is a universally accepted truth. It works in virtually every realm: politically, economically and, as Jesus went on to emphasize, spiritually.

Both dictators and slave-holders know that to keep large numbers of people subservient, it is necessary to keep them ignorant. One of the first things a new dictator will do in attempting to gain absolute power is seize control of radio, television, newspapers, and other news outlets. The truth makes men free.

However, citing the statement of Jesus in that way leaves off half of what Jesus said and greatly changes its emphasis. As cited, there is one condition, "know the truth," and one promise, "be set free." The whole statement reads, *"If you abide in my word, you are truly my disciples, and you will know the truth, and the truth will set you free"* (John 8:31-32). It still has one condition, but a different one, "abide in my word." On meeting that condition, there are three promises: "you will be my disciples," "you will know the truth" and "the truth will set you free." Jesus not only stresses the value of truth, He tells us where truth is: "in His word."

Some of the Jews who heard Him did not understand the freedom of which He spoke. They answered him, *"We are offspring of Abraham and have never been enslaved to anyone. How is it that you say, 'You will become free'?"* Jesus answered them, *"Truly, truly, I say to you, everyone who commits sin is a slave to sin"* (John 8:33-34).

Throughout the gospels, the Jewish leaders reject Jesus as the Christ, because they wanted freedom from Roman rule in a physical kingdom. Jesus came to grant them freedom from sin, death and Hell in a spiritual kingdom. *"If the Son sets you free, you will be free indeed"* (John 8:36).

Today, I will...live by Jesus' words and be free indeed.

Tuesday
The Man Born Blind

Today's Scripture John 9

The man Jesus healed in John 9 is an intriguing fellow. He knows one fact: "I was blind, and now I see." He stubbornly maintains that fact.

Some questioned whether he was ever blind. His parents assured them he was. They asked. "How does he now see?" His parents declined to answer, but he said, "Jesus put mud on my eyes, and I washed, and I see." They asked, "What do you say about him, since he has opened your eyes?" He said, "He is a prophet"–that is, He speaks for God (ESV throughout, paraphrased by CMJr.).

Jesus did not keep their obscure Sabbath rules; so they said Jesus is a sinner. The formerly blind man said, "One thing I know, though I was blind, now I see." They asked him twice, "What did he do to you? How did he open your eyes?" He said, "I have told you already. Why do you want to hear it again? Do you also want to be His disciples?"

They angrily replied, "You are His disciple, but we are disciples of Moses. We know that God has spoken to Moses, but as for this man, we do not know where He comes from." The once blind man stuck to his one fact: "Why, here is the wonder: you cannot figure out where He came from, and yet He opened my eyes!"

If you cannot answer a person's arguments, attack the person. They answered him, "You were born in utter sin, and would you teach us?" And they cast him out.

Jesus found him and said, "Do you believe in the Son of Man?" Knowing that Jesus is a prophet, he answered, "You tell me who he is and I will believe." Jesus said, "It is He who is speaking to you." He said, "Lord, I believe," and he worshiped Him.

Anyone who gets up and walks out of His own grave is whoever He says He is!

Today, I will...resolutely proclaim that Jesus is risen and is my Lord.

Wednesday
The Good Shepherd

Today's Scripture John 10

In John 10 Jesus presents Himself as the Good Shepherd who, in contrast to a hireling, "lays down his life for his sheep" (10: 11–13). As "the Good Shepherd" He is the model for the work of shepherding. In the Jewish dispensation, the kings, priests and prophets were to "shepherd" God's people (Ezekiel 34). In the New Testament it is the elders to whom both the title (Ephesians 4:11) and work (Acts 20:28) are ascribed. However, preachers, teachers and other leaders/workers do some shepherding. We can all learn to do it better by observing our "chief shepherd."

He loves His sheep and is willing to lay down His life for them. The elders with whom I serve show that kind of sacrificial love for the people of our congregation. They would, I believe, if necessary, give their lives for the souls and lives of those they shepherd.

Though we do not at this time face that kind of persecution, elders today (as well as dedicated preachers and other workers) lay down their lives for the church, a few days or hours at a time. Time that could be spent with family, recreation or personal business advancement is instead spent in visiting, preparing, teaching, counseling and in meetings discussing matters that impact the church. Love is their motivation.

"I am the good shepherd. I know my own and my own know me" (10:14). A vital part of shepherding is mutual knowledge and appreciation. In large congregations elders must spend time and effort learning all under their charge in order to shepherd them.

Members should also get to know their leaders so as to have confidence in their faithfulness and to be willing to follow their leadership.

Today, I will...model my life and leadership after that of Jesus Christ, the chief shepherd.

Thursday
Jesus Wept

John 11:35 is widely known as the "shortest verse in the Bible" (Actually, it is the shortest verse in the English Bible; in the Greek text it has 14 letters; whereas I Thessalonians 5:16, "Rejoice always," has only 13).

Why did Jesus weep? He arrived in Bethany just as Lazarus, "he whom you loved" had died. It is unlikely however, that it is for the loss of friend Lazarus that Jesus cried. He knew ahead of time that Lazarus was sick. The text indicates He deliberately waited until Lazarus died so that people could see the glory of God in Jesus the Son of God.

Jesus loved Mary and Martha and their brother Lazarus. They were an important part of His ministry. He often spent time at their house. Though He knew He was about to raise Lazarus, Mary and Martha did not. He met Mary and Martha separately as He come to Bethany. Each of the sisters said exactly the same words when they saw Him: "Lord, if you had been here, my brother would not have died."

When He found Mary, Martha and other friends with them weeping, "he was deeply moved in his spirit and greatly troubled" (11:33). "Jesus wept" (11:35). I am of the conviction that Jesus was weeping because of love and empathy for those who loved Lazarus, as He did. They were sad; so He was genuinely sad with them.

I am reminded of a little girl who was befriended by an elderly couple who lived next door. One day the wife died. The girl and her mother saw the old man sitting on his porch with his head in his hands. The little girl went over to join him and sat with him for a time. Later the mother asked her what she had said to the man. "I didn't know anything to say. I just sat with him and helped him cry."

Today, I will...find someone lonely or distressed and, if possible, I will console them and help them cry.

Friday
The Triumphal Entry

When the king, the president or a governor comes to town, he (or she) is likely riding in a Cadillac limousine. Centuries ago Zechariah prophesied the coming of King Jesus to Jerusalem, not with pompous ceremony but humbly, not in a limousine (horse and chariot), but in an old Chevy (on a donkey).

Rejoice greatly, O daughter of Zion! Shout aloud, O daughter of Jerusalem! Behold, your king is coming to you; righteous and having salvation is he, humble and mounted on a donkey, on a colt, the foal of a donkey. (Zechariah 9:9)

Zachariah's prophecy is in the line of "suffering servant" prophesies of Isaiah and the Psaltery. The King is coming meek and lowly, to die for our sins, not to be victorious in a carnal war of liberation, and to be raised to reign over a spiritual kingdom, not a "kingdom of this world."

In John 12 the time of His crucifixion is at hand. Jesus makes His "triumphal entry" into Jerusalem.

The next day the large crowd that had come to the feast heard that Jesus was coming to Jerusalem. So they took branches of palm trees and went out to meet him, crying out, 'Hosanna! Blessed is he who comes in the name of the Lord, even the King of Israel!' And Jesus found a young donkey and sat on it, just as it is written, then quoting Zechariah (John 12:12–14).

A conspicuous theme of the Synoptic Gospels is Jesus trying, generally unsuccessfully, to convince both His disciples and the public that He did not come to free Israel from Roman oppression, but to die on a Roman cross. To His disciples, "Don't tell them I am the Christ" (Matthew 16:20); so the people will not raise an army. Jesus came to die on a cross for us. Whoever, then, would be His disciple, "let him deny himself and take up his cross and follow me."

Today, I will...take up my cross, find someone outcast, lonely, sick or hungry, and relieve their burden.

Week Seventeen
John 13–17

Steve Bailey

Monday
The Great Servant

In John's writing, he shares the account of The Lord's Supper. He begins by reminding the readers of the Feast of The Passover. The Passover is a much-loved feast that reminds the Jews of the Passover recorded in Exodus 12: 42-51.This feast is most certainly a "foreshadowing" of the Christians remembrance of The Lord's Supper.

In verses 1-4 John shares how the devil had entered into Judas' heart to betray Christ. This was one of the first steps in the process of Christ's death that would come as He physically died on the cross.

Jesus begins the time with His disciples by washing their feet. This of course was the ultimate act of servanthood. As Jim McGuiggan so profoundly stated, "Our Lord—He took a towel; then He washed the disciples' feet." In just a simple act, Jesus showed the entire world how to be a servant. In verses 12-20 Jesus asks the question: "Do you know what I have done to you?" He then said, I have washed your feet, you should wash others feet." He further stated a slave is not greater than his master; neither is the one who is sent greater than the One who sent him.

Jesus then gives us insight into the work of Judas. In verse18 he says so the scripture may be fulfilled. Jesus further predicts his betrayal in vs 21-27 with pin point accuracy.

Thoughts: Do I have the heart of a servant? Have I even remotely demonstrated the spirit Christ had in serving others? A cup of water given in His name? A brief visit to the grieving? A spoken or written word to give encouragement?

Today, I will...do one thing to serve someone who needs the love of Jesus who first loved me.

May God bless you today!

Tuesday
I Go and Prepare a Place

Verses 1-6 are some of the most loved passages in the entire Bible. It is filled with great hope and promise. Jesus said in the previous chapter that He was going away and the disciples could not go at the present time. Jesus then said that they would come to a place that He was preparing. This is a great promise to Christians regarding our future in heaven. Do you long for that day? There are many rooms in that mansion.

Over the years, there have been long discussions on how "Three are One" (meaning God, Jesus and The Holy Spirit), and the One (meaning the Godhead) is Three. Jesus addresses how He and The Father are One. Christ said, "If you have seen Me, you have seen The Father."

In verses 15-31 Jesus begins by stating that if we love Him, we will keep His commandments. Jesus follows with the promise that He will ask The Father to give another Helper that is the Spirit of Truth. We may ask, "Why didn't Jesus come back and remain on earth as an example for all truth?" We know He could have, but He chose to send a Helper to assist, comfort, and strengthen the disciples.

God has sent His Spirit to indwell Christians to help and comfort us. The Bible tells us in Acts 2:38ff when a person is baptized into Christ, that person receives the gift of The Holy Spirit. The NASB uses the word "Comforter" to describe The Holy Spirit. In verse 23 He will make His abode in us. Now that's comforting!

Today, I will...ask The Lord to help me to be a comfort in this world of trouble, pain and sorrow. "Thank You for leaving Your peace with us and teaching us not to be afraid. Thank You for Your Holy Spirit. In Jesus Name, Amen."

Wednesday
Jesus Is the Vine

Today's Scripture John 15

When I was a young boy one of my favorite songs was "I Am the Vine and Ye Are the Branches" written by Knowles Shaw. I love that song to this very day. The message seems simple, but in reality it has a deep message. It teaches us if we (the branches) are not attached to the vine (Christ) we do not abide in Christ.

If the vine does not bear fruit, it is to be thrown away, then dried up, and cast into the fire. These are very sobering words to hear as a child. To the adult, however; these words should give us greater pause. Are we bearing fruit? Am I living my life attached to the true source of life? How long have I been a Christian? Have I taught anyone the gospel? Have I led one soul to Jesus? Am I bearing fruit for the vinedresser, God the Father? Suddenly, a song that touched us as a child, now causes us as adults to think deeply about our purpose and mission in life.

The rest of the chapter deals with the subject of love. As Christians we are to love one another; and love so deeply that we would lay down our life for others. Jesus says in John 15:17 *"These things I command you, so that you will love one another."*

In verses 18–27 Jesus speaks of our relationship with the world. He states the world will hate us. Hate is a strong word. Jesus then gives hope and reminds us that The Helper will come from the Father.

Today, I will...pray for one person that I can teach the gospel. Today I will make it a point to not be separated from the vinedresser. I will do my best to bear precious fruit for the Savior.

Thursday
Jesus' Warning

Today we hear Jesus' warning about persecution. Early Christians were persecuted and Jesus warns them to not fall away or "stumble." The persecution may come in many forms, such as mocking, rejection, torture, or even physical death.

Today, many Christians are being persecuted in this present world. The very threat of persecution could cause us to fall away from Christ's teachings, perhaps deny Christ publically, and at the very least cause one to doubt Christ and be weakened in faith. In Matthew 5:11-12, Jesus said, *"Blessed are you when others revile you and persecute you and utter all kinds of evil against you falsely on My account. Rejoice and be glad, for your reward is great in heaven, for so they persecuted the prophets who were before you."*

There may come a time that we as Americans will suffer for our faith. The key is preparation in strengthening our faith so we can withstand the insults, the imprisonment, and the possibility of death.

We can take great comfort in The Comforter, The Holy Spirit that abides in us as faithful Christians. We may suffer for being a Christian, but God is the God of all comfort and blesses us beyond measure.

Jesus turns His attention in vs 16-33 stating that He is going away. The disciples would mourn, but could rejoice because of His resurrection. We too have great joy as we can rejoice in the resurrection day at the end of time on earth. Christians have a hope that many of the world do not have. We can rejoice in the "here and now" as well as the future. As Christians we can go and be with The Father as Jesus promised in John 14:1-6.

It is great to be a Christian!

Today, I will...be thankful for the forgiveness of sin, The Holy Spirit that dwells in me, and the blessed promise of Jesus in knowing I have a home prepared in heaven!

The Glorified Christ

Today's Scripture John 17

Today we hear Jesus make the great statement that He must be glorified. Jesus states His hour has come. He is speaking of His physical death, but now He must be glorified over this physical death and return to the Father in His former glory. Jesus existed before the creation of the world, and now is going to return to that pre-existent exalted place.

Jesus prays for the disciples that they may be kept together as one and not be divided as the world is divided. On earth the disciples were bonded together, all except Judas, the son of perdition (see John 13:18ff).

In verse 13 Jesus prays that the disciples would have joy as He had joy. But then Jesus prays for their protection against the evil one. He prays that they would be sanctified/set apart from the world as they were sent into the world to save men, and then Jesus prays for unity of the believers. God the Father and Jesus are One, and He prays that all believers will be one as well.

May God help us to be servants that pray and honor the request that Christians be one in unity and love, share in the efforts against things that divide the body of Christ, and share in evangelism efforts to preach the saving gospel to a lost world. It is truly this unity that comes from knowing and following Jesus' teachings that will unite us. May God bless us one and all in our diligent efforts.

Today, I will...be thankful for Jesus who intercedes for me as I pray. I will rejoice in knowing that Jesus has been glorified and sits at the right hand of God and prays for me. I am thankful to be a Christian.

Week Eighteen
John 18–21
Acts 1

Ed Gallagher

Monday
Not of this World

According to early reports, in AD 312 Constantine was waging a war with his rivals for the purpose of securing the Roman throne, when he experienced a vision of a cross and heard a voice saying, "In this sign, conquer." He took this vision to mean that he would achieve victory if he marched under the Christian symbol. He defeated his enemies, reigned for twenty-five more years, and legalized Christianity. However one interprets Constantine's conversion to Christianity, his rule appears little different from that of other kings of this world.

Not so in the case of Jesus, as His conversation with Pilate makes clear (John 18:33–38). Jesus confirms in this conversation that He is a king, one unlike any the world had ever seen (cf. 6:15). Like Constantine, Jesus knows that He will conquer through the cross, but his method of conquest would be much different from that of the Roman emperor. Every earthly kingdom (whether in antiquity or today) is established and sustained by violence. Certainly Peter was anticipating that Jesus was going to establish just such a kingdom, and He was ready for the fight (18:10). General George Patton said that no one ever won a war by dying for his country but by making his enemy die for his country—a true statement as applied to earthly kingdoms. If this were the kind of kingdom Jesus envisioned, then His servants would fight (18:36). But Jesus had in mind a completely different kind of kingdom, and He established his kingdom through His own death. Jesus himself is not of this world (1:1–3; 6:41–42), and neither would His kingdom be.

Jesus behaved "not of this world:" He served others (13:1–11) and sacrificed Himself on their behalf. He also expects His kingdom to be "not of this world." Have we—Christ's followers—failed to abandon our worldly lusts and behaviors? Do we still think of success and failure as defined by this world? Jesus demonstrates the other-worldly lifestyle to which He calls us, a lifestyle defined by self-sacrifice and love.

Today, I will...live not of this world.

Tuesday
Jesus' Glorification

The crucifixion of Jesus in John 19 appears as the climax of the narrative to which everything has been leading. The cross fulfills not just the story told by John but the entire story of Israel, as this moment fulfills Scriptures going back to Israel's origins (v. 36; cf. Exodus 12:46). Nay, rather, the cross fulfills the entire story of creation (John 1:1–3); everything has been pointing to this moment.

Certainly Jesus Himself was anticipating this moment. He had been telling people that He was going away and they could not follow Him (7:33–34; 8:21; cf. 14:2; 16:5; etc.). More specifically, He indicated the type of death He would die (12:33) when saying: "I, when I am lifted up from the earth, will draw all people to Myself" (v. 32). We recognize here a reference to the crucifixion, when Jesus would be literally lifted up from the earth, and Jesus used this same Greek word (hypsoō) about Himself also at 3:14 and 8:28. But almost every other time this word appears in the NT, it is translated "exalted" (cf. Matthew 11:23; 23:12; Luke 1:52; 18:14; Acts 2:33; 5:31; 2 Corinthians 11:7; James 4:10; 1 Peter 5:6). Jesus is ironically referring to His own crucifixion as the moment of His exaltation. The previous verses confirm this interpretation: at 12:23, Jesus says, "The hour has come for the Son of Man to be glorified," and the context (vv. 24–27) makes clear that He refers to His death.

The reader is thus prepared to see in the events of ch. 19 the moment of Jesus' exaltation/glorification. The crown and the robe (v. 2), the "confession" of Pilate (v. 14), the sign above His head (vv. 19–22)—all demonstrate that this act of torture and humiliation exalts and glorifies Jesus as the true king appointed by God. Followers of Jesus understand that He came to bring a new world order, and that those who are last in human terms are first in God's eyes. Our lowest moments of humility may be our greatest moments of glory.

Today, I will...seek to be last.

The Family of Jesus

Today's Scripture John 20

After Mary Magdalene recognizes the risen Jesus, He commissions her to "go to My brothers and say to them, 'I am ascending to My Father and your Father, to My God and your God'" (v. 17). Who are these "brothers"? Mary correctly interprets Jesus's statement to mean that she should go to the disciples (v. 18), but, in fact, this is the first time in the Gospel that Jesus refers to them as "brothers." Elsewhere in the Gospel, the word "brother" signifies a purely physical relationship (cf. 1:40−41; 6:8; 11:2; etc.). Before ch. 20, when the Gospel mentions the brothers of Jesus, it is the physical brothers of Jesus that are intended (2:12; 7:3, 5, 10).

Previous to this resurrection Sunday, these new "brothers" of Jesus had been labelled his "disciples" (78x in John; cf. 2:2, 12; etc.), or, less commonly, His "servants/slaves" (cf. John 13:13−16; 15:20). Jesus had announced, however, that He would no longer call them servants/slaves, but instead "I have called you friends, for all that I have heard from My Father I have made known to you" (15:13−15; cf. 11:11). Surely to be called a "friend of Jesus" is a high honor entailing a lofty position. We know how important friendship is, how precious, and most of us have friends with whom we want to share the highs and lows of life.

Usually there is no stronger bond than friendship except for family (but cf. Proverbs 18:24). Whereas friendships might last years, even decades, the family connection is even stronger. You're not friends with people you don't like, but you're always family with people you don't like. The bond goes deeper than shared affection or common interests. This bond now joins Jesus to his disciples, because through His atoning death and victorious resurrection, they have been made His brothers, and they now share with Him the same Father. Indeed, now all of those who have believed without seeing (cf. v. 29) have become a part of the family of Jesus and are rightly called His brothers and sisters (21:23).

Today, I will...live like I'm in God's family.

Thursday

Come and Have Breakfast

Today's Scripture John 21

The Gospels show Jesus serving meals to His disciples or other people on several occasions. He instituted the Lord's Supper by distributing bread and wine (Mark 14:22–25). He broke bread with the two disciples who were traveling to Emmaus (Luke 24:28–35), when Jesus "was known to them in the breaking of the bread" (v. 35). Jesus also fed thousands of people on multiple occasions (Matthew 14:13–21; 15:32–39). Such depictions of Jesus—which connect to some OT prophecies (cf. Ezekiel 34:11–16)—show Him providing for the basic needs of others.

John contains one of these feeding stories, the feeding of the 5000 (John 6:1–13), along with an additional one, not contained in the other Gospels: the story in ch. 21, where Jesus fixes breakfast for His disciples. Jesus appears here in the role of cook, serving His followers. Matthew (20:28) and Mark (10:45) both have a well-known saying in which Jesus declares Himself to be a servant, but John contains the most extensive passage on this theme. In John 13, Jesus washes the disciples' feet, explaining that He is providing an example (v. 15).

Now, after the resurrection, when He is about to ascend to the right hand of the Father, Jesus again serves His disciples. This final act of Jesus' earthly career, this last memory of the master in this final Gospel, portrays Him in the familiar posture of the servant. Before the disciples can get their enormous catch of fish to shore, Jesus already has some fish cooking and He has brought some bread (v. 9). After their fruitless night on the water (v. 3), Jesus invited them to breakfast (v. 12) and He distributed the food (v. 13). These very disciples had mostly abandoned Him in his hour of trial (Mark 14:50), or denied Him (John 18:17, 25–27), but Jesus provides, along with the fish and bread, an opportunity for reconciliation and renewed friendship. Fixing a meal for His disciples exhibits the character of Jesus and the character he hopes to instill in His followers.

Today, I will...serve someone with whom I need to be reconciled.

Friday
Testifying About Jesus

Today's Scripture Acts 1

People who played for the legendary UCLA basketball coach John Wooden love to tell stories about their former coach and talk about the lessons they learned from him. Especially his famous centers Kareem Abdul-Jabbar and Bill Walton routinely share wisdom derived from Wooden. Abdul-Jabbar has even written a book on *Coach Wooden and Me*. These men spent a few years of their young adulthood witnessing the life of a great teacher, and then they devoted a portion of their remaining lives to testifying about what they had seen and heard.

The apostles were witnesses of Jesus. They had spent a few years of their young adulthood with this great teacher, and they were now specially appointed to testify about what they had seen and heard. They had been with Jesus "beginning from the baptism of John until the day when He was taken up from us" (1:22). They were to be Jesus' "witnesses in Jerusalem, in all Judea and Samaria, and to the end of the earth" (v. 8). They particularly needed to testify about His resurrection (v. 22; cf. Luke 24:46–48). Acts stresses this role for the apostles throughout the book (2:32; 3:15; 4:33; 5:32; 10:39, 41; 13:31; 22:15; 26:16). At the beginning of this ministry, the apostles appoint a fellow apostle to take the place of Judas so that the church could begin with the full complement of twelve apostles (1:15–26), paralleling the twelve patriarchs of Israel (cf. v. 6; Luke 22:29–30).

We cannot be witnesses in the same way the apostles were, because we were not privileged to be with Jesus during the time before His ascension. But just as they were given the task of testifying to what they had seen and heard, so also we can bear witness to what God has done for us, to the positive role of the church for our families, to the hope that Christianity provides us. We can testify to God's grace in our lives.

Today, I will...testify about God's work in my life.

Week Nineteen
Acts 2-6

Russ Crosswhite

Monday
Get What They Got

Today we are looking at Acts chapter 2 which has been called "the hub of the Bible." In this chapter there are many "firsts." People are hearing the gospel message preached in its fullness for the first time and people are responding to it and becoming Christians for the first time. Also, we read of Christianity being lived out for the first time and that's what we want to focus our thoughts on today.

"So those who received his word were baptized, and there were added that day about three thousand souls. And they devoted themselves to the apostles' teaching and the fellowship, to the breaking of bread and the prayers." (Acts 2:41-42)

Those first Christians "devoted themselves." Worshipping God and living for Him was a way of life for them. They continued in the word by following the teachings of the apostles. They loved the fellowship they had among brethren of like precious faith. They remembered what Jesus had done for them as they ate the Lord's Supper on the first day of the week. Also, prayer was very important to them.

They were a committed group of folks. They were dedicated to the one who has saved them from their sins. That example should encourage us to "devote ourselves" to Him also.

A few thoughts: First, I must want to know and obey God's word. I can do that by keeping my head in the book. Second, I must treasure the sweet Christian fellowship I have with other disciples of Christ. This is something that must never be taken for granted. Third, communion with the Lord each Sunday in worship as I remember His death for my sins ought to move me to be more determined to live for Him during the upcoming week. Fourth, every day I need to make time for prayer.

Today, I will..."do what they did, so I can get what they got."

Listen to the Great Prophet

Today's Scripture Acts 3:22-23

Today we are looking at Acts 3 when Peter and John go up to the temple at the hour of prayer. Many people will be there and that might present an opportunity to teach the gospel of Christ. By the power of God, Peter heals a lame beggar and that naturally draws a lot of attention. Peter then takes advantage of the situation and teaches them about God's scheme of redemption. He tells them about Jesus and how He was put to death and was raised from the dead. After telling them what God had provided through Jesus, he then tells them about their need to respond to the Lord (vs. 19, 20).

"Moses said, 'The Lord God will raise up for you a prophet like me from your brothers. You shall listen to Him in whatever he tells you. And it shall be that every soul who does not listen to that prophet shall be destroyed from the people.'" (Acts 3:22-23)

Note that Peter pointed the people to Jesus. He told them what Jesus had done and how He was the one the prophets said was coming. Peter's messaged focused on looking to Jesus. He was that prophet like Moses and they were to listen to Him.

A few thoughts: First, we must teach the same message that Peter did. Jesus' death and resurrection is the foundation or ground of our salvation. Second, we must continue to listen to and obey Jesus after becoming a Christian. "Listen to Him in whatever He tells you" Peter declared. He "tells us" through the New Testament. So we must grow in our knowledge and application of Jesus' teachings. Third, like Peter, let's take advantage of opportunities to tell as many people as we can the gospel message of salvation.

Today, I will...listen to Jesus through the written word (New Testament) and tell someone about that great prophet.

Wednesday
We Cannot but Speak

Today's Scripture Acts 4:19-20

Today our reading is from the fourth chapter of Acts. The Lord's church is on the move. In chapter two we read about three thousand being baptized into Christ and by Acts 4:4 the text says "But many of those who had heard the word believed, and the number of the men came to about five thousand." Think about that. And that does not even count the women and young people that might have obeyed the gospel.

This draws the attention of the Jewish Council and therefore Peter and John are arrested because "they were teaching the people and proclaiming in Jesus the resurrection of the dead" (v. 2). They were challenged to explain themselves and they do so effectively. As a side note, they were simply practicing the principle that Peter would later write about in 1 Peter 3:15 by making a defense of what they believed and why they believed it.

This resulted in the Jewish rulers acknowledging the boldness of Peter and John and were amazed and "recognized that they had been with Jesus" (v. 13).

"But Peter and John answered them, 'Whether it is right in the sight of God to listen to you rather than to God, you must judge, for we cannot but speak of what we have seen and heard." (Acts 4:19-20)

A few thoughts: First, Peter and John were determined to obey God even if it cost them their lives. Following the will of God was more important to them than following the will of man. Second, they had to tell others about Jesus and the salvation He has made available through His death, burial, and resurrection. Third, they could explain what they believed and why they believed it.

Today, I will...do like Peter and John. I will obey God's word, tell others about Jesus, and explain from the Bible what I believe and why I believe it.

Thursday

In the Temple and House to House

Today's Scripture Acts 5:41-42

Today's thoughts are from Acts chapter five. Three main points can be made from this chapter. First, there is the deception of Ananias and Sapphira (vs. 1-11). Second, there is the account of the apostles performing "many signs and wonders" (vs. 12-16). Third, the apostles are arrested, beaten, and set free (vs. 17-42). For our thoughts today we want to focus on this third section.

"Then they left the presence of the council, rejoicing that they were counted worthy to suffer dishonor for the name. And every day, in the temple and from house to house, they did not cease teaching and preaching that the Christ is Jesus." (Acts 5:41-42)

Beginning in verse seventeen, we read about the apostles being arrested, threatened, beaten, and set free. On several occasions after they were freed they were told to tell others about Christ. In other words, they were to keep on keeping on telling the gospel message. For example, after their first release by an angel they were told to "Go and stand in the temple and speak to the people all the words of this Life" (v. 20). And they did that very thing (v. 21). They were accused of filling Jerusalem with their message about Jesus. When the council asked them about it they said they must "obey God rather than men" (v. 29). Then the genuineness of their faith comes forth. They rejoiced in their suffering and then went out and told everybody they could about the gospel of Jesus Christ.

A few thoughts: First, I must believe in the gospel as much as the apostles did. Second, I must look at trials as an opportunity to serve the Lord. Third, telling people about Jesus ought to be a major priority in my life.

Today, I will...be bold like they were and teach what they taught everywhere I have the opportunity so I can please the Lord like they did.

Friday
The Word of God Continued to Increase

Today our thoughts are from Acts chapter 6. Two primary things stand out from this chapter. First, seven men are chosen to serve those with physical needs. These men could very well be deacons that are functioning in an official capacity. Secondly, Stephen is seized for preaching the gospel of Christ.

"And the word of God continued to increase, and the number of the disciples multiplied greatly in Jerusalem, and a great many of the priests became obedient to the faith." (Acts 6:7)

The Hellenists, that is, Greek-speaking Jews "were being neglected in the daily distribution" (v. 1). That was a legitimate need but it was not the number one priority of the apostles. They said preaching the word of God was their main concern. The word has to be taught before people can be saved from their sins. But in order to take care of those with physical needs, seven men were chosen to help in this regard. The apostles were then able to focus on their primary work, which was prayer and teaching the word of God.

A few thoughts: First, this does not say we are not to be concerned with material needs. Second, it does teach that the spiritual welfare takes priority over physical needs. Third, when God's word is taught souls are saved. Fourth, if there is an increase in teaching God's word then there will be an increase in the number of disciples made. Fifth, there is a response on the part of the one being taught the word of God. One must be "obedient to the faith." Salvation is conditional.

Today, I will...focus on the most important work I can be engaged in and that is the teaching of God's word. If we do what they did, we'll get what they got. They sowed the "seed" of God's word and the increase came. The question I need to ask myself is "who am I going to teach the gospel to this week?"

Week Twenty
Acts 7-11

Jason Moon

Monday
A Hard Heart

Today's Scripture Acts 7:54-60

Have you ever seen a bunch of religious people get stirred up? You may be thinking about a time when there was a great response to a sermon and many were baptized or restored. You may be thinking about a time when a church was challenged by her leaders to rise to an occasion and do something great.

But in Acts 7, a bunch of religious people got stirred up for all the wrong reasons. This was not just your average group of religious people. This was the Sanhedrin Council! The Sanhedrin was supposed to be one of the most religious groups among the Jews, headed by the High Priest and patterned after the 70 elders of Israel established by the Lord under Moses (Numbers 11:16). These men were referred to as "the assembly of the elders" (Luke 22:66).

Yet, after they heard a sermon straight from God spoken through Stephen's mouth, these religious people show us the example of A HARD HEART.

A hard heart is mad (Acts 7:54). Luke says "when they heard these things they were enraged." The word "enraged" is translated as "cut to the heart" in other translations. It probably refers to being "mad" and "mentally vexed or divided." A hard heart will cause good, religious people to not hear what God plainly states. It will cause those people who know the truth to get mad when the truth confronts them and challenges them.

A hard heart is moving (Acts 7:57). Luke says "they rushed together at him." A hard heart acts impetuously. Exodus 23:2 says, "You shall not fall in with many to do evil." The NIV says, "Do not follow the crowd in doing wrong." A hard heart causes us to move quickly toward sin.

A hard heart is morally-corrupt (Acts 7:58). The law said, "You shall not murder" but these religious men, led by Saul of Tarsus "cast him out of the city and stoned him."

Today, I will...Examine my heart and challenge it to hear truth and respond with God-pleasing obedience.

Tuesday
A Searching Heart

Today's Scripture Acts 8:26-39

Let's be honest. Sometimes we question if anybody cares about spiritual things anymore. We know the Lord said to "Go into all the world" but we wonder if there's anybody left who wants to hear it.

Reality check: Even if no one shows an interest in the Gospel, we are still charged to preach it. We don't live in the days of Noah, the Judges or in Nineveh. Sure, those were times and places when nobody seemed to care anymore. But as bad as things seem to be, if we'll open our eyes we might just find "A Searching Heart."

The wonderful story of the conversion of the Ethiopian Eunuch shows us some of the things for which we should be looking:

Look for those who still value worship. The Ethiopian had travelled many miles and many days to get to Jerusalem to worship. The distance was roughly 130 miles and it would have taken about 6 days to navigate. Travel in those days was hazardous so the fact this man took going to worship in Jerusalem so seriously indicates he had "a searching heart."

Look for those who are reading their Bible. As the Eunuch travelled he was reading from Isaiah. It's encouraging to occasionally see someone reading their Bible (or maybe some other religious material). This indicates a person has a searching heart. I know of a preacher today who was converted because a Christian saw him reading his Bible and the Christian said, "Do you understand what you are reading?"

Look for those who are humble. Perhaps the most overlooked aspect of this conversion story is that the Eunuch wasn't so caught up in himself that he believed he knew it all. When Philip asked him "Do you understand what you are reading?" his response was "How can I, unless someone guides me?"

Today, I will...Remind myself there are still people searching for Jesus and I will pray to God to help me see them and share with them!

Wednesday

A Changed Heart

Today's Scripture Acts 9:1–22

It's the kind of heartwarming story that makes the headlines or evening news. A man who was filled with hate suddenly has a changed heart. But the conversion of Saul of Tarsus probably didn't make the headlines of the Jerusalem Times (at least for any celebratory reason).

Saul was a man who stood by when Stephen was stoned and oversaw a terrible persecution of early Christians. He hated Christians and wanted them eradicated. But the story in Acts 9 tells of a man who had "A Changed Heart." What made the difference?

Saul needed to meet Jesus. God took care of that when he sent Jesus to appear to him on the road to Damascus. Today, God depends on Christians to share Jesus with others.

Saul needed to know Jesus as Lord. Saul knew Jesus was a teacher and motivator of those of "the way" (those associated with first century disciples). But he needed to know Jesus was "the way" to God (John 14:6). When Saul asked, "Who are you Lord?" he needed to know that he was "Jesus," the only name associated with salvation (Acts 4:12).

Saul needed to know the plan of salvation. Jesus told Saul to "rise and enter the city, and you will be told what you are to do." Acts 9 tells us about a disciple named Ananias. He was the one commissioned to go visit with Saul and share the plan of salvation with him. Acts 22:16 says that Ananias told him, *"And now why do you wait? Rise and be baptized and wash away your sins, calling on his name."*

Saul needed to share his faith. We sometimes overlook the fact that Saul demonstrated his changed heart by sharing the good news with others. This is the only evangelistic program God ever created (Matthew 28:18–20, Mark 16:15–16, 2 Timothy 2:2).

Today, I will...Examine the conversion story of Saul and compare my life with his. I'll make sure my heart has changed according to God's revealed Word.

Thursday
A Softened Heart

Today's Scripture Acts 10:9-35

It's unimaginable that an apostle of God could have been guilty of racism. But according to Acts 10, Peter struggled to view Gentiles as his equal. But an amazing thing occurs. God shows Peter his way of thinking was not God's way of thinking.

Today, so many struggle to see others beyond their physical characteristics. Let's see how Peter transformed his thinking to God's thinking to have "A Softened Heart."

Peter needed to pray. Isn't it interesting what can happen in our lives when we pray? God knows our hearts are usually transformed by prayer. No wonder Paul would say "pray without ceasing." The transformation that takes place in Peter's life is preceded with prayer!

Peter needed to to see things differently. Sometimes what seems so clear to us can be transformed with looking at it differently. Jesus used parables to cause people to see things differently. The trance allowed Peter to see God had made all animals clean or worthy to be eaten. "What God has made clean, do not call common." His perspective was changed by seeing a side of the story he'd never considered. If you struggle with racism perhaps you should try to consider what others are seeing or saying.

Peter needed to spend some time with others. Peter was called to go to a Gentile's house to teach Jesus. While the extraordinary event of the Holy Spirit falling on them is important in this story, the fact that it took Peter going to a Gentiles house shouldn't be overlooked. The only way to truly overcome subjectivity is through objectivity. If you don't know someone or like someone, perhaps the thing you need to do is go and sit a while with them. You'll likely be reminded that it's the "human condition" that will unite you with them.

Today, I will...Try to walk in someone else's shoes. I'll try to understand how other people feel. I'll take the time to talk to someone who is not like me.

119

Friday
An Encouraging Heart

Each person needs a Paul, Timothy, and Barnabas in his/her life. You need a mentor, like Paul. You need a mentee, like Timothy. But you also will need an encourager, like Barnabas.

Barnabas is first introduced to us in Acts 4:32-37. His given name was Joseph, but the apostles started calling him Barnabas, which means son of encouragement. In Acts 4, Barnabas sold some land and gave the money to the apostles to use to take care of others.

In Acts 11, Barnabas reappears and lives up to his lofty new name. Not surprisingly, he shows us how to encourage others.

Barnabas encouraged some new Christians. After the Gospel had started to be preached to Greeks, some of them believed and turned to the Lord. When the news of this came back to Jerusalem, Barnabas was sent to them to "exhort them all to remain faithful to the Lord with steadfast purpose" (Acts 11:23). Realize that a new Christian needs encouragement. Someone needs you to be their Barnabas!

Barnabas encouraged people to become Christians. Barnabas is said to be "a good man, full of the Holy Spirit and of faith" (Acts 11:24). The verse goes on to say "And a great many people were added to the Lord." By Barnabas' very presence in Antioch, the inference is that others also became Christians. It should not surprise us the Barnabas' encouraging spirit attracted the lost to Jesus.

Barnabas encouraged a great preacher. After Barnabas left Antioch, he went to Tarsus to look for Saul. Saul had only very recently been converted and started to preach. When he found him he brought him back to Antioch and for a whole year they met with the church and taught others. I can only imagine the encouragement the new preacher of the Gospel received during that time from one of the great encouragers of the early church. Somebody needs you to encourage them in their faith today!!!

Today, I will...Be positive. I'll try to be an encourager rather than a complainer!

Week Twenty-One
Acts 12-16

Kevin Langford

Monday
The Power of Prayer

Today's Scripture Acts 12:5-15

Our text finds Peter in Prison but Luke adds the encouraging note of the church in earnest prayer for him (vs 5). The word translated "earnestly" (ektenos) means "to stretch out". This idea of earnestness comes from the motion of hands stretched out to God in fervent supplication. It also gives the impression of wholehearted, urgent pleading to God. While Peter was asleep between the two guards, the church was engaged in prayer for him.

In verses 9-11, 15; we find Peter and the church in disbelief to learn that their prayers had been answered! This came after God; through an angel, released Peter from imprisonment (Acts 12:6-8). When the servant girl, Rhoda learned of Peter's deliverance from prison she was overjoyed over the answer to their prayers. However; when Rhoda shared the good news with the number gather together, they thought she was out of her mind.

Within these verses, we are given a powerful example of community prayer. When believers come together to petition our Father, powerful things can occur. It is true that we do not always receive the answers we ask for (cf. the contrast between James's death in Acts 12:1-2 and Peter's release), but the Bible is clear that, "the prayer of a righteous man is powerful and effective" (James 5:16).

A few thoughts: First, when was the last time you gathered with fellow believers to petition God to provide safety for a fellow brother or sister in Christ? Secondly, are you more like Rhoda or those gathered in the house when God demonstrates his power within the lives of others? Thirdly, prayer has the ability to change things. Prayer may not change the outcome of the situation to be what we want, but it does change us. We are strengthened and comforted in our walk with God when we pray.

Today, I will...consider ways the Lord has accomplished His will and not diminish His ability to work within my life.

Tuesday
Sending Missionaries

One of the greatest needs in the world today is the sending of missionaries to help in our commission to spread the gospel of Jesus Christ. In today's reading, we have some simple, yet powerful truths given to us to aid us in our mission efforts.

Luke lists five of the outstanding teachers of the church in Antioch. They are probably listed in the order of their importance, as this was the Jewish custom (13:1). It is significant that the church in Antioch had such a culturally diverse leadership in keeping with the diversity of the population of the city.

The Holy Spirit sent a message probably to one of the other prophets who relayed the message to Barnabas, Saul, and the church "while they were worshiping the Lord and fasting" (13:2). The church's prayer was accompanied by fasting, both when the church received the message and when they sent off the missionary team (13:2-3).

The sending-off ceremony included the laying on of hands which was for the purpose of separating them as they had been commanded to do. Here, this action was not to receive spiritual gifts for only the apostles could do this (Acts 8:14-19). It was not to ordain them. There is no divine command for ordination and these men had served as preachers and teachers for quite some time. It was simply a method of commending a man to God for the work God had already commissioned him to do.

A few thoughts: First, notice the message the church received was to release their best preachers and teachers for missionary service (13:2) and they were willing to do so. This is a trait that effective churches with missionary vision do and maintain. Secondly, clarity for missions and ministry often occur when we practice spiritual discipline. Through disciplines such as prayer and fasting, we become more attune with what is occurring in the mission field.

Today, I will...Spend time in prayer and fasting for our mission efforts (Domestic and Foreign).

Responding to Opposition

As Paul and Barnabas arrive in Iconium, they went to the synagogue to preach. A great multitude of Jews and Gentiles believed (became Christians) (vs. 1). Sadly, a group of disobedient Jews stirred up the souls of the unbelieving Gentiles against the Christians. (vs. 2)

Luke does not state how long they stayed (vs. 3) but does convey that they were opposed but not to the point they needed to leave the city. Paul and Barnabas spoke boldly, meaning they were not going to be intimidated by those who opposed them. God blessed them with the ability to do many signs and wonders, thus, confirming their message was from God. However, the city was still divided (vs. 4).

As tension mounted, a mob formed and began looking for Paul and Barnabas. They were thinking of insulting them and stoning them (vs. 5). These men were warned of the pending danger and left the city in a hurry. They traveled some forty miles to the surrounding cities who had synagogues so they could continue to preach the gospel (vs. 6-7).

A few thoughts: First, just as this community was divided over the gospel (vs 4), communities today can also be divided when we share the gospel with them (Matthew 10:34). Secondly, A mob can be swayed from adoration to contempt in a short time (vs. 11-19). Another example took place in Jerusalem when the crowd worshipped Jesus as the king (Luke 19:37-38) then shouted, "Crucify Him!" less than a week later. Thirdly, although Paul and Barnabas "spent considerable time there speaking boldly for the Lord" (vs. 3), there was a time for them to take evasive action by fleeing from this place of danger (vs. 6, 20). Though Paul left Lystra, we know the church survived when he visited them on his way back and during future missionary journeys (14:21; 16:1). While boldness is a prerequisite for evangelism; wisdom may suggest we flee from a harmful situation.

Today, I will...Choose to be gentle in the face of opposition while boldly proclaiming His truth.

Thursday
Opposing False Teaching

Today's Scripture Acts 15:1-21

As Paul and Barnabas returned from their first missionary journey, they preached in Antioch. While there, brethren came down from Judea teaching the Gentiles had to be circumcised in addition to obeying the gospel (vs. 1). Paul and Barnabas refuted this claim but were opposed by some former Pharisees who had become Christians (vs. 5).

The apostles and elders met together (vs. 4). Peter reminds them how God had opened doors to the Gentiles and that they should not bind the law of Moses on these Gentile believers (vs. 7-11). James shared how the Old Testament prophets declared the gospel was to go to the Gentiles. He concluded they should stay away from idols, fornication, and things strangled and from eating blood. The apostles and elders accepted this recommendation (vs. 13-20).

A few thoughts: First, we live in a time of pluralism in which we can agree to disagree and everything will be ok. Yet in this passage false teaching was not tolerated. God is not the author of confusion (1 Corinthians 14:33). He has given us His definite and eternal word of truth though the Word (John 17:17). All believers are to contend for the truth (Jude 3,4). Any teaching contrary to what the Scriptures clearly state must be debunked and removed with urgency. Secondly, when opposition occurs, the Word of God must be the sole source for authority. Too many times, when a disagreement arises you will hear the statement, "Well, I feel..." followed by the person's position.

Paul makes it clear in 2 Timothy 3:16-17 that our source for authority is to be the Word alone. For within it, we do not have the imagination of men but words men wrote as they were carried along by the Holy Spirit (2 Peter 1:20-21). Thirdly, it can be difficult to confront doctrinal error. Because of our love for God and His church, we must be willing to confront error and pay the price of it.

Today, I will...Strive to be like the Bereans by examining the Scriptures daily to see if what I am being taught is true (Acts 17:11).

Friday
A Response to Suffering

Today's Scripture Acts 16:25-29

Strange sounds could be heard throughout the prison as evening came. There were curses and vile language to accompany the familiar tones of weeping and gnashing of teeth. Yet, through all of the cries of despair a new sound could be heard from God's two missionaries, Paul and Silas. No doubt, the emotions of these men were affected by the pain, humiliation, and injustice they had experienced yet they resorted to a time-tested method of responding to suffering by lifting their voices in praise to God and the prisoners heard them. Paul and Silas knew the Lord was with them and the joy of the Lord burst forth in these songs in the night.

Numerous psalms have been written from the hearts of men experiencing the depths of despair (Psalm 27, 42, 43). James wrote, "Is anyone among you suffering? Let him pray. Is anyone cheerful? Let him sing songs of praise" (5:13). Singing helps us focus on the eternal which may be clouded by our temporary reality.

Singing psalms, hymns, and spiritual songs help us when we cannot produce words on our own, to utilize the words written by others. Consider a time when you were down, what song came to your mind to help convey the heartache and despair you were experiencing?

While these men were worshipping, the doors were opened; the bonds of the prisoners were loosened and these men were set free. A note of interest; a Roman prison was often built in excavations in a rocky hillside. This was a district where earthquakes were by no means uncommon. The door was locked by a wooden bar falling into two slots, and the stockers were fastened. The earthquake shook the bar free and the prisoners were freed from their chains as the door was open.

A few thoughts: First, no matter where you are; the Lord and Jesus Christ is always with you. Secondly, instead of complaining, cursing their captors, and planning their vengeance, they worshipped God.

Today, I will...Realize that I am never alone, that when times get tough, I will choose to glorify the name of Jesus through songs of praise.

Week Twenty-Two
Acts 17–21

Keith Parker

Monday

Turn or Burn

Today's Scripture Acts 17:30-34

The title of this chapter is not encouraging. It's not pleasant or positive. In fact, it's not a title that I like or that fits my nature. But it is a title that tells the truth. Turn or burn. Repent or perish.

The apostle Paul put it in these words in Acts 17:30: "The times of ignorance God overlooked, but now he commands all people everywhere to repent." Jesus put it in these words: "But unless you repent, you will all likewise perish" (Luke 13:5). What is Jesus saying? Repent or perish. Turn or burn. Change, sinner, change!

And it's not easy to change, is it? Just look at where you sit in church. Most of us sit in the same pew Sunday after Sunday. We have our favorite "spots" in church. We feel comfortable in "our place." The sad thing about it is, some of us feel comfortable in our sins. Perhaps it's a habit that we have had for years—cursing, lying, cheating, stealing, or adultery. Maybe it's the harsh and unpleasant way that we treat a family member or a co-worker. Perhaps it's a sin of the heart—envy, jealousy, lust, greed, or racial prejudice. It's hard to give up old habits, isn't it? It's difficult to turn from something that we've been doing for years. But God commands (not suggests) all of us to change.

How did the people of Athens respond to Paul's preaching? Acts 17:32-34 says that some laughed (sneered or mocked). Some lingered (waited or hesitated). And some loved the message (believed or obeyed). Jesus said, "If you love Me, you will keep My commandments" (John 14:15). And one of these commandments is to repent.

How will you respond?

Today, I will...acknowledge one thing in my life that I need to change, confess it to God and start in a different direction than I have been going.

What Must I Do To Be Saved?

Today's Scripture Acts 18:5-11

If you were to ask ten different preachers what a sinner must do to be saved, you perhaps would get ten different answers. One preacher might say, "Just ask Jesus to come into your heart." Another preacher might say, "Trust in the Lord and turn from your sins." Another preacher might say, "A sinner doesn't have to do anything because God does it all." And on and on the answers go.

Let's look at scripture. Let's see what the Corinthians did to be saved. Paul went to Corinth and reasoned in the synagogue with the Jews and Greeks. *"Crispus, the ruler of the synagogue, believed in the Lord, together with his entire household. And many of the Corinthians hearing Paul believed and were baptized"* (Acts 18:8)

Observe what Crispus did: "He believed in the Lord." What does that mean? Keep reading. The first part of Acts 18:8 is explained in the last part of Acts 18:8: *"And many of the Corinthians hearing Paul believed and were baptized."* Crispus did what the Corinthians did and the Corinthians did what Crispus did. Crispus (and the other Corinthians) believed in the Lord. What does that mean? First, they heard the message of the Lord. Second, they trusted the message of the Lord. And, third, they obeyed the message of the Lord by being baptized. In other words, they did what Jesus said in Mark 16:16: *"Whoever believes and is baptized will be saved, but whoever does not believe will be condemned."*

The truth of God is often in conflict with what men (including preachers) say. But Jesus said that the truth will set us free (John 8:32). Seek truth. Study truth. Obey truth. If we walk in harmony with the truth of God, God says to us as he said to Paul, "Do not be afraid, but go on speaking and do not be silent, for I am with you..." (Acts 18:9-10).

Today, I will...examine "my salvation story" and see if it is in harmony with the truth of God.

Wonderful Words of Life

Today's Scripture Acts 19:1–10, 20

"So the word of the Lord continued to increase and prevail mightily" (Acts 19:20). Is God's word increasing and prevailing mightily in your life?

First, have you been listening to God's word? That's how faith comes. Faith comes by hearing the word of God (Romans 10:17). Paul preached in Ephesus for over two years. The result? "All the residents of Asia heard the word of the Lord, both Jews and Greeks" (Acts 19:10). Have you heard God's voice today? Are you like the people of Berea? Have you received the word of God eagerly and are you searching the scriptures daily (Acts 17:11)?

Second, are you living God's word? When the twelve disciples in Ephesus heard the truth about baptism, notice how they responded: "On hearing this, they were baptized in the name of the Lord Jesus" (Acts 19:5). They didn't just brag on the sermon. They didn't just hear the message, shake the preacher's hand and say, "I enjoyed the sermon." They did something about it. They put the message in their lives. They did what wise people do: listen and obey (Matthew 7:24).

Third, are you leaving the word of God with others? Are you sharing his message? Have you told anyone about the Lord lately? Paul did. "And he entered the synagogue and for three months spoke boldly, reasoning and persuading them about the kingdom of God" (Acts 19:8).

The B–I–B–L–E: Basic Information Before Leaving Earth. Let's be "people of the book." Let's listen to it, live it and leave it with others. *"I have stored up Your word in my heart, that I might not sin against You"* (Psalm 119:11).

Today, I will...memorize one verse from the Bible and apply it to my life.

The 20/20 Vision of the Church

Today's Scripture Acts 20:20

What is the purpose of the church? Why do we exist? We live for one reason: to bring glory to God. We exist to "fear God and keep his commandments, for this is the whole duty of man" (Ecclesiastes 12:13).

One of the primary ways that we make God happy is by bringing others to him. How do we do that? By teaching and preaching God's word. In Acts 20:20 Paul said to the elders of the church of Christ at Ephesus, "I did not shrink from declaring to you anything that was profitable, and teaching you in public and from house to house." And that, my friend, is the 20/20 vision of the church. If the church is going to see spiritually and grow numerically, we must teach people privately and in public.

First, we must teach people in public. Paul did at Ephesus. "Therefore be alert, remembering that for three years I did not cease night or day to admonish everyone with tears" (Acts 20:31). Paul went about "proclaiming the kingdom" (Acts 20:25) and "testifying both to Jews and Greeks of repentance toward God and of faith in our Lord Jesus Christ" (Acts 20:21). There's still a place for gospel preaching. There's still a need for gospel meetings and city-wide revivals. When was the last time that a preacher came to your city and "preached Jesus and him crucified?"

Second, we must teach people privately. Most of our teaching and preaching are done at the church building. I have an idea: Go to someone's home. Invite someone to your home. Have someone over for dinner and a Bible study. Baptize a sinner on a Monday night or Thursday afternoon after you have studied one-on-one with him. Do what the apostles did: "And every day, in the temple and from house to house, they did not cease teaching and preaching Jesus as Christ" (Acts 5:42).

Today, I will...think about one sinner who needs to be saved, pray for him and invite him to my house for a Bible study.

The Power of Prayer

Today's Scripture Acts 21:5

Most of us have memorized our favorite phone numbers. Those that we haven't memorized, we have stored in our phones. Do you realize that God has a phone number? Have you memorized God's number? It's easy. God's number is 3-3-3. In Jeremiah 33:3 God said, "Call to me and I will answer you."

The apostle Paul called to God in the city of Tyre. "When our days there were ended, we departed and went on our journey, and they all, with wives and children, accompanied us until we were outside the city. And kneeling down on the beach, we prayed." First, observe the people. The disciples of Tyre with their wives and children joined Paul and Luke (the writer of Acts) for prayer. One of the best things that we can do with our mates and children is to pray. Families that pray together, stay together.

Second, observe the place. They were on a beach "outside the city." They were secluded, away from the crowds and the noise. Jesus talked about the importance of the place when he said, "But when you pray, go into your room and shut the door and pray to your Father who is in secret" (Matthew 6:6). Do you have a favorite prayer-place?

Third, observe the position. The disciples knelt to pray. There is something special about someone who bows his body in conjunction with his heart. Paul penned, "For this reason I bow my knees before the Father" (Ephesians 3:14). With the elders of Ephesus, "he knelt down and prayed with them all" (Acts 20:36). Have you knelt before the King this week?

Fourth, observe the performance or action. Luke simply says, "We prayed." Why pray? "The prayer of a righteous person has great power" (James 5:16). Call to God. Why? He answers.

Today, I will...go to a secret place, get down on my knees and pray.

Week Twenty-Three
Acts 22-26

James Hayes

What Is Your Story?

Years ago I was teaching a group of young men the basics of preaching. Many of them had not yet overcome their fear of public speaking, so I asked one of them who his favorite baseball team was. He said it was the Braves. "Fine," I said. "Stand up here and talk to us for five minutes about the Braves."

"But I haven't prepared anything," he said.

"That's okay," I said. "You don't need to prepare. You've watched their games all year. You know all the players. You know their stats. You could probably talk about the Braves for an hour. I just want five minutes."

It was easy for the apostle Paul to explain the events of his conversion. It was a dramatic event, for sure, but it was also personal. He lived it. He felt it. It was the most important event of his life, so it was easy for him to share that story.

All of us have a story to tell. You can tell anyone about the day you decided to obey the gospel and be baptized for the forgiveness of your sins. You know who baptized you. You know what the weather was like. You know how you felt when you came out of the water. More importantly, you know how it changed your life. You know the feeling of conversion and repentance. What may seem like an ordinary story to you might be a dramatic, awe-inspiring story to someone else.

Evangelism does not require a Ph.D. in Biblical Studies or a Masters degree in communication. Evangelism is simply sharing the good news of Jesus with those around you. Your story is not like the apostle Paul's, but it does not have to be. It is your story, and the world is waiting to hear it.

"Oh give thanks to the Lord; call upon His name; make known His deeds among the peoples!" (Psalm 105:1)

Today, I will...share my conversion experience with one person.

Tuesday
The Anonymous Faithful

Hebrews 11 is one of my favorite chapters. It begins with a definition of faith and then lists hero after hero from the Old Testament who did mighty things "by faith." Most of those names are familiar: Noah, Abraham, Moses, and Joseph. But then the Hebrew writer stops naming names and starts focusing on the deeds. He writes about people who were stoned and sawn in two. Some lived in caves. Others were destitute. They endured the world's worst treatment for the sake of faith. I call these people "The Anonymous Faithful." We do not know their names, but we know their faith.

In Acts 23, we encounter another anonymous faithful person. He is Paul's nephew. After Paul defended himself before the Sanhedrin, the Jewish ruling council, about forty men plotted to kill him. Paul's sister's son heard about the ambush and immediately told his uncle. Paul informed the commanders about the conspiracy and Paul was later moved to Caesarea.

What was Paul's nephew's name? We do not know. But we do not need to know. All we should know is that Paul's nephew saw an opportunity to help his uncle, and he took it. Surely he figured that his own safety might be compromised by informing on the conspirators, but that did not matter: He simply did what was right.

Every day you are presented with opportunities to do the right thing. Those seemingly ordinary acts will not get your name on the evening news, but it might change someone else's life forever. It has been said that Christians are God's hands and feet on earth. We are the tools He uses to carry out His will. To neglect those opportunities is to sin—we miss the mark of service. And we miss the lesson of the Good Samaritan.

"So whoever knows the right thing to do and fails to do it, for him it is sin." (James 4:17)

Today, I will...call a shut-in and give them a word of encouragement.

Wednesday
I'll Do It Later

Mark Twain once said, "Never put off till tomorrow what may be done day after tomorrow just as well." As funny as that is, it seems to be the motto of many people. Everything is pushed to the future. They'll save money after the kids are grown. They'll change the oil in the car after they drive another 1,000 miles. They'll clean the garage next week. And so on. Putting off worldly tasks is one thing, but delaying obedience to God could have eternal consequences.

Paul was in Caesarea defending himself before a governor named Felix when an interesting exchange took place. Paul preached boldly about righteousness, self-control, and judgment to come. Felix responded with a 21st century-type answer: "Go away for the present. When I get an opportunity I will summon you" (v. 25). The text also teaches us that Felix was hoping Paul would offer him a bribe, which shows how corrupt Felix's heart was. Paul stayed in Caesarea two more years, but we are not told if Felix was ever converted.

As you evangelize, you should share the gospel with a sense of urgency. You have heard the phrase, "Almost saved is completely lost," and it is true. The sinner cannot be made to think that obedience is optional. You should not mold the gospel into a take-it-or-leave-it, "It doesn't really matter," politically correct fable. The word must be presented as powerfully as it is revealed (Hebrews 4:12).

Jesus taught us to seek first the kingdom of God (Matthew 6:33). His will should be your first priority every day. You should think good things so that you will do good things. Your light should never go out. Procrastination is not a fruit of the Spirit. This is the day the Lord has made, and you should not only rejoice in it, but you should also use this day to grow closer to the likeness of His Son.

Today, I will...pray for three friends who are not Christians.

Thursday
Defend Yourself

When Samuel was considering David to be the next king of Israel, he said, *"For the Lord sees not as man sees: man looks on the outward appearance, but the Lord looks on the heart."* (I Samuel 16:7)

So God is the only other person who really knows you. Your mother probably claims she knows you better than you know yourself, and that's true; but she does not know you better than God does. Therefore, your friends and family only know so much about you. They do not know everything. They can only judge your actions (your fruit), but they cannot judge your intentions with 100 percent certainty.

So, at times you must defend yourself. You must speak up. If you are being falsely accused, it is not a sin to say, "I did not do it." And you should do it without being defensive—there is a difference. You can see the difference in Paul's statements to Festus.

After defending himself to a Jewish mob, the Jewish Sanhedrin, and Felix, Paul defended himself to Festus, Felix's successor. Paul claimed that he had done nothing wrong to the Jews, and then stated, "If then I am a wrongdoer and have committed anything for which I deserve to die, I do not seek to escape death. But if there is nothing to their charges against me, no one can give me up to them. I appeal to Caesar" (v.11). Paul did not rant and rave—he was not defensive. But he also did not wilt in the face of powerful men. He simply told the truth and submitted himself to the government of the land.

Someone once said, "You are never as bad as people say you are, and you are never as good as people say you are." Since that is true most of the time, you must be sure that the people around you know the truth. Never bear false witness, especially of yourself.

Today, I will...be sure I speak the truth about myself.

Friday
Best Wishes

Maybe the most challenging command Jesus ever gave was, "But I say to you, love your enemies and pray for those who persecute you" (Matthew 6:44). To love someone is to want the best for them. When you love your spouse, you want to do whatever it takes to make his/her life better. The same goes for your children, friends, and fellow Christians. But do you always want what is best for your enemies? After all, they are your enemies—the word itself means you are at odds with them. But Jesus commanded us to disregard our feelings and choose to love all people.

After Paul presented the gospel to King Agrippa, the king said, "In a short time would you persuade me to be a Christian?" (v. 28). Keep in mind, the king is not Paul's friend in any way. He is just the next Roman official Paul must confront in the judicial process. So how would you respond to Agrippa? Would you say, "I don't care if you become a Christian or not." Would you say, "Are you stupid? What more do I need to say? Why haven't you already been persuaded?" Paul did not respond that way. He said, "Whether long or short, I would to God that not only you but also all who hear me this day might become such as I am—except for these chains" (v. 29).

What a statement of love! Paul said that no matter how long it took, he wanted Agrippa to be like him in all the good ways. He did not want Agrippa to be in chains. He did not wish any harm to come to Agrippa. He just wanted him to be saved.

How do you think of your enemies? Do you want them to be punished? Do you want them to hurt? Do you want revenge? Or do you want them to be faithful? Do you pray for them? Do you love them?

"Do not be overcome by evil, but overcome evil with good." (Romans 12:21)

Today, I will...seek to repair a broken relationship.

Week Twenty-Four
Acts 27-28
Romans 1-3

Tim Gunnells

Monday
Forsaken Advice

Today's devotional could have been entitled: A Sail, A Storm, and A Shipwreck. However, we will boil it down to one principle to consider.

What should I do when someone forsakes sound spiritual advice and ends up suffering the consequences? Do I say, "I told you so!" and leave the person to suffer. Do I pretend like nothing happened and enable them to keep making poor choices? Do I ignore them? When certain people scorned Paul's advice and wound up in a storm that left them in grave danger, Paul did not simply say, "I told you so!" He did not enable them to continue to make poor choices. Nor did he ignore their pleas. Let's pick up the text to see what he did.

"Since they had been without food for a long time, Paul stood up among them and said, 'Men, you should have listened to me and not have set sail from Crete and incurred this injury and loss. Yet now I urge you to take heart, for there will be no loss of life among you, but only of the ship. For this very night there stood before me an angel of the God to whom I belong and whom I worship, and he said, 'Do not be afraid, Paul; you must stand before Caesar. And behold, God has granted you all those who sail with you.' So take heart, men, for I have faith in God that it will be exactly as I have been told. But we must run aground on some island." (Acts 27:21-26)

The situation was dire, but Paul knew that God was still involved. When people don't heed sound spiritual advice there are consequences. However, to simply repudiate them, enable them, or ignore them is not right. Like Paul, we help them see their mistakes and learn from them while helping them to move forward.

Today, I will...consider how to help someone to overcome their mistakes.

Tuesday
Giving and Receiving Help

In Acts 27, Paul and his companions are in a ship that runs aground. In Acts 28, they go ashore on the island to seek solace and shelter, and to regroup. They find themselves both giving and receiving help from the people of the island. There are principles at work here that we should seek to emulate. Luke records how Paul handled himself among a strange people who did not know the Lord.

"Now in the neighborhood of that place were lands belonging to the chief man of the island, named Publius, who received us and entertained us hospitably for three days. It happened that the father of Publius lay sick with fever and dysentery. And Paul visited him and prayed, and putting his hands on him, healed him. And when this had taken place, the rest of the people on the island who had diseases also came and were cured. They also honored us greatly, and when we were about to sail, they put on board whatever we needed." (Acts 28:7-10)

While we cannot heal people of their diseases like Paul, we can help people in need. We often find ourselves among people who are very different than us religiously, racially, or philosophically. What do we do in these situations? Do we ignore their needs? Do we start preaching to them right away and try to "straighten them out?" Paul did neither of these things. Instead, he offered the aid that he was able to provide, and he received the aid he needed.

We are quick to dismiss those who are different. We ignore their needs and shun their offers for help. We put up roadblocks instead of building bridges. Becoming involved in the lives of people who are different will help us to grow and will also make roadways for the Gospel of Jesus to be spread.

Today, I will...look for ways to help someone who is different than me and be open to receiving help from them in return.

Wednesday
The Power of God for Salvation

Romans 1 is full of important spiritual truths. Some of those truths are positive, and some are negative. Some are about God's power to save and humankind's right way to live. Some are about humankind's foolish choices where God is denied and humanity is elevated, thus bringing about sin and death. When the chapter is weighed, the gospel remains the shining bright point, and to that point of light we must turn our eyes.

"For I am not ashamed of the gospel, for it is the power of God for salvation to everyone who believes, to the Jew first and also to the Greek. For in it the righteousness of God is revealed from faith for faith, as it is written, 'The righteous shall live by faith.'" (Romans 1:16-17)

In Romans 1, Paul contrasts things that are shameful to that which is the opposite of shame: the gospel. How so? We make sinful choices that alienate us from God and lead to our spiritual (and sometimes emotional, mental, or physical) demise. God made another choice. God chose to provide a way of salvation for us. Salvation that we did not deserve, that we did not earn, and that we did not create. The salvation is from our own foolish choices and for our own best interest. It originates from the heart and mind of God, and it is by His power. It is His righteousness in contrast to my unrighteousness, yet I have an ongoing decision to make and an ongoing path to take: the path of faith.

Paul is very clear that "The righteous shall live by faith." Put another way, the one who lives by faith will be righteous and live. We make the choice not once, but daily, to walk in the way of faith with the Father and live in the light of the gospel given to us by His Son.

Today, I will...decide if I am ashamed of the gospel or if I am thankful for my salvation.

Thursday
Patience in Well-Doing

Today's Scripture Romans 2:6-10

When Peter, in 2 Peter 3:16-17, says that the Apostle Paul wrote some things that are hard to understand, he was probably talking about Romans. Much of Romans 2 must be read and reread. Certainly much of it pertained to the Jewish believers at Rome but many of the things of which Paul writes are meaningful and important for us. Consider our text in Romans 2:6-10.

"He will render to each one according to his works: to those who by patience in well-doing seek for glory and honor and immortality, he will give eternal life; but for those who are self-seeking and do not obey the truth, but obey unrighteousness, there will be wrath and fury. There will be tribulation and distress for every human being who does evil, the Jew first and also the Greek, but glory and honor and peace for everyone who does good, the Jew first and also the Greek." (Romans 2:6-10)

If I am being open and honest, I sometimes get weary of always, in every single circumstance, trying to seek God's will above my own. My experience tells me that I am not alone and that you are like me in this regard. Always humble, always serving, always seeking the needs of others above your own is not easy but it is right. I do not mean acting in a codependent way that is unhealthy, but in a spiritual way this is unselfish and humble. Paul speaks of those "who by patience in well-doing....he will give eternal life." On the other hand, the "self-seeking" and disobedient will feel God's "wrath and fury."

God promises good things to those who are patient in well-doing. In Galatians 5, Paul gives credit to the Holy Spirit for producing fruit in us that is extraordinary. Doing the right things that bring glory and honor to God and that demonstrate love for other people is not always easy, and often requires sacrifice, but it is worth it.

Today, I will...ask God to help me to be patient in well-doing.

Friday
The Righteousness of God Through Faith

Today's Scripture Romans 3:21-26

In Romans 1, Paul says he is not ashamed of the gospel and in this passage he gives us a better understanding of the gospel and of its magnificent power. Sin, grace, redemption, righteousness, and faith are all on display in today's text.

"But now the righteousness of God has been manifested apart from the law, although the Law and the Prophets bear witness to it—the righteousness of God through faith in Jesus Christ for all who believe. For there is no distinction: for all have sinned and fall short of the glory of God, and are justified by his grace as a gift, through the redemption that is in Christ Jesus, whom God put forward as a propitiation by his blood, to be received by faith. This was to show God's righteousness, because in his divine forbearance he had passed over former sins. It was to show his righteousness at the present time, so that he might be just and the justifier of the one who has faith in Jesus." (Romans 3:21-26)

The Law given through Moses cannot deliver the righteousness of God to humankind. The righteousness of God can only come through faith in Jesus Christ. There is no person who is righteous apart from Jesus Christ. Jesus Christ was put forth by God as the only way to satisfy the penalty that sin requires (propitiation literally means satisfaction). We can be the recipients of God's grace through faith. God is the just one. We do not have it within us, by our own actions, to be just or righteous. So the power of the gospel steps in and we can be redeemed.

I am not good. I fall short of God's glory. Jesus, the glorified One, provides a way for me to be good in God's eyes and be glorified with Him.

Today, I will...praise God for the salvation that comes through Jesus Christ.

Week Twenty-Five
Romans 4-8

Barry Throneberry

Monday
Our Spiritual Father

When we think of forefathers, we often think of the great leaders who shaped significant portions of history: the Washington's and Lincoln's of America's past, the Plato's and Aristotle's of Western thought, or the Peter's and Paul's of the church in the New Testament. In Romans 4 the apostle Paul takes us to the spiritual forefather of the faithful, Abraham.

The church in Rome was struggling with incorporating Jewish and Gentile believers. Paul begins his great letter by reminding both the Jews and Gentiles that all are in sin apart from Christ (Romans 1:18-3:20). However, even the sinfulness of man cannot overcome the grace of God (3:21-26). Jesus was sent to earth and died to secure our justification, or right standing, before God. Abraham stands as Paul's model of how both the Jews and Gentiles find salvation. What he displayed, when he received the promise of an heir, stands as the exact thing that secures justification for both Jew and Gentile alike.

What Abraham displayed was faith in God's promises (Genesis 15:1-6). Faith, or belief (they come from the same Greek word), is at the heart of what makes one right with God. Abraham had faith that God would keep his promise to give him and Sarai an heir, even in their old age. This faith "was counted to him as righteousness" (Romans 4:22). Before circumcision was commanded (Genesis 17) or the Law of Moses was given on Sinai (observance of both was a requirement for Jews), Abraham displayed faith in the promises of God and that is what made him right with God. Jews and Gentiles believed God like Abraham believed, and it is belief in Jesus' death and resurrection that makes us right with God today (Romans 4:24-25).

Today, I will...remember that Abraham's faith secured the promises of God and that my faith does the same. While we will see what all being made right with God entails in the coming chapters, it is faith in Jesus and what he has done that makes us right.

Tuesday

We Are at Peace

There is something beautiful about a bridge. The engineering and construction are fascinating when you study them, and the fact that they connect what was previously unconnected stands as a great metaphor for many things. Paul, in Romans 5:1–11, seems to be writing a bridge text connecting the first four chapters with the next four. It also contains themes that Paul will explore further in Romans 5:12–8:39. The one I want us to focus on in this devotional is peace.

After explaining that we are all in sin and that it is faith that makes us right with God (Romans 1–4), Paul tells us that this right standing gives us peace with God. Being at peace with God stands at the beginning and end of our text (5:1, 11). The theological word Paul uses in 5:11 is reconciliation, which means a removal of hostilities between two parties or to make peace. It is the death of Jesus that makes this reconciliation a reality—the death of Jesus.

It is hard to overstate the importance of Romans 5:6–8. There Paul paints a picture of the love that God has for us as it is displayed in the death of Jesus. It is his death on the cross that makes peace with God a reality. It is the bridge humanity needed to gain access to God. The death of Jesus reaches out to those who do not deserve God's love (sinners and enemies, 5:8, 10), and it saves them from the wrath of God that they deserve (5:9). In one text Paul includes the love of God, grace, justification, reconciliation, and salvation. All of this is seen in Jesus' death on a Roman cross. It stands as the bridge between God and sinful mankind.

Today, I will...thank God for the death of Jesus. While I used to be an enemy of God because of my sin, I will rejoice that I am at peace with God because of his love for me.

147

Dead to Sin, Alive to God

Today's Scripture Romans 6:1-11

Christianity has as its heart the death, burial, and resurrection of Jesus. Jesus came from heaven to live and die only to be raised to life (Mark 10:45; 8:31). Paul tells us in today's text that baptism, or immersion in water, is the act of faith that unites us to the death, burial, and resurrection of Jesus (Romans 6:3-4). For Paul and the early church, faith culminating in baptism marks the time where our sins are forgiven (Acts 2:38) and we are joined to Jesus Christ (Galatians 3:26-27). It is a physical picture and daily reminder that we have died to sin and have been raised to live a new life in Christ.

This new life is to be seen in how we live today. This is Paul's point in Romans 6:5-11. Paul tells us that if we have died with Christ (6:5), then we are set free from sin and we are called to live for God (6:6-11). He goes so far as to use the language of slavery—we were slaves to sin and now we ought to be slaves to God. We used to live under the domain and power of sin, now we ought to live under the banner of grace and obedience to God. Paul reminds us that what matters is not only what we believe (which he has taught in Romans 3:21-6:2), but also how we live. Our Christian baptism is to manifest itself in a new life of obedience.

However, it is not looking back to Christ's death, burial, and resurrection alone that Paul wants to use as motivation for our obedience. He always reminds us that we live in light of our coming resurrection (6:5, 8). Paul speaks of our resurrection in the future tense. Yet this great future event is also to be lived out now!

Today, I will...look at the reality of the death, burial, and resurrection of Jesus. I will use its past reality to realize I am a slave to God and I will live now in light of the coming resurrection of believers.

Thursday
The Life of Sin

Today's Scripture Romans 7:7-25

Today's text is one that has puzzled many believers since it was written. Paul is trying to unite the Romans church by telling them that all have been made right by the love of God seen in the work of Jesus Christ on the cross. In Romans 7 he goes back to the theme of Romans 1:18-3:20, Sin. Here he is talking about the power of sin. How can a man who wrote Galatians 1:14 and Philippians 3:4-6 write Romans 7:7-25? Well what if Paul switched to speaking as if he was currently living under power of sin and not as one who is living for Christ? That is what he appears to be during here. He reminds his readers of what life was like apart from Christ. What should we remember about that life today?

First, we should remember that the problem is not law, but sin (7:7-12). The Law was a good thing given by God since it revealed his will for us (7:12). It even gave the conditions Christ fulfilled in becoming our perfect sacrifice (Galatians 4:4).

Second, Paul tells us that Sin is a powerful force in itself (7:13-20). There is a power to Sin that Paul has recognized since Romans 1 (Go back and read it through to our text and you might be surprised to see this!). It controls many and causes them to live in disobedience to God's will. To Paul, Sin uses the Law to name sin and to increase it in the world. Sin has taken what God has given us for our good (the Law) and turned it into something evil. That is its power and why God, through Jesus, had to conquer Sin.

Third, humanity is now enslaved to sin and needs to be redeemed from it (7:14, 25), and that is exactly what Jesus has done! Romans 8 will be Paul's grand description of what God has done to defeat Sin and Death.

Today, I will...recognize the power that Sin has, and I will focus more intently on what Jesus has done to save us from it.

Is There Anything Greater Than God's Love?

Today's Scripture Romans 8:31-38

Is anything greater than God's love? In a very short answer, NO! There is nothing greater than God's love as it has been shown in Jesus. If you ever wonder if you are forgiven, if you are loved, or if you will be a conqueror over sin and death, then meditate often on Romans 8 (For the record, it is this author's favorite chapter in all of Scripture!). So what is something from this rich text that we can meditate on today? It is simply that no matter what the world, or the devil, or sin throws at you, God's love is greater and more powerful.

Paul employs the scene of a courtroom to sum up what he has written so far in Romans. He seems to bring his entire argument to a head and fitting conclusion here before he addresses another issue facing the Roman church. In Romans 8:31-38 he asks seven rhetorical questions that find their answer in Christ's sacrifice on the cross. He then quotes Psalm 44:22 in Romans 8:36 to remind us of the level of commitment we are to show to Christ as well. Though the world may want to put us on trial for our faith in Christ, we see that nothing the world can throw at us is as powerful as God's love in Christ Jesus.

Nothing is as powerful because all those things are not the Lord of heaven and earth. Jesus himself is the one who is greater than the things of this world—even spiritual forces (Colossians 2:15). In Christ Jesus we must never forget that God is for us (Romans 8:31). We stand confident and sure that those things in this world (sin and death) and even spiritual beings against us cannot overcome God's love as it is seen in Christ's work for us in his death, burial, and resurrection.

Today, I will...remember the love of God as it has been displayed in Christ. I will stand confident in being forgiven of my sin and in being secure from all evil forces in this world.

Week Twenty-Six
Romans 9-13

Ralph Gilmore

Monday
The Potter and the Clay

Today's Scripture Romans 9:19-24

My dad was a carpenter. When I was a boy, I would play in Dad's workshop nailing together pieces of scrap wood into whatever I wanted. Usually, I just started nailing and I did not know what I was building. God never does this. He is the Potter and we are the clay. Often, I don't know what I will become when the Potter finishes with me—but He does. According to the text, I may comply or I may resist what the Potter is fashioning in me, but God always has the right of disposition because He is the Potter. The Scripture for today is a segue into the topics Paul wants to address, i.e., the sovereignty of God and choices of the Jews and the Gentiles in their relationship to God.

Romans 9-11 is known to many as the hardest section of the New Testament. However, it also paints a multi-layered picture of God's covenantal love for both the Jews and the Gentiles. Paul uses the interrogative approach in Romans 9-11 in that he asks a series of five questions to organize his thoughts, though guided by the Holy Spirit.

Question 1 (in Romans 9:14) is "Is there injustice on God's Part?" Many of the Jews in Rome could have easily thought that God favored the Gentiles since the Jews were expelled by Claudius from Rome in 49 AD.

Question 2 (in Romans 9:19) is "Why does he still find fault? For who can resist His will?" Since God is sovereign, ultimately, as the Potter, none of us as His clay can ever testify against Him.

Question 3 (in Romans 9:30) is "What shall we say then (about the Gentiles)?" If God did not predestine the Jews to reject the gospel, then how can one explain how the Gentiles entered the picture?

The thread that ties together all these three questions is that Paul is proclaiming the sovereignty of God. He is the Potter—we are the clay.

Today, I will...accept that God knows what He is doing. Although I am free to choose, God can know what I freely choose to do. I can never play "hide and seek" with an omniscient God.

Tuesday
Paul's Heart's Desire

Today's Scripture Romans 10:1-4

When I was in high school, my "heart's desire" was a blond girl who was head majorette. I knew God meant her for me, although we had different religious backgrounds. When we broke up, I felt that my "heart's desire" was lost. Of much more serious importance to the Hebrew nation, why did so many Jews in Paul's day not accept the gospel of Jesus? Paul affirms his love for the Jews and his respect for their zeal for God, though it was not based on knowledge. His "heart's desire" and prayer to God for Israel was for their acceptance of the true Messiah, and yet many Jews had not accepted Jesus.

It prompted Paul to ask the fourth of five questions in Romans 9-11, "Lord, who has believed what he has heard from us?" (Romans 10:16), as Isaiah also asked in Isaiah 53:1-3. However, a significant difference in Isaiah and Paul is that Isaiah is asking the question preparatory to the coming of the messianic age, and Paul is asking the question after the true Messiah has come.

So, Paul's "heart's desire" was to help people find the Messiah—not because they were predestined or privileged, but because they found Jesus with free will and full responsibility for their actions. Paul wanted the Messiah to be found not only by the Jews, but by all people. Everyone should have known that Paul really did love his own people. Even though Paul was appointed by God to be an apostle to the Gentiles (Acts 26:16-18), it took a while for Paul to bring this to fruition. In Acts 13:46-47, Paul felt the time was right to turn to the Gentiles although, as he said, it was appropriate that he should begin with the Jews.

So, who has believed God's report? Belief in Jesus as Messiah is an individual decision, not a national one. I make the decision for myself; I do not make it for my country or my nationality.

Today, I will...honor my individual commitment to Jesus as Messiah. I will try not to form stereotypes about any national group based on their non-commitment to Jesus. I will focus on confirming my own calling and election (2 Peter 1:10).

Our Unsearchable God

Today's Scripture Romans 11:33

I never have liked anything I could not figure out. Later in our marriage, I have given in to depend on my wife as navigator rather than to depend on my own sense of direction. I have spent hundreds of hours trying to "figure out" God, but full comprehension of God and His attributes still alludes me. In concluding this difficult section, Romans 9-11, Paul, even aided by the gift of Holy Spirit inspiration, willingly concedes that he does not understand everything about our God who is inscrutable, unfathomable, and unsearchable. Who can know the mind of God except God? (1 Corinthians 2:11).

To illustrate, Paul asks his final of five questions: "Did they stumble in order that they might fall?" (11:11). Did God foredestine Israel to fall for the purpose of "grafting in" the Gentiles? (11:22). Did Israel as a nation have no choice except to fall away from God since God foreknew that this would happen? It is perhaps a disservice to the subjects of predestination and foreknowledge to even bring them up in our current devotional setting. However, I do so purposefully. It is not logically impossible for our God to foreknow that something will happen without forcing it to happen. Jesus knew that Judas would betray him (Matthew 26:23), yet Judas made his own decision willingly (Acts 1:25). In order to disprove a theory, one need find only one exception. Yet there are hundreds in Scripture. God can know something that I will decide without forcing me to conform to His knowledge. Thus, God knew that many in Israel would not accept Jesus, so he planned what would happen when that occasion eventuated.

How does this affect my life with God? My God does not assign an eternal destiny for me—I chose that myself. I have plenary power over my own destiny, yet God is still Sovereign. It does not matter to me whether God can know whether I will be saved or lost in the end—I don't know.

Today, I will...believe in a God who loves me. I will believe in a relational God because I cannot really have a relationship with a God who manipulates my final sentence at the judgment.

Thursday
Christ Over Culture

Today's Scripture Romans 12:1-2

Romans 12 was my Dad's favorite passage. He thought every Christian should memorize this chapter. Once when he had to have an MRI, he and I quoted parts of Romans 12 together to help him keep calm during this test requiring confinement.

Romans 12 is known as the Magna Carta of Christianity in that it sets the pattern for servant living for every Christian. It has brought comfort and guidance to millions over the years. The key to all that follows in the chapter after verses 1 and 2 is the concept of "transformation or conformation" in verse 2. Individual transformation occurs as a Christian walks with Jesus. Individual conformation occurs when a Christian gives in to the world. Therefore, the option for each of us is whether we will choose Christ over culture.

We live in a time where culture sways in many religious discussions. Twenty years ago, I would never have thought that matters of basic Christian doctrine, such as baptism and the Lord's Supper, would have been seriously challenged among us by cultural considerations. But, the time has come. It seems we live more in a time of conformation than transformation. The remainder of the content of Romans 12 appears irrelevant to the reader if the reader prefers culture over Christ.

Everything that is written in Scripture occurs in a cultural context. Even the account of the creation and the Garden of Eden is in a cultural context because Moses was writing from within the culture of the Ancient Near East when he penned the Torah. So, I am not saying to ignore culture. However, I am saying to seek to find the principle(s) of the text under consideration in order to ascertain what God is trying to say to us in the twenty-first century. Thus, in a text that appears heavily embedded in culture (e.g. 1 Timothy 2:8-9), examine the text for language that brings the text home to me in my culture. For instance, if any of the passages relative to the role of women are tied to creation, then the principle involved is not going to change.

Today, I will...seek to hear God's voice in Scripture by looking for divine principles in Scripture whenever I study the Bible. Thus, I will intentionally choose Christ over culture.

Go Debt Free

I know this will date me some, but my wife and I have paid off the first mortgage on a house. It took twenty-seven years, but we did it. However, the goal of being debt-free has not been achieved. But in a biblical sense, I can be "debt-free" spiritually if I extend love to those around me (Romans 13:8-10).

Romans 12 begins the section of Romans I call the "Nurturing Section." Paul has explained the need of the gospel in chapters 1-3 and the nature of the gospel in chapters 4-11. Now he demonstrates how the gospel looks when properly practiced.

In the past, I thought verses 1-7 of Romans 13 just did not fit with the remainder of the chapter. How can one move seamlessly from a discussion of a Christian's individual responsibility to the government (12:17-21), to a discussion of a Christian's group responsibility (13:1-7), to a discussion of a Christian's being indebted to love each other? I believe that the concept tying them together is "fulfilling the law" (13:8). Doing what God says, whether individually or as a group, is exactly what God wants from His church and from me.

The Roman christians in the first century naturally wanted to know if they owed anything to the corrupt Roman government abusively run by Emperor Nero. Surely Christians owed nothing to them. However, Paul extends our spiritual indebtedness to all people, reminiscent of Jesus' command to love even our enemies (Matthew 5:43-48). Does everyone "deserve" my love? This question represents a misunderstanding of my own spiritual condition. I did not "deserve" for Jesus to die for me. I did not "deserve" to have the love I have received from countless people. So, why should I expect this condition to be met if I am to love someone? Perhaps that is why this concept is referred to as the "acid test of Christianity."

Today, I will...extend love to someone who I used to think does not "deserve" it. Today, our country is going through some tough times—mass shootings, hurricanes, wild-fires, etc. Maybe there are many things I cannot do, but I can extend love. It would be best for us not to let this "debt" go unpaid. We can go debt-free.

Week Twenty-Seven
Romans 14-16
1 Corinthians 1-2

Jacob Hawk

Monday
Pursue Peace

Jesus, our Savior, can silence any storm as the "Prince of Peace" (Isaiah 9:6). In His famous Sermon on the Mount, Jesus promised the masses, *"Blessed are the peacemakers, for they will be called sons of God."* (Matthew 5:9)

Harmonious peace strokes the chords of God's song, but God's people destroy the calm through their own calamities.

Questions about life and its choices echo from the hearts and walls of churches around the world. Not every social matter is "black" and "white." Words like "expediency" and "judgment" turn the shades to gray. When we set standards based on our experiences, we confuse someone else's business for ours. We step into shoes we were never called to wear. That's exactly why the apostle Paul, in a chapter of "hot topics" such as worldly holidays and habits, wrote these powerful words in Romans 14: 13, "...let us not pass judgment on one another any longer..." Yet many view Paul's words as permission to follow the path they prefer. Quite the contrary. Paul's point doesn't end there. It really didn't even begin there.

Because as soon as Paul says to stop passing judgment, he then says, "...decide never to put a stumbling block or hindrance in the way of a brother." And again in verse 19, "...let us pursue what makes for peace and for mutual up building." Do we hear his exhortation? His main point? Just because we have the right, that doesn't make it right; but what is always "right" is pursuing peace—honoring our brethren above ourselves—sacrificing what we want for the betterment of the Kingdom.

Today, I will...consider how my choices not only affect me, but my brethren as well. I will stop passing judgment on others, but I won't force my freedom on others either. Above all, I will pursue peace.

Tuesday

Welcomed Welcomers

Today's Scripture Romans 15:5-7

"It's impossible for the church to be one." A common, condemning phrase from the insiders and outsiders of religion's mighty arm. Churches of every brand displayed on every corner, like fast food restaurants and coffee shops, certainly doesn't help the perception of division; but when it comes to true, New Testament Christianity, the impossibility of unity is a false platform. Jesus would have never prayed for unity (John 17) if it wasn't attainable.

To be fair, disagreement within the body of Christ is common—like the air we breathe and the water we drink. In this great chapter, Paul prays for the church in Rome to have a "spirit of unity" (verse 5) and to praise God with "one heart" (verse 6) and "one mouth" (verse 6), yet even the most passionate idealist will join hands with the most convicted realist and admit oneness of mouth and heart is rare.

But in verse 7, the apostle pulls back the curtain and provides a powerful glimpse of unity's aura—"welcome one another as Christ has welcomed you, for the glory of God." Paul urges us to be "welcomed welcomers." We're to welcome each other as Christ welcomed us. Not for our glory, but for the glory of God.

How did Christ welcome us? When Christ welcomed us through His blood in baptism, He didn't hold the magnitude of our sin over the top of our heads. He didn't reach back into the "slop bucket" of our past, reminding us of every mistake in our existence. Christ said, "We're forgetting about your past so we can focus on your future." This is the spirit in which Paul urges us to welcome our brethren, for unity's sake and for God's glory. Will you accept His divine challenge?

Today, I will...thank Christ for the way He welcomed me into His Kingdom. I will strive to welcome others the same—for the glory of God and for the unity of His people.

Wednesday
"Watch Out!"

"But their intentions are pure!" They don't mean any harm!" It doesn't matter. When it comes to the pure message of Jesus Christ, we don't have the luxury of listening to error even from sincere voices.

Many congregations of the Lord's people have journeyed on the edge of the abyss, disguised by the best of intentions. These diversions are due to "compromise"—a refusal to "stand firm"—all to become more "appealing" and "appetizing" to a biblically illiterate culture.

Unfortunately, this is nothing new. The apostle Paul told the church at Rome—a church absorbed and infused by pagan culture—"I appeal to you, brothers, to watch out for those who cause divisions and create obstacles contrary to the doctrine that you have been taught; avoid them. For such persons do not serve our Lord Christ, but their own appetites, and by smooth talk and flattery they deceive the hearts of the naïve" (Romans 16: 17-18). Did you catch the seriousness and somberness of Paul's voice? I "appeal to you." Some translations render it, "I urge you." It's the same seriousness, the same wording, by which he urged the Romans to become "living sacrifices, holy and pleasing to God" (Romans 12: 1-2). Paul goes so far as to say, "...avoid them..." Strong words from the pen of the apostle who provided the original church discipline pattern.

Paul even reminds us deception stems from confident, talented speakers who can effectively capture the attention and stroke the ego of their listeners. They attack those who are weak—the "naïve"— who don't know any better. Yes, when it comes to restoring New Testament Christianity, we can't be too selective regarding the voices we hear. We must "watch out" for words that would lead us astray.

Today, I will...yearn for the simplicity and beauty of New Testament Christianity. I will acknowledge Jesus and His word as the ultimate authority. I will "watch out" for those who cause me to think or believe differently.

Sent with a Purpose

Today's Scripture 1 Corinthians 1:13-17

"How many people did your church baptize last year?" "Now I don't have to worry about my children—they've been baptized." "If we could just get them into the water, their lives would change forever."

How often have you heard one, if not all of these statements from brethren? Throughout our history, churches of Christ have prominently and passionately preached the essentiality of baptism. This is a tremendous reputation to hold as the church has been preaching this message from God since Pentecost. Baptism is the method and moment where we receive the forgiveness of sins and the gift of the Holy Spirit (Acts 2:38). Nevertheless, if we aren't careful, we can convert people to baptism more than we convert them to Christ.

This was a problem in Paul's day just like in ours. That's why Paul told the church at Corinth he was glad he only baptized two brothers and one household in Corinth (1 Corinthians 1:13; 16). Paul explained his reasoning. First, people were beginning to follow WHO baptized them rather than WHO they were baptized into (1 Corinthians 1:13-15); but more importantly, it was also his God given purpose. "For Christ did not send me to baptize but to preach the gospel..." (1 Corinthians 1:17).

Was Paul saying baptism wasn't part of the gospel? Had Paul changed his mind about the essentiality of its role in salvation? Of course not. Paul was simply saying, "My job is to convert people to Jesus—not to the baptistry." When we truly get Jesus, that's when we get baptized. We are called to produce disciples immersed in the blood of Jesus—not spectators dunked in a Jacuzzi. This was not only why Paul was sent, but why we're sent as well.

Today, I will...thank God for His plan of salvation which includes baptism, but I will also remember I was converted to Jesus, not to the baptistry.

The Cream of the Crop

"He's the best preacher I've ever heard." "I just wish our preacher could preach like that congregation's preacher." "Did you hear that sermon? Now THAT's gospel preaching!"

Every ear demands a different criterion for effective preaching. That's understandable. While every preacher should strive to be better, he must remember people learn in different ways and enjoy different styles. There isn't one "perfect" way to preach, and it certainly isn't a competition.

The apostle Paul knew that better than anyone else. He ministered in a time when exceptional oration was a profound and respected gift, especially in the city of Corinth. Every corner of the metropolis boasted effective communicators, displaying their gifts in philosophy, history, and other disciplines, entertaining the citizens walking and standing nearby. Consequently, many of the town discounted and degraded spiritual teaching because their presentations didn't portray the same excitement and wonder of ancient philosophers. For them, public speaking was entertainment more than it was education. Unfortunately, this describes the modern day church in too many ways.

Yet Paul defended the foundation for true, biblical preaching. He told the church at Corinth, *"My speech and my message were not in plausible words of wisdom, but in demonstration of the Spirit and of power, so that your faith might not rest in the wisdom of men but in the power of God"* (1 Corinthians 2: 4-5).

This type of preaching, according to Paul, was the "cream of the crop." It was preaching that paved the path to the forgiving blood of Jesus and the gracious heart of God. It was preaching grounded in the power of the Holy Spirit, not in the persona of men. That same preaching is desperately needed in the Lord's church today. "Cream of the crop" preachers will always be messengers of God, not of themselves.

Today, I will...thank God for true, biblical preaching. I will remember effective preaching is about God's education and exhortation, not man's entertainment.

Week Twenty-Eight
1 Corinthians 3-7

Matthew Morine

Foolishness of Following Men

Today's Scripture 1 Corinthians 3:4-7

People lead the majority of church divisions. Brother Bart is opposed to some change or lack of change, so he goes on the offensive to secure the support of others in the congregation. Sister Mary is upset because someone changed the paint color of her grade 5 classroom, so she talks with Martha, who is married to Mark, who is best friends with Cecil, who is an elder. Cecil tells Mark, to tell Martha, to tell sister Mary, to get over it. So sister Mary calls the remaining elder's wives to complain about how she was treated. One can see how this small disagreement can escalate into a full-fledged church fight in which people start to take sides.

Paul warns of the foolishness of following men in 1 Corinthians 3:4-7, *"For when one says, 'I follow Paul,' and another, 'I follow Apollos,' are you not being merely human? What then is Apollos? What is Paul? Servants through whom you believed, as the Lord assigned to each. I planted, Apollos watered, but God gave the growth. So neither he who plants nor he who waters is anything, but only God who gives the growth."*

Paul warns the Corinthian congregation about dividing over personalities. Sometimes we can forget that we are all in the church together. We start to base what we believe on the people connected to us. Typically, none of us would be that emotionally involved over the color of paint in a room, but once it upsets one of our friends or family members, all of a sudden that color on the wall represents egregious sin. We become angry at Cecil.

Instead of following the emotions of people, we need to follow the great commission of God. It is not about you, or me, or them, or some people, it is about helping the Lord grow His congregation.

Today, I will...refuse to get involved in a church disagreement.

Tuesday
Suffer for Success

The Christians in Corinth struggled with pride. Pride is a dangerous attitude because arrogance blinds people to reality. It creates the mindset of feeling perfect while one's heart is empty. Satan uses this tool to create spiritual stagnation.

In 1 Corinthians 4, Paul contrasts the mindset of the Corinthians with the attitude of the Apostles. The Corinthians feel filled, rich, and kingly, while the Apostles feel condemned, embarrassed, and foolish. The Corinthians are concerned with honor and strength which causes them to reject Paul's instructions.

In contrast to the haughty nature of the Corinthians, Paul is not concerned with the public perception of the Apostles. 1 Corinthians 4:11-13 says, *"To the present hour we hunger and thirst, we are poorly dressed and buffeted and homeless, and we labor, working with our own hands. When reviled, we bless; when persecuted, we endure; when slandered, we entreat. We have become, and are still, like the scum of the world, the refuse of all things."*

Instead of worrying about image, the Apostles are concerned about taking the right action. To often we are caught up in how we might look, instead of thinking about what is the right action.

When we ask ourselves, "What will people say?", or "What will people think?" We are making choices with the wrong audience in mind. The world has shifted from character development to image development. We say, "How do I look to others on Facebook?" instead of, "Does God see me having a pure heart?" A man looks on the outside, but God sees us for who we truly are. We should care less what the world thinks because we care what God thinks.

Today, I will...do the right thing, regardless of how I might look.

Wednesday
Tolerance Overload

The greatest virtue in the world's eyes is tolerance. No matter what someone does or thinks the progressive left demands tolerance. There is some wisdom in practicing patience and tolerance, but there comes the point in which people must act to protect others. The Corinthian congregation was tolerating a man that was in sexual sin. He was having an illicit affair with his father's wife. The Gentiles did not even tolerate this behavior, but the Christians were putting up with this sin in the name of love.

There is a balance between tolerance and church discipline. After a certain point, tolerance becomes wrong because it is infecting the rest of the body of believers. Paul makes this point in 1 Corinthians 5:6–8, *"Your boasting is not good. Do you not know that a little leaven leavens the whole lump? Cleanse out the old leaven that you may be a new lump, as you really are unleavened. For Christ, our Passover lamb has been sacrificed. Let us, therefore, celebrate the festival, not with the old leaven, the leaven of malice and evil, but with the unleavened bread of sincerity and truth."*

Too much tolerance merely allows sinful cancer to spread in the congregation. It emboldens others to sin because of the lack of consequences.

All Christians sin and have fallen from the glory of God. We are patient and loving to one another through various struggles, but when a church is hosting sin without denouncing its destructive force, that church is creating a sewer, not a hospital. The only way to treat sin is to stop the spread. A church must isolate it. Love is not mere tolerance, but the courage to correct that which is wayward.

Today, I will...pray for someone that is struggling with sin.

Bigger Than a Wrong

Today's Scripture 1 Corinthians 6:7-8

Years ago, two brothers in Christ started fighting over a fax machine. One brother owned a fax machine business, while the other brother owned a pizza shop. Both of the brothers were part of the same congregation, so when the brother with the pizza shop needed a fax machine, he knew who to call. The deal was quick because of the trust between the two. After a month, the fax machine broke. The brother with the fax machine business arrived to fix it, but there would be a cost of a few hundred dollars for a new part. The pizza owner was upset and accused the other brother of selling him a junky machine. The disagreement escalated until a court date was set. Neither brother was willing to give up a few hundred dollars in the name of maintaining a healthy relationship. Both of these men could have easily written off the cost as a business loss, but instead each wanted the other person to pay in the name of justice, and perhaps a little vengeance.

Disputes among Christians are notorious for being ugly. This commentary is a heartbreaking concerning the church. Instead of going to battle in the worldly court systems, Paul advises the church members to be defrauded. 1 Corinthians 6:7-8 says, *"To have lawsuits at all with one another is already a defeat for you. Why not rather suffer wrong? Why not rather be defrauded? But you yourselves wrong and defraud—even your own brothers!"*

Too often, the desire to prove oneself right overcomes feelings of grace. Even though the person might be in the wrong, sometimes it is best to drop the matter and absorb the cost.

Everyone should deal with others with integrity. Realistically, there will be times in which both parties will feel right. A Christian must fight the prideful response of taking his brother to court. Harsh disputes only cast shame on the Lord's church.

Today, I will...be quick to forgive someone who recently wronged me.

Friday
Follow God's Plan

The church has done an excellent job of standing against illicit sexual expression. The church has been clear—sex outside of marriage is sinful. The Bible is clear—one man for one woman for life. This pattern is the ideal for all marriages. But has the church been as adamant about encouraging Christians to fulfill one another's sexual needs within the covenant of marriage?

Paul realized that humans would want to get married. In marriage, there is a mutual submission to one another. He provides the principle in 1 Corinthians 7:4-6, *"For the wife does not have authority over her own body, but the husband does. Likewise, the husband does not have authority over his own body, but the wife does. Do not deprive one another, except perhaps by agreement for a limited time, that you may devote yourselves to prayer; but then come together again, so that Satan may not tempt you because of your lack of self-control."*

The church must restore the conversation concerning a healthy sex life to counteract the overwhelming flood of sinful sexuality, and to fight against the spread of pornography, homosexuality, and adultery by holding up the beauty of a fulfilling sexual life in a healthy marriage.

Paul notes that each party in the marriage is under the submission of the other in regard to his or her body. Each party must not deprive the other of sexual contact. A marriage in which the husband refuses to fulfill the wife's sexual needs is an unhealthy marriage. According to Paul, the wife has the right to ask for her physical needs to be met. Of course, there are times in which a break might be necessary, but this is for only a season because of the strong temptation to find sexual gratification somewhere else. Sex is part of a healthy marriage.

Today, I will...obey God in every aspect of my marriage.

Week Twenty-Nine
1 Corinthians 8-12

Robert Hatfield

Monday
What Would Love Do?

At the beginning of 1 Corinthians 8, Paul begins a discussion about meats that were offered to idols. Modern readers must remember that, to the original readers, this was a complicated issue. A portion of the meat from animals that were sacrificed in pagan temples would be burned on the altar, another part would be eaten in idolatrous ceremony, and another part would be sold in the marketplace for people to eat at home.

Paul said that, as long as one was not participating in the idol worship, Christians were not sinning by eating meat offered in the temples before it was purchased in the marketplace. Some Christians, however, struggled to divorce the idolatry from the food. In so doing, they violated their consciences (1 Corinthians 8:7).

In response, Paul said there is nothing sinful about eating meat (1 Corinthians 8:8), unless doing so would cause the "weak" brother to stumble (8:9). If one Christian ate meat in the presence of a weaker Christian, doing so could cause the weaker brother to lapse back into idolatry, destroying "the brother for whom Christ died" (8:11). This is serious because to sin against a brother is to sin against Christ. Therefore, it is better to abstain from meats than to cause a Christian to stumble.

What can we learn? First, we should treat other Christians with love (8:3). Love is always the appropriate response. Jesus teaches us to put others before ourselves, serving them. Second, we may have the right to do something, but that doesn't mean we should do it. Scripture reminds us to think of others before ourselves (Philippians 2:3-4; Matthew 7:12). Jesus taught us to serve other people (Matthew 20:28). Your personal rights are not more important than your brother or sister in Christ. It would be better to give up a liberty than to cause a brother or sister to become unfaithful to the Lord.

Today, I will...consider the needs and thoughts of others before thinking of myself.

Tuesday
A Servant to All

Some areas of life are morally neutral. These are areas about which God has neither given a command nor a condemnation. In these situations, Christians are at liberty to choose what they will or will not do. In chapter 8, the choice was between eating meat or not eating meat. In today's text, Paul appeals to his own example and shares how he conducts himself in order to promote peace among Christians and share the gospel with the lost.

Though it would have been appropriate for Paul to be paid for his ministry in Corinth (9:14), Paul had "not made use of this right" because he did not want to "put an obstacle in the way of the gospel of Christ" (9:12). Apparently some people had accused Paul of being motivated by money. He proved himself to be above reproach.

By studying this apostle's great example, modern Christians can learn how to promote the gospel of Christ and properly unify the body of Christ, the church. First, Paul chose to serve other people, reaching out to them from their perspectives, for the sake of the gospel (9:18-23). Paul voluntarily altered his behavior to bring people to Christ. Second, he exercised strenuous self-discipline by sacrificing his own opinions and feelings for the sake of the gospel (9:24-26). Third, Paul continually reminded himself that his brethren were worth the extra effort − for the sake of the gospel (9:27)! He knew that to sin against a brother is to sin against Christ. He would not "be disqualified" from the Christian race!

As Christians, we like to know that we're on the right track. With our Bibles in hand, we studiously seek authority for all that we do. But when we reach an area about which God has not legislated, we should follow Paul's example. My personal rights are not more important than the gospel of Christ. Never hinder the gospel.

Today, I will...put the gospel of Christ ahead of my personal rights or opinions.

Wednesday
Not All Things Build Up

Today's Scripture 1 Corinthians 10

1 Corinthians 8-10 form one discussion on matters of religious liberties (matters about which God has not spoken, therefore we are at liberty to choose our own course of action). The main issue he addresses has to do with eating meats offered to idols.

Paul begins chapter 10 by referencing the example of the Israelites during the wilderness wandering. He emphasizes that these Old Testament references are examples for us (10:6, 11). They prove that even the mighty can fall (10:12), and remind us that God provides us ways to escape spiritually dangerous situations (10:13).

Those were needed reminders in light of Paul's earlier warning: "'Knowledge' puffs up, but love builds up" (8:1). Just as the Jews lost their focus, so Christians could lose their focus on what really matters. Twice in this chapter Paul specifically warns them of idolatry (10:7, 14). While it was true that idols were fake, and eating meats that had been offered to them was not anything (10:19), some Christians could become arrogant in their knowledge, causing them to let down their guard and slip into idolatry.

What does all of this mean for the church today? Paul's final charges in the last 10 verses of the chapter summarize the issue of eating meats offered to idols. They also provide five principles we should remember today.

[1] Seek to build up the church (10:23-24). [2] Don't worry about whether someone's conscience is bothered by a matter of Christian liberty (10:25-27). [3] However, if they bring up the issue, then refrain from that activity for their sakes (10:28-30). [4] Never intentionally offend another Christian (10:31-33). [5] Ultimately, this is about helping our brothers and sisters in Christ to go to heaven (10:33-11:1).

Today, I will...carefully consider whether my actions build up the church or tear it down. I will be intentional about encouraging and strengthening God's people.

Imitate Christ

Paul's example was worth following because of the One whom he followed – Jesus (11:1). His appeal to the Christians in Corinth to follow Jesus gave way to a two-part exhortation in chapter 11: words of commendation, and words of censure.

The commendation is based on their willingness to "maintain the traditions even as [Paul] delivered them" (11:2; compare 2 Thessalonians 2:15; 3:6). It is an important reminder for us to hold tightly to God's word as it has been revealed to us by inspiration and preserved for us by providence.

What follows is a difficult section of scripture regarding men, women, and head coverings. It helps to know that Corinth was home to the temple of Aphrodite, which included one thousand temple harlots. These women were identified by their shaved heads. Women with shaved heads (or short hair) could have easily been mistaken as temple prostitutes in that day.

For those reasons, Paul reminds them of principles that we need to remember, too. First, there is an order of authority given by God (11:3). We must respect the divine arrangements for submission. Second, our influence is to be guarded (11:6). Third, each person should pursue God's plan for his or her gender (11:14-15). Men and women have different responsibilities in the church and in the home. We should respect those roles, and seek to thrive in them.

The second main section of the chapter deals with words of censure. It seems that the Corinthians had allowed their custom of love feasts (2 Peter 2:13; Jude 12) to mix into their observance of the Lord's Supper (1 Corinthians 11:20). As a result, they were to consider the command from the Lord (11:23-26) and the consequences of diluting the Lord's Supper (11:27-34).

This chapter reminds us that it is important to preserve and obey the commands of God as He revealed them through His word. In everything, follow Christ.

Today, I will...recommit to following Jesus, wherever He leads.

Friday
Unified

Unity is a wonderful word with huge implications (Psalm 133:1). That is undoubtedly why Jesus prayed that all of His disciples would be one (John 17).

As Paul wrote to a church that struggled with division (1 Corinthians 1:10), he included several appeals for unity. Today's scripture is one of them.

The apostle began by emphasizing a unified message. Having come from a pagan background, these Christians needed to be reminded of the simplicity and singularity of the God they served and the message He had given them. Paul affirms that the Holy Spirit would never speak against Christ (12:3). We know Jesus said the same thing to His disciples (John 16:13-15).

One of the ways they could know that they were hearing the true message from God was through the spiritual gifts that they received from the Holy Spirit. There are nine gifts mentioned in 12:8-11. These were miraculous signs given for the purpose of confirming the word of truth (Mark 16:20; Hebrews 2:3-4). Further, at the end of the chapter, Paul listed nine positions that were held in the church during the time of the apostles (12:28-30). These, too, seem to be tied to the miraculous spiritual gifts. Chapter 13 will tell us that such miraculous signs served a temporary purpose, and that they no longer exist today.

We can get so caught up in the gifts themselves that we lose sight of their purpose. The Corinthian Christians had the same problem. The purpose of the miraculous signs was to promote unity.

With that in mind, Paul emphasized the unity of the church (12:12-27). Though there are many Christians, we are all one in Christ. Though we have differing abilities, our differences contribute to a stronger unit. Each Christian is vitally important.

The question you have to answer is this: Do you contribute toward the unity of the body or toward the division of the body?

Today, I will...do my part to work for unity.

Week Thirty
1 Corinthians 13–16
2 Corinthians 1

Terry Edwards

In Praise of True Love

Today's Scripture 1 Corinthians 13:1–8

"Love is patient and kind; love does not envy or boast; it is not arrogant or rude. It does not insist on its own way; it is not irritable or resentful; it does not rejoice at wrongdoing, but rejoices with the truth. Love bears all things, believes all things, hopes all things, endures all things. Love never ends." (1 Corinthians 13:4–8a)

If it is true that 70% of all lyrics of secular songs are about love, this is added proof that it is a vital force of men of all times and all cultures. But it does need to be clearly defined, as the word is used in so many different and confusing ways.

True love is greater than any charismatic gift from God, better than speaking in tongues, or prophesying. To be motivated by it, is far more rewarding than possessing all knowledge, or the ability to move mountains. Nothing compares, in a sense, nothing else matters.

True love shuns personal pride, is incapable of self-interest. It requires putting others first, mourns at all injustice, pursues only Truth. It is all encompassing, truly far-reaching, and the purest of motivators; it can be as powerful as a hurricane, but as gentle as a breeze.

It lasts for more than a season, or a century. It is timeless, seamless, has no expiration date, and cannot be consumed by moth or rust. The meaning of the word is permanent, eternal, written on a cross at Golgotha, the standard for all men.

True love summarizes/condenses all the virtues of a godly person: faithfulness, kindness, gentleness, patience, peacefulness, goodness and self-control. It is the defining evidence of maturity, which is achieving the goal for which men were created. This kind of love is the mark of excellence within the Creator's masterpiece (you).

True love is an attribute of the very heart of God.

Today, I will...strive to be a perfect mirror of the heart of God which is in me.

Tuesday
A God of Peace

"For God is not a God of confusion, but of peace." (1 Corinthians 14:33)

True worship involves both the heart and the mind. All of the worshipper is involved. The emotions and the intellect, energy and thought, passion and meditation–all are important in the act of worship. It seems today that many go to one extreme or the other, celebrating confusion in the name of God, or, conversely, apathy in the presence of God.

In the early days of the Way of Jesus of Nazareth, in Corinth, one of these was becoming the norm. They were exciting times, as the Holy Spirit had bestowed through the apostle Paul various charismatic gifts to certain members, including prophecy & speaking in a foreign language. There was a problem, however, with pride, and a sense of spiritual entitlement. The result was a cacophony of sound in the public worship, with prophecies overlapping, and voices colluding, and no one understanding.

But God is not a God of confusion. He created us to be both intelligent and emotional beings, and He knows we need to both feel and understand. He is the God who says, "Be still, and Know I am God" (Psalm 46:10). He is a God of peace. He offers peace between Himself and men, and peace between men. But He also offers inner peace. True worship should bring with it a sense of calm, awe, respect, and order.

A believer recently confessed to me that he did not retain much from his years of worship experiences, because the roar of joyful, yet conflicting expressions of praise and approval, left him dazed. He experienced sensory overload. Good intentions do not excuse our dismissal of the divine instructions given through Paul: the end result of worship is "that you may learn and all be encouraged"(v. 31).

Today, I will...strive to grow in my need to meditate on God's Word, so that I can better experience His peace.

Wednesday
Either There Is, Or There Is Not

Today's Scripture 1 Corinthians 15:20

"But in fact Christ has been raised from the dead..." (1 Corinthians 15:20)

The fundamental question we must answer is whether there is life after death or not. Two buttons on a desk: press one or the other. It is not a somber subject; it is actually liberating to choose, commit, and live thereby.

In Paul's day, the man-made pagan gods were of no comfort in addressing this human existential dilemma. Most believed that there was something beyond this earth, but it was a gloomy world of shades. Only the best were allowed in a corner of Hades, but it was still sad, and worse than being alive. The idea of a bodily resurrection was totally foreign.

That is why the Way of Jesus of Nazareth, with its promise of eternal life and a home in heaven, was so attractive. And it clearly hinged on the historical reality of the resurrection of Jesus Christ. Hundreds of reliable witnesses saw Him again, three days after his death, the first ever to resurrect himself. Paul received his own, personal appearance of the resurrected Jesus, and lived the rest of his life proclaiming this undeniable fact (and died for it).

So, here are the parameters of the debate. If Christ was not raised, disciples of His are all false witnesses, personal faith is vain, you are still in your sins, we are all lost, and Christians are of all men most to be pitied.

But since Christ was raised from the dead, His empty tomb is a guarantee that all shall be made alive at His return. Death will be defeated for good, and those whom He claims will be welcomed to recline at the table of Abraham, Isaac, and Jacob (Matthew 8:11).

Today, I will...strive to make clear to all who know me that there is abundant life after death, but only in Christ Jesus.

Thursday
A Church in a House

Today's Scripture 1 Corinthians 16:19

"Aquila and Prisca, together with the church in their house, send you hearty greetings in the Lord." (1 Corinthians 16:19)

The only apostle to not be married, Paul will outright say that he wished everyone could be single as he is (I Corinthians 7:7). He does clarify that he does not say so as a command. Yet surely he will never forget the first time he met an extraordinary married couple by the name of Aquila and Priscilla (alternate version of Prisca). It was likely in the year 50 AD, as he sat cross-legged sewing tents for a living in the market of Corinth, the third largest city in the Roman Empire.

He was single, yet gregarious like all of us. He suffered while being deprived for months of Timothy and Silas' company. Thus I imagine the thrill of discovering shared faith in Christ with the young Jewish husband and wife before him: God had sent "family members" to encourage him, just as he felt lost in a hostile crowd. They were very well traveled: originally from the Black Sea, they had come lately from the capital of Rome, expelled by an edict of the emperor. They will bless the missionary work of Paul in the following months in Corinth.

And now they are in Ephesus, across the Aegean Sea from Corinth, and there is a church in their house. Wherever they went, they took their faith with them, set up house, and there was a church that met in the living room. Of course there were no church buildings till after the year 313 AD, and thus all churches were in a house in early Christianity. Still, this couple stands out in their passion to teach and encourage communities of faith.

Which brings up an interesting question: would our homes be a welcome site for a church? What matters not at all, of course, is the physical cleanliness. What does matter, instead, is the spiritual atmosphere. Is God welcome in our living rooms? Is the relationship of husband and wife/parents and children such that a church could meet there and feel at home? Are the words spoken, attitudes shown, and the actions taken, blessed by love of righteousness and holiness?

Today, I will...strive even more to make my home worthy of His presence, and that of His children.

Friday
Comfort Under Siege

Today's Scripture 2 Corinthians 1:3

"Blessed be the God and Father of our Lord Jesus Christ, the Father of mercies and God of all comfort..." (2 Corinthians 1:3)

It is so rare for Paul to share a pronounced personal element in his writings. He dislikes the pronoun "I," always choosing "you" instead. He prefers to focus on the blessings and needs of his recipients.

Yet here he is, clearly emotional, explaining his delay in coming, in self-defense mode. He is under siege by opponents within the church, having to assure the Corinthians he tells it like it is, and does not have a crafty bone in his body. He is like a father whose children have been led to mistrust the very one who gave them life. Unjustified criticism is always most hurtful when it comes from brothers and sisters in Christ.

Have you ever been under siege by "friendly fire?" Have you ever poured out your soul to believers who are woefully of the world and twist every word? Here is the Pauline prescription, derived from personal experience: get your comfort from the God of all comfort. He sprinkles the word ten times in a context of five verses, 20 times in the letter. He has learned to trust in Him who raises the dead. As he looks back on the many crises he has experienced, Paul finds that God always rewarded his trust in Him by giving him deliverance in one way or another.

I like to imagine Paul is the writer of Hebrews, and thus pens these words: _"For because He himself has suffered when tempted, He is able to help those who are being tempted."_ (Hebrews 2:18)

The ability to give comfort is a precious gift indeed, and it can be learned only in the crucible of suffering, anguish and despair. We learn to comfort when we reach for it day after day from the God of all comfort.

Today, I will...choose to comfort those in need, as I acknowledge God's loving hands around me.

Week Thirty-One
2 Corinthians 2-6

Gantt Carter

Monday
The Fragrance

In the letter we call 2 Corinthians, the apostle Paul holds his hearts out to reach the heart of the Christians in ancient Corinth. He is often "defensive" of himself and others, but certainly not in some egotistical manner. He writes for the sake of Jesus and for the sake of the Christians themselves.

Paul explains his actions (his visits and letters) toward Corinth and the sin within (2 Corinthians 2:1-11). He always wanted repentance from a heart of love—love for God and love for others. The inspired apostle did not want to make their sorrow worse than it had to be, and he wanted them to fully forgive and fully welcome the brother that had repented. He tells them about his troubled mind at Troas (vs. 12-13), but then breaks out into a defense of his ministry that continues until 7:5.

"But thanks be to God, who in Christ always leads us in triumphal procession, and through us spreads the fragrance of the knowledge of Him everywhere. For we are the aroma of Christ to God among those who are being saved and among those who are perishing, to one a fragrance from death to death, to the other a fragrance from life to life. Who is sufficient for these things? For we are not, like so many, peddlers of God's word, but as men of sincerity, as commissioned by God, in the sight of God, we speak in Christ." (2 Corinthians 2:14-17)

King Jesus led His apostles as His captives in a fragrant victory march. Paul and the others were sincerely relying on God in His power to spread His words through them like incense – a bitter stench of decay and death to those who rejected Him, but a sweet aroma of life to those who receive Him.

Knowing God is the fragrance of triumph over death. Only in this procession, is life. We must strive to know Him through His truth and serve to spread His greatness to all.

Today, I will...seek to take the fragrance of God everywhere.

Tuesday
The Glory

Today's Scripture 2 Corinthians 3:16-18

Paul had done a wonderful work preaching Jesus and building relationships among the Corinthians (see Acts 18:1-18). But sadly, some were beginning to question the credibility of Paul and his fellow-workers. He informs them that they are the letter of recommendation, their own Christianity demonstrated the successful work of Paul (2 Corinthians 3:1-36).

"The letter kills, but the spirit gives life" (v. 6). Mentioning stone tablets, the apostle then compares the glory of the Mosaic covenant with the glory of the Messianic covenant. Paul explains his boldness toward them by sharing this hope for life in the new covenant (2 Corinthians 3:7-12). The temporary covenant pales in view of the covenant of righteousness that is here to stay! The old covenant was important, but the Messiah and His work is even greater. However, the heart of the failings of the old was the hard hearts of the people (2 Corinthians 3:13-15). Many in ancient Jews were unable to see the true fulfillment and meaning of the Law in the Messiah.

"But when one turns to the Lord, the veil is removed. Now the Lord is the Spirit, and where the Spirit of the Lord is, there is freedom. And we all, with unveiled face, beholding the glory of the Lord, are being transformed into the same image from one degree of glory to another. For this comes from the Lord who is the Spirit." (2 Corinthians 3:16-18)

Toughened by tradition as they may be, our hearts are melted when we are converted to Jesus. In this text, Paul gives new meaning to Exodus 34:34. The Holy Spirit was working through the apostles just as Moses saw the Lord at Sinai. Now, as we see the glory of the Master reflected in the faces of our fellow Christians, we can all be transformed to be like the Master. May we note that this conversion after our initial salvation is a continuing growth in heart and in life.

Today, I will...seek to be transformed to be more like Jesus.

Wednesday
The Unseen

In this section of 2 Corinthians, Paul continues his discussion about seeing the glory of God and the sincerity of the ministers of the cross. Even in the face of intense persecution and incredible problems, Paul remained joyfully steadfast in heart. Paul's motivation was multifaceted: the ministry of God's mercy (vs. 1-7); the Corinthians (vs. 12-15a); and the glory of God (v. 15b).

Paul was about Jesus (v. 5). Ultimately, Christianity is about seeing "the light of the glory of God in the face of Jesus Christ" (v. 6). God commanded the light into existence in Genesis 1:3. Some Jewish traditions explain that light as the light of His law or of His righteousness. The law and the righteousness of God are most powerfully and distinctly seen in our Master, Jesus.

"So we do not lose heart. Though our outer self is wasting away, our inner self is being renewed day by day. For this light momentary affliction is preparing for us an eternal weight of glory beyond all comparison, as we look not to the things that are seen but to the things that are unseen. For the things that are seen are transient, but the things that are unseen are eternal." (2 Corinthians 4:16-18)

Building on his words about the resurrection (vs.13-14) and the grace/ glory of God (v. 15), the apostle continues to explain why he doesn't lose heart. Our bodies may be deteriorating due to the trials, the troubles, and the tribulations of life. In contrast, our hearts and minds can be renewed every day, if we are looking to God and the eternal blessings that await us. If we are not careful, life can easily and quickly drag us down. Paul wants us to see the bigger picture: That the difficulty of this life is easy and brief when compared to the unseen hope of endless life with God. But alas, this hope is so wonderful that it is truly beyond any real comparison.

Today, I will...be renewed on the inside by focusing on the unseen glories to come.

Thursday
The Reconciled

Today's Scripture 2 Corinthians 5:20-21

Continuing his encouragement regarding our glorious future (see 2 Corinthians 4:13-18), Paul refers to our bodies as tents pitched in this current world (2 Corinthians 5:1-5). While we are in our mortal/earthly home, we are painfully awaiting our glorified body, which will be our eternal home or tent (see also 4:11). Paul longs for the resurrection body and living forever with his God.

In a play on words, Paul states that he confidently makes his primary goal to please his Master (vs. 6-9). The judgment day of the King is coming (v. 10), and that should cause us to pause and reflect on our attitudes and on our actions (vs. 11-13). May we then, like Paul, be totally controlled by the love of the Messiah (vs. 14-16). So, we are new creatures in Him and a part of the new creation. The old is passed away, and the new is here to stay!

Paul then concludes that this work is all from God who reconciles people to Himself through the work of Jesus (vs. 18-19). The apostles had been reconciled to God and given a ministry of helping others to also be reconciled to God.

"Therefore, we are ambassadors for Christ, God making his appeal through us. We implore you on behalf of Christ, be reconciled to God. For our sake he made him to be sin who knew no sin, so that in him we might become the righteousness of God." (2 Corinthians 5:20-21)

The apostles are designated as ambassadors sent forth on the King's behalf to bring communion back to His creation. Reconciliation is about renewed friendship and closeness with our Creator. As we read the words of the apostles, we are also being called to be reconciled to our God. Only by the Savior's powerful redemptive sacrifice and His people's repentance is reconciliation possible. Contextually, we then can be sure of our resurrection hope because of the reconciliation we may now enjoy.

Today, I will...be fully controlled by the love of Jesus to draw nearer to God.

Friday
The Grace

Today's Scripture 2 Corinthians 6:1-2

"Working together with him, then, we appeal to you not to receive the grace of God in vain. For he says, 'In a favorable time I listened to you, and in a day of salvation I have helped you.' Behold, now is the favorable time; behold, now is the day of salvation." (2 Corinthians 6:1-2)

After describing himself as God's representative, Paul now urges the Corinthians to appropriately receive the grace of God. God's grace is perhaps the most delightful, stirring, and glorious aspect of God.

Inherent within God's grace is that we never deserve or earn such. However, we must receive His grace. A key point in our text is that it is possible to receive His grace in vain or without His grace reaching its true purpose and power for us, and within our daily lives.

The quote in the second verse is from Isaiah 49:8, a verse showing our God running to our cry for help. Given the context of the passage, Paul is further emphasizing that the day of the Messiah's deliverance for His people is here (compare 5:17-21). Today is the day!

One continuous theme of this letter is that appearances are often deceptive. In the middle of this section, we discover further defense of the ministry and a fascinating list of paradoxes within the lives of these workers (vs. 3-12a).

Perhaps due to a false impression, the Corinthians had distanced themselves from Paul, and therefore, from God. They are warned not to join up with those standing against Paul, unbelievers and idolaters (vs. 12b-18). By referencing several ancient texts, he says to them and to us: You can become friends with God again. Do not destroy that communion by communing with Satan's followers. Be holy and separate as His reverent child (compare 7:1). Remember: Through His grace, God promises to live with us (Leviticus 26:12-13). Truly, the Messianic exodus is upon us (Isaiah 52-53). Receive this grace in its fullness!

Today, I will...let His grace work in me by seeking to live as His holy child.

Week Thirty-Two
2 Corinthians 7-11

Justin Guin

Monday
Widen Your Hearts

In 2 Corinthians 7:2, Paul exhorted the church to "make room in their hearts" for Titus and him. Previously, he instructed them to close their heart to anything which polluted their lives. They were to "bring their holiness to completion in the fear of God" (7:1). Dealing with sin is never an easy task because Satan does not give up easily. The apostle dealt with the problem and sent them a bold letter (7:8). How would they respond? Paul's credibility was already being questioned by those who opposed him. This influential minority caused Paul much grief. Would they heed the apostle's exhortation?

The Corinthians followed Paul's instruction, and Titus' report concerning the situation brought Paul comfort "from God" (7:6-7). The Corinthians longed to see Paul. Even better, they were moved by "godly grief" to repentance (7:9-10). This led to their salvation, and Paul rejoiced at the news of their penitence (7:16). Their grief blessed both Paul and them spiritually because it produced necessary change.

Grief is not often viewed as a positive thing. We must understand the difference between "worldly grief" and "godly grief" (7:9-10). Worldly grief is self-centered and focuses on the loss or denial of something we want for ourselves. It leads to despair, bitterness and paralysis (David Garland, 2 Corinthians, Nashville: Broadman). On the contrary, godly grief is caused by meditating on God's will. It motivates us to change our direction away from sin and towards the Father. An excellent illustration of godly grief leading to repentance is the prodigal son. As he took inventory of his situation, Jesus stated the son "came to himself" and went home to his father. Godly grief recognizes what our choices do to our relationship with God. It motivates us to amend it. Making room for Paul and Titus was deeper than the Corinthian's reconciliation with them. It was reconciliation with God and opening their hearts to His will.

Today, I will...widen my heart to God's instruction, and if I need to repent I will make the necessary changes.

Tuesday
Prove Your Love

In 2 Corinthians 8, Paul exhorted the Corinthians to help with the collection for the poverty-stricken Christians in Jerusalem. He did not command them to be generous since generosity cannot be coerced (8:8). So, he gave them two examples to follow. First, he noted the generosity of the Macedonians. Even though in affliction Paul stated they "overflowed in the wealth of their generosity" (8:1-2). McCord states they "begged" Paul to "earnestly allow them the privilege of sharing in the needs of the saints" (vs. 4, McCord). What a generous heart and proof of agape love for the Corinthians to follow!

Second, Paul referred to the example of Christ. God's marvelous grace enabled the Corinthians to become rich through Christ's poverty (8:9). Note the paradox Paul presents here. How can a person become rich through another's poverty? Only through Christ's vicarious, atoning death is this possible. Christ laid aside His divine privilege to become a man and die on a cross (cf. Philippians 2:6-8). It was rightly stated that Christ is "the supreme and inescapable incentive of all Christian generosity" (Philip E. Hughes, "2 Corinthians," in NASB Study Bible: Zondervan). The Corinthians had two examples of generosity set before them. Would they follow them and prove their love?

2 Corinthians 8 provides the same spiritual challenge for us today. Will we prove our love through generosity? We must not love in "word or talk but in deed and truth." God's love does not abide in a person who has the ability to help someone in need but chooses to close his heart to him (1 John 3:17-18). Constant reflection on Christ's example of love motivates us to give of ourselves to God and others (2 Corinthians 8:5). This chapter challenges us to have the mind of Christ (Philippians 2:5), and this mindset develops a compassionate heart.

Today, I will...have the mind of Christ and strive to develop a compassionate and generous heart. I will seek to help one person who is in need.

The Blessings of a Generous Heart

Today's Scripture 2 Corinthians 9:8-14

At a banquet honoring a highly successful fundraiser for colleges and universities, the person who presented him said, "Here is the greatest beggar in America!" Not pleased by the unintentional misconception of his host, the honored guest replied, "I am not a beggar. I have never begged from anyone. But I have given a lot of people opportunities to be of service to their fellows in this world" (Curtis G. Jones, 1,000 Illustrations for Preaching and Teaching; Broadman and Holman).

Paul was not a beggar on behalf of the Christians in Judea. He offered the Corinthians an opportunity to be of service to other believers. In 2 Corinthians 9, Paul reminded them of the blessings of Christian charity.

First, a generous heart relies on God's strength and resources (9:8-10). God was the source of the Corinthians' efforts. His grace gave them the resources needed to abound in every good work (vss. 8-10). Remember, as the church serves God strengthens and provides.

Second, a generous heart overflows with thanksgiving to God (9:11-13). Both Paul and the Judean Christians offered thanks to God because of the Corinthians' generosity. Their offering was a reminder that God is the source of everything good (cf. James 1:18). Much like the Corinthians, we need to be reminded that God makes us sufficient for ministry. Thus, our service to others flows from a heart of gratitude to Him.

Third, generous hearts advance the well-being and solidarity of the worldwide Christian community (9:13-14). The Judean Christians glorified God and prayed for the Corinthians. The Corinthians' assistance demonstrated their mutual love and concern for the Judeans. This is a beautiful picture of unity and love (cf. Psalm 133:1). The church must do good for all people, but especially those of the household of faith (Galatians 6:10).

Today, I will...remember the church is the hands and feet of God and he makes us sufficient for ministry. As a part of the church, I will abound in every good work endeavoring to serve others.

Commendation That Matters

"Let the one who boasts, boast in the Lord." This was a familiar biblical principle to the Corinthian church. In his first letter to them, Paul referenced this exhortation, which is rooted in Jeremiah 9:23–24, in 1 Corinthians 1:31. He returned to it in 2 Corinthians 10:17. Paul spent much of this letter defending his ministry. He was not a peddler of God's word who deceitfully handled the truth (2:16–17). He preached it with sincerity (2 Corinthians 4:2). Consequently, his ministry was commended by Christ. For Paul, only Christ's commendation mattered (10:18). Note Paul's description of a servant who is commended by Christ.

First, a servant of Christ is characterized by humility and gentleness (10:1). Paul comforted, commanded, and even condemned some of the Corinthians in this letter. Yet, in all of his instruction, he approached them with meekness and gentleness. Jesus described himself as one who was "gentle and lowly" (Matthew 11:29). Paul followed the example of his Lord. A faithful servant is characterized by these qualities. This disposition seeks the best for others in all circumstances (cf. Philippians 2:1–4).

Second, a servant of Christ engages in spiritual warfare (10:3–6). Paul's used the image of spiritual warfare often in his letters (cf. Romans 13:12; Ephesians 6:11–18; 1 Thessalonians 5:8). Here he reminded the Corinthians of their spiritual struggle. The goal of spiritual warfare is to take every thought captive under the lordship of Christ (10:5). We are called to arms against our adversary. He uses every resource at his disposal to draw us away from God. We must stand our ground and pray that our influence is increased. This is not for self-promotion but to spread the knowledge of Christ to a lost world (10:15–16).

There is only one commendation that matters for a Christian. We strive to abound in the Lord's work so we may hear, "Well done, good and faithful servant."

Today, I will…serve Christ with greater gentleness and humility. I will endeavor to take every thought captive to obey Christ so His influence may spread throughout the world.

Friday
Divine Jealousy

2 Corinthians 11 uses an interesting metaphor to describe Paul's work in Corinth. Paul played the part of matchmaker. The bride-to-be was the Corinthian church and the groom, Jesus Christ. Paul spent eighteen months preaching the gospel in Achaia (Acts 18:11). During this time, the church was planted and grew. Problems accompanied the work in Corinth, and Satan tried to destroy the church. Now, three letters later Paul passionately pleads with the Corinthians to rid their lives of Satan's influence. Paul felt "divine jealousy" for them, and he wanted to present them as a pure bride before their Husband (11:2-3).

However, Paul had serious concerns. As Eve was deceived, he was afraid the Corinthians were too. He feared they were led away from their "pure devotion" for Christ (11:3). They must not be deceived by Satan's false preachers (11:13-15). These must be exposed for what they were—Satan's pawns used to destroy the church. This is why Paul responded so strongly to the problems in the Corinthian church. Paul was motivated by divine jealousy.

Let's take a moment to focus on the phrase divine jealousy. "Jealousy" is translated from the word zelos. It refers to an intense positive interest in something or someone (William Danker ed., A Greek-English Lexicon of the New Testament and other Early Christian Literature; University of Chicago Press). Here it refers to God's demand for the church to be exclusively His. The church belongs to Christ, and Paul passionately pled with them to remain faithful.

I love Paul's example in this chapter. Are we motivated by divine jealousy for the Lord's church? When we see worldliness creeping in, do we respond with complacency or conviction? When we hear false doctrine, are we zealous to defend the truth? We need more Christians who are motivated by divine jealousy.

Today, I will...seek to grow in my love and zeal for the Lord and his church. I will do my part to expose the attempts of Satan to hurt the bride of Christ.

Week Thirty-Three
2 Corinthians 12–13
Galatians 1–3

Wayne Jones

Monday
The Power of Sufficient Grace

Today's Scripture 2 Corinthians 12:1-21

Self-promotion should be difficult for God's humble servants. Even filling out a resume or taking an aggressive stance in a job interview might feel too self-serving for most.

Paul seems to struggle with this internal battle throughout the book of 2 Corinthians. His reputation had been tarnished by unsubstantiated rumors and his only recourse was to give his apostolic resumé. That resumé comes to a close in the opening verses of today's reading. Paul acknowledged that these discussions made him look foolish (12:6,11), but they were necessary for the sake of the Corinthian church.

Today's reading takes an important turn when Paul reveals that God allowed an agonizing struggle to be introduced into and remain in his life. The reason? In Paul's words it was to, "to keep me from becoming conceited" (12:7). Paul had an impressive resume and that resume might have become a source of personal pride. Paul desperately and repeatedly sought for the removal of this physical hindrance, but God simply and powerfully responded, "My grace is sufficient for you, my power is made perfect in your weakness" (12:9). Due to the power of God's sufficient grace, Paul was confident that he would be able to fulfill his ministry among the Corinthians (12:14-23).

We, as God's servants today, would do well to appreciate this same principle. It might be tempting to pray and long for the removal of every physical trial and difficult situation of our lives. Yet, God might be using those very things to show His power in our weakness while still providing His grace for our endurance.

While man's words might tend to over inflate our egos or discouragingly suppress our abilities, God's sufficient grace is powerful enough to keep us humble and supply our confidence, all at the same time. Thanks be to God for His sufficient grace.

Today, I will...consider my physical challenges as an open door for God's grace to supply my every need.

Tuesday
Aiming for Restoration

Like the last piece of a jigsaw puzzle or the last drive of the Super Bowl, the last words a New Testament letter can bring everything into focus and cement the message intended throughout. This is especially true in today's reading.

Paul addressed some tough issues, moved out of his comfort zone by boasting of his credentials, and even exposed the greatest burdens of his heart in this intensely personal epistle. What was the point of it all? Perhaps that question is best answered and brought clearly into focus in this last chapter.

So what was Paul's point? Here it is, in his own words: "Finally, brothers, rejoice. Aim for restoration, comfort one another, agree with one another, live in peace; and the God of love and peace will be with you" (2 Corinthians 13:11). Earlier he wrote, "Your restoration is what we pray for" (13:9). Paul had visited Corinth at least twice and written them as many as four letters at the time of this writing. He did all of it – every step and every word – in the pursuit of reconciliation and unity. It was not about personal vindication or the popularity of his ministry. It was about repairing relationships that meant so much to him. It was about the restoration of fellowship, trust, and love that are the staples of the Christian religion (John 13:35).

At the heart of this discussion is the oft-quoted command to "examine yourselves" (13:5). The connection between self-examination and the pursuit of reconciliation should be clear. Broken relationships are generally not one sided nor are they repaired without introspection. Even Jesus taught such in the familiar text of Matthew 7:1-5.

How are your relationships? In the ones that are strained or broken, have you reflected on your role in the problem and in the potential solutions? Are you aiming for restoration?

Today, I will...begin praying for one relationship in my life that needs mending with the determination that it will be restored in the near future.

Wednesday
Because of Me

"Carve your name on hearts, not on tombstones."

Legacies can be a funny thing. At this point in time, we are witnessing in our own country that legacies can change and how we are remembered can fluctuate from generation to generation. Due to social, political, and personal issues, how we are remembered is subject to amendment through the years.

However, in our lucid world, there are some things that never change. There are some legacies that are forever cemented. One such legacy is found in the words that close today's reading. Paul declared, "They gloried God because of me." Can you think of a better legacy than this? Could you imagine words more powerful than these? Can you imagine an impact with more eternal significance than someone glorifying God because of me?

A careful reading of Galatians 1 will highlight some of the reasons that Paul's life was an occasion for others to glorify God. For example, Paul respected the word of God more than another message every delivered (Galatians 1:6-8). Also, Paul's life reflected a strong desire to please the Lord even if it meant displeasing men (1:10). Again, Paul was willing to admit that his former measurement of success was inaccurate (1:13-17). Finally, his life was a living example of the power of the Gospel to change the hearts of men; even the most religiously stubborn men (1:23).

There is no way to insure that history will be kind to our reputations. Since people are imperfect, then their recollection of our deeds will also be imperfect. However, we can control what people see while we are living. We can choose to let Christ shine through us and to let God be seen in our actions. We may not know if 50 years from now they will recall it, but we can do something today that causes others to glorify God because of us.

Today, I will...measure my words, my actions, and my attitudes so that others might glorify God because of me.

The Gospel Is For All

Despite its intended design some have used religion and the church for their own selfish purposes through the years. To some it is another way of controlling others. For some the church is a business wherein they seek to turn a profit. Still others consider the church as a place to jockey for position. In the church and through the church, they attempt to move up the proverbial ladder.

As a result of these perversions, some have developed a self-inflated view of their roles in the church. Rather than being humble servants whose actions are for the good of all who have been saved by faith to the glory of God, they consider themselves on par with God deciding who is worthy of fellowship and who is not. Today's devotional text actually reveals that such attitudes were present in the early church.

This chapter gives us a glimpse into 1st century church tension. Specifically, certain Jews from certain congregations were unwilling to accept and include Gentiles into the church based solely on their conversion to Christ. Like the Pharisees of the Gospels, Even Peter was carried away by the influences and "stood condemned" for it (Galatians 2:10). These hypocritical overtones threatened to compromise influence of the church in a pagan world and even worked to "nullify the grace of God" (2:21).

From this text we learn that when we draw our own lines of fellowship that we can threaten the unity of the church (Galatians 2:14); deny the doctrine of justification by faith (15-16); and supplant the importance of the conversion to Christ (17-20).

We should embrace the diversity of persons that make up the Lord's body. Rather than drawing lines based on our preferences and alienating brethren based on our non-doctrinal difference, we should be thankful for the fact that the Gospel is for all.

Today, I will...thank God that He has saved all men in one body and that He has trusted us to love each other in it.

Father Abraham Had Many Sons

From Vacation Bible Schools of my childhood the words of the song that titles today's thoughts echo in my head. Although the hand motions and body movements that accompany this VBS favorite make you feel like you are doing the Hokey Pokey, the words of this song are deeply imbedded in Scripture. The lyrics include the following: "Father Abraham had many sons and many sons had Father Abraham. I am one of them and so are you. So let's just praise the Lord."

"Know then that it is those of faith who are the sons of Abraham... And if you are Christ's, then you are Abraham's offspring, heirs according to promise." (Galatians 3:7, 29)

It might seem difficult for us to answer that question because the story of Abraham goes all the back to a promise made Genesis 12. The antiquity of the occasion alone can make that promise seem distant and unrelated to our walk with God today. Added to that promise was the law that contained no less than 600 commands to keep (including yearly feast days, animal sacrifices, and mandatory, week rest period).

Yet, the point of Galatians chapter 3 is that it is not law that saves or even promises that make men acceptable in God's sight. Living by faith in Jesus is the key. Abraham had faith before Jesus came and we have faith after His time here on earth. Either way, we are all saved by faith in Him.

Where do you put our faith? Is it in a system of rules that allows you to complete obedient act after another, thus building your case for your own faithfulness? Is it in a religious system God has not authorized, but that others have championed? Or is it the person, power, and promises of Jesus Christ?

Today, I will...do my best to be obedient to my Lord and Master, Jesus Christ. While doing so, I will remind myself that living by faith is the only way to be an heir of that great promise.

Galatians 4-6
Ephesians 1-2

Mike Vestal

Monday
Don't Turn Back

Nothing in the world is more important than a deep, rich knowledge of God. To know Him and to be known by Him is the very essence of eternal life (John 17:3; 2 Timothy 2:19). In this passage, Paul reminds these Christians of their former condition. They "did not know God" and were "enslaved" (vs. 8). What a powerful way of speaking of one's background before coming to Christ!

Then God's word speaks concerning their present condition. "But now that you have come to know God, or rather to be known by God'"(vs. 9). These people had come out of slavery into the family of God! (4:1–7). They had heard and embraced the saving message of Jesus and His gospel (Galatians 1:4; 4:4). They had come to realize something of the richness of being in Christ (Galatians 3:26–29).

Also, this passage speaks of their possible future condition. Notice the use of a rhetorical question: "how can you turn back to the weak and worthless elementary principles of the world, whose slaves you want to be once more?" (vs. 9). The world at times can seem so appealing, but Paul indicates that all it really offers is "weak," a term meaning inefficient, helpless and without strength. He further speaks of this possibility of turning back as being "worthless." Such a return would result in spiritual poverty and deprivation! By returning they would again be "slaves." Paul was so concerned about this possibility that he was afraid that he might have labored over these Christians in vain (vs. 11).

Today, I will...think about my own past before coming to Jesus and focus on the true blessedness of knowing God. I will think about what possible "fatal attractions" are out there that might cause me (and others) to lose sight of the true knowledge of God.

Tuesday
The Freedom to Love

Today's Scripture Galatians 5:13-15

Four expressions help us appreciate the over-all message of this chapter. They are "freedom," "slavery," "the Spirit," and "the flesh." There is marvelous freedom in Christ, and walking in the way of the Spirit will keep us from the works of the flesh, which often enslave. The chapter indicates that those belonging to Christ have resources to help battle Satan, the world's enticements and the flesh!

The emphasis in verses 13-15 is on the the place of God's people (the church) in making it easier to live as God desires. Note the stress on "brothers" (verse 13) and the expression "one another," found three times in this brief section (13, 15). The family of God should make it easier to walk as children of God. The encouragement of Christ's church helps us "stand firm" (5:1) and to pursue life in God (5:25).

Consider four observations from this text. First, there is a calling. Christians have been called to freedom in Christ (vs. 13). This freedom is a release from the bondage of sin due to what Christ did at the Cross on our behalf (John 8:31-36; Romans 6:16-18). Second, there is a practice. The practice is stated negatively, then positively. "Only do not use your freedom as an opportunity for the flesh, but through love serve one another" (vs. 13). Next, there is an explanation or expansion of the thought. "For the whole law is fulfilled in one word: 'You shall love your neighbor as yourself'" (vs. 14). God truly is honored when His people properly love and serve others! Christian love is not to be self-indulgent, but love with Christ's love in serving others. Finally, there is a warning. Do not "bite and devour one another" (vs. 15).

Today, I will...remember that my calling as a Christian must result in the practice of loving, selfless service. Such service may well cause others to know the freedom Jesus gives!

Wednesday
The Necessity of Being Christ-Centered

Today's Scripture Galatians 6:11-18

The book of Galatians was written in the heat of controversy. There were some who were trying to coerce Christians to be circumcised and to observe various aspects of the Jewish law. Paul saw this as a threat to the very nature of the gospel (Galatians 1:6-9) and said "to them we did not yield in submission even for a moment, so that the truth of the gospel might be preserved for you" (Galatians 2:5). This was a critical matter that could have threatened the life and health of the early church! But even then, Paul kept Jesus preeminent. No matter what the circumstance, there is an amazing Christ-centeredness in Paul that is well worth our contemplation. Here are three questions from this text to think about.

Am I Christ-Centered When Persecuted and Hurt? (vs. 12 and 17). When we go through times of intense, unpleasant controversy and suffering, when things get both personal and hurtful, does Jesus shine in us? You can tell a lot about a person by what and how they suffer! (John 16:33; 1 Peter 4:12-19). Paul was willing to suffer for the cross of Christ. He bore the "marks" of Jesus. Will we?

Am I Christ-Centered When Boasting or Glorying? (vs. 14). To Paul, there simply were no personal grounds for boasting or pride; there only was legitimate reason for glorying in Christ and His cross. Sadly, we often struggle here. We can boast of personal accomplishments, abilities, opportunities and possessions—but fail to exult enough in what God has done through Jesus.

Am I Christ-Centered In Encouraging Others? (vs. 18). Paul was quick to encourage others in requesting that "the grace of the Lord Jesus Christ be with your spirit." Through grace, we all can become more Christ-centered. Grace ever reminds us of His sufficiency, goodness and mercy!

Today, I will...seek to be Christ-Centered in how I think, speak and act.

202

Thursday
Blessed, Blessed, Blessed!

Today's Scripture Ephesians 1:3-14

Blessed, blessed, blessed! That is how today's Scripture begins (Ephesians 1:3). Then the apostle Paul unpacks a truckload of truth as it concerns the vocabulary of victory and salvation. He indicates what God has done "in Christ" (notice how often this is repeated) for us to be saved.

God has "chosen" (vs. 4), "predestined" and "adopted" us (vs. 5) and extended to us "glorious grace" (vs. 6). In Christ, there is "redemption" by His "blood," allowing us to experience "the riches of his grace" (vs. 7-8). In Christ God has "made known" the "mystery" of His counsel and "will" regarding man's salvation—along with how "all things" can be united (vs. 9-10). In Christ, an "inheritance" can be obtained, "hope" has been given, the good news of the "gospel" is made known, the "word of truth" has come and the Spirit has been given as a "seal" (vs. 11-13). Now, that is being blessed!

Even more, this passage speaks of the involvement of the Trinity in blessing. The Father (vs. 3-6), the Son (1:7ff) and the Holy Spirit (1:13) all are mentioned. What an amazing thought to realize that there is a God in Heaven, and that God Himself wants to have a rich and eternal relationship with us! But more—think of His plans and actions in making such a relationship possible in Christ!

This passage overflows with theology; it is absolutely breathtaking as it speaks of God and the things of God concerning salvation. True biblical theology is not dull and lifeless, but inspires and instills greater love, devotion, worship and service. Paul himself shows us how theology should lead to doxology and praise. Three times in this passage, Paul bursts into praise (vs. 6, 12, 14). By being "in Christ," one can find incredible blessing and riches.

Today, I will...seek to have a mind that has thought deeply about God and His will and a heart that reflects worship, praise and devotion.

Friday
Jesus — Bringer of Peace

In five short verses, grand themes such as Christ, the cross, race relations, the taking away of the Old Testament, unity and the removal of hostility, the gospel, the church, reconciliation, access to God and the Trinity all are beautifully and powerfully linked. As crucial as are all these themes, "peace" dominates this passage both explicitly (vv. 14, 15, 17) and implicitly. Here both the horizontal and vertical dimensions of peace are treated within the framework of God's saving plan in Christ. In this marvelous section, there are four great truths to remember about peace.

Remember Jesus Is the Embodiment of Peace. "For he himself is our peace" (Ephesians 2:14). The personal pronoun "he himself" is at the beginning for the sake of emphasis. The point simply must not be missed; there was hostility but now the One who brought us near is "our peace." Paul seeks to connect Jesus and peace as comprehensively as possible. Without Jesus, there is no peace.

Remember the Means of Peace. The question now turns to "how." How did Jesus bring peace to us? The text yields three expressions that provide insight. They are that Jesus "has made us both one" (vs. 14), "has broken down in his flesh the dividing wall of hostility" (vs. 14), and that he has "abolished the law of commandments expressed in ordinances" (vs. 15). These were done by means of His death.

Remember the Purpose of Peace. But why? The purpose of Christ's removing the hostility by bringing to an end the old law was twofold: (1) "To create in himself one new man in place of the two" (vs. 15); and, (2) To "reconcile us both to God in one body through the cross" (vs. 16).

Remember the Result of Peace. Verse 18 says, "For through him we both have access in one Spirit to the Father." Jesus provides us access to God!

Today, I will...be an instrument of Christ's peace in a fractured, often hostile world.

Week Thirty-Five
Ephesians 3-6
Philippians 1

Jay Lockhart

Monday
A Prayer for Ministry

The apostle Paul was thankful he was privileged to be a preacher and he considered himself to be a steward of the gospel of God's grace (3: 1-2). He spoke of the gospel as God's "mystery," something unknown to anyone until God revealed it "to His holy apostles and prophets by the Spirit" (3: 3). As an apostle, Paul received the gospel he preached by revelation and inspiration (see 3: 4-6; I Corinthians 2: 7-14) and, thus, became a minister to proclaim the message (3: 7-9). All of this was according to the eternal purpose of God, and God's purpose included the work of the church in making the message known (3: 10-13).

God is depending upon the church to get the message of the gospel to the world. To accomplish its mission, the church must not only have the will to do it, but the blessings of God to accomplish it. Therefore, immediately after speaking of the mission, Paul prayed for the Ephesians that God would help them to succeed.

Three petitions were made by the apostle, each one introduced by the conjunction, "that", implying "purpose, design, and result" (Bullinger, A Critical Lexicon and Concordance to the English and Greek New Testament, p. 836). First, there is the request for power to do the job by the indwelling Spirit of God and the Christ who dwells in our hearts. We know that God (2: 22), the Holy Spirit (3:16), and Christ (3:17) dwell in us "by faith" (3: 17). Second, there is the request for motivation to do the job by the love of Christ (3: 17-19). Although we cannot fully comprehend the great dimensions of heaven's love for us, the fact, of this love is the motivation for doing the Lord's work (2 Corinthians 5: 14). Third, there is the request for the fullness of God (3: 19). The passive voice of this request suggests that it is for something done to us as we yield to God.

Today, I will...ask God to help me be bold in inviting three people to attend worship with me this Sunday.

Tuesday

Walking Worthy of the Calling

The theme of Paul's letter to the Ephesians may be stated in this way: The Eternal Purpose Of God In Christ and The Church. The letter divides itself into two parts: The Doctrinal Section in which the apostle develops the theme; and the Practical Section in which he gives the practical application of the theme as it is lived out in the lives of members of the church. The verses under consideration today emphasize the importance of walking (living) according to who we have become in Christ. Paul said, "Walk in a manner worthy" of those who have become "the saints" of God (1: 1).

There are six words in this section that describe how we can be successful in this walk: "humility" (our attitude toward self – 2); "gentleness" (our attitude toward others—2); "unity" (our attitude toward the truth of God's word – 3–6, 13 "love" (for self, others, and the word of God – 2, 15-16); "grow" (our maturity in Christ – 15); and "working" (each member doing his part – 16).

As we set our minds upon "walking worthy of the calling," we should remember that God helps us in becoming what we are to become (7-12). God has always given the church what it needs. Before there was a completed New Testament, God gave "the apostles and prophets," inspired men to speak and then to write down the message of the New Testament. With the completion of the New Testament their work was done and there remained no need for successors. Further, God gave the church "the evangelists, the shepherds, and teachers," those who would always be needed to advance the cause of Christ until He comes again. God's gifts to the church are for the purpose of providing the church with what is needed in order that each individual member may "walk in a manner worthy" of the purpose for which we have been called (2 Thessalonians 2: 14) into the church, the body of Christ.

Today, I will...use God's resources in order to neither speak a work or perform an action until I ask: "What would Jesus do?"

207

Wednesday
Be Filled with the Spirit

Today's Scripture Ephesians 5:15-21

Paul urged the Ephesians to walk "carefully" and by so doing, to demonstrate that they were truly "wise" (15). Wisdom is deep knowledge, moral insight, and enlightened understanding. If one is unwise, he lacks knowledge, insight, and understanding. In the midst of the paragraph under consideration, he said, "Be filled with the Spirit" (18). Man is controlled by that with which he is filled. If he is filled with wine, he will be controlled by wine, and that is a wasted, foolish, out-of-control life (the meaning of "debauchery"). On the other hand, when one is filled with the Spirit of God he lives a controlled, productive, wise life. Notice that being filled with the Spirit is an imperative and is not optional.

So, how can I know when I am "filled with the Spirit," and, in God's sight, being "wise"? First, the Christian's life begins when, as penitent believers, we are baptized into Christ and receive "the forgiveness of sins" and "the gift of the Holy Spirit" (Acts 2:38). This gift of the Spirit is the Spirit Himself (Acts 5:32; I Corinthians 6: 19), who helps us in living the Christian life (Romans 8: 13, 26-27; Galatians 5: 22-23). Therefore, if one is to "be filled with the Spirit, he must be in Christ. One may ask, "I have been baptized into Christ, but how can I know I am filled with the Spirit? Here are five clues from our text:

1. Take advantage of your opportunities to do good (16).

2. Understand the will of God through study (17).

3. Worship faithfully with the church (19).

4. Be thankful (20).

5. Submit to one another (21) by being more concerned about the welfare of others than about yourself.

Today, I will...spend time in the study of scripture, and then find an opportunity to do something nice for someone else.

Thursday
The Whole Armor of God

Today's Scripture Ephesians 6:10-20

There is a spiritual war going on in the universe. It is a war between God and Satan, light and darkness, good and evil, and right and wrong. This war is unseen, but real. It is being fought in the spiritual realm (12) and with spiritual weapons (see 2 Corinthians 10: 4). It is the battle for the minds of men (2 Corinthians 10: 5) and every member of the church must be engaged, unless we have already surrendered.

What are the prospects for victory? The people of God are going to win. First, there is the power of God (10). Second, there is the cross and the empty tomb of Christ who has already won the war with evil (Revelation 12: 11). Third, there is the encouragement of the church as each member is fully engaged and doing his part (Ephesians 4:16), and as each member reaches out to other members when we worship as the church (Hebrews 10: 24-25). Fourth, there is the legacy left by other servants of God who have gone on before us (Hebrews 12: 1). Fifth, there is the Christian armor that helps us stand against the devil's plans and tricks (11). There is the belt of truth (God's word manifested in flesh in the person of Christ); there is the breastplate of righteousness (relationship with God); there are the shoes of peace (the gospel of peace); there is shield of faith (which absorbs the evil darts of Satan); there is the helmet of salvation (protecting our minds from onslaughts of error); there is the sword of the Spirit, the word of God (our offensive weapon against every false teaching). Take the armor and win! And don't forget to pray (18).

Today, I will...be aware of the battle for the minds of men and I will seek to think as Christ would think, talk like Christ would talk, and act like Christ would act.

Approve What Is Excellent

Today's Scripture Philippians 1:3-11

It is wonderfully encouraging to have someone say to us, "I am praying for you." That, in effect, is what Paul was saying to the Philippians in our text. The church at Philippi was loved in a special way by Paul. He had planted this church, as the first congregation in Europe, on his Second Missionary Journey. He wrote his letter to the Philippians, in part, to thank them for their encouragement and financial support in his work. From the very first, they had supported Paul (1: 5). Having lost track of him, they had not supported him for a while, but having learned of his state, they had begun their financial support again (4: 10). Paul thanked them for what they had done for him in the past and for what they would yet do for him (4: 14-20). The letter Paul wrote was a letter of joy, summarized in 4: 4: *"Rejoice in the Lord always; again, I say, Rejoice."* Paul loved the Philippians and for them he prayed.

What did Paul pray? That their love might overflow, that their insight would grow in the things of God, that discernment would be clear, and that they might "approve the things that are excellent" (1: 9-10). He wanted them to choose good over bad, but also to choose better over good, and the best over better. In encouraging the Philippians to choose the best, Paul wanted them to make the best choices possible so that they might be the best people possible. All of this was to prepare them for the coming of the "day of Christ," the second coming of Christ and the final judgment (1: 10). So, let us today choose the best!

Today, I will...weigh my choices and settle not for the good, or even the better, but the best.

Week Thirty-Six
Philippians 2–4
Colossians 1–2

Kurt Montooth

Shine As Lights In the World

We know from history and the whole of scripture that the church in Philippi was under heavy persecution, just like Paul was when he wrote the book from jail in Rome! Most Bible commentaries and scholars teach that when Paul wrote the letter to the Philippians that he had four reasons for writing. Two of those motives were to encourage perseverance in the church during the persecution they were under, and to encourage unity in the church. That's the theme which is on display in Philippians 2. While it is very clear that Paul wanted the church to accomplish both of those things, I think it's a mistake to separate the two as if they are unrelated.

The Philippians lived in a time where it was extremely difficult to be a Christian, and they needed one another if they were going to both make it through life faithfully and have a positive impact on a lost and dying world. Paul understood that perfectly! Take time today to read what he writes about Christian unity in Philippians 2:1-14 as leading into what he says in v.15-16: *"that you may be blameless and innocent, children of God without blemish in the midst of a crooked and twisted generation, among whom you shine as lights in the world, holding fast to the word of life, so that in the day of Christ I may be proud that I did not run in vain or labor in vain."*

Today, just like in Paul's day, the world desperately needs faithful Christians shining light into the darkness. Only together can we do those things effectively! The church is vital and necessary for Christians to make it through a difficult life, but it's also vital and necessary as God's chosen vehicle for sharing the light of the gospel. The church can accomplish nothing for the kingdom unless it is united in Christ. Take time today and this week to pray for the congregation where you attend, and make a list of actions you should take to help build unity among the brethren.

Today, I will...Focus on helping bring unity to the church, understanding that the salvation of many depends on it!

Tuesday
Passionate Faithfulness Is Not Optional!

Today's Scripture Philippians 3

The Philippian letter is especially powerful because of the circumstances in which it is written. Paul writes about all the blessings found in Christ and the joy he has despite his persecution and imprisonment! In fact, even though Philippians is written under some of the harshest circumstances, its message is so positive that false teachers of the prosperity gospel frequently pervert parts of Philippians to justify their false doctrine. One of the things Paul says gives him great joy in Philippians is his hope of eternal life. In Philippians 3:7-14 Paul lays out what he would do to have eternal life: Anything. There Paul writes that he counted his former life as garbage, and that he would gladly given up everything he had and every ounce of his effort one day to receive the heavenly prize!

This would be no surprise to the Philippian church—not only had they been associated with one another for over a decade, but Paul had already told them in Philippians 1:20-26 that he was going to be delivered from his troubles, either by being released from prison or by being executed and going to be with Christ! In fact, he even mentions that he would prefer execution so he could go be with Christ but he plans to make his best effort to stay on earth in order that he might continue to serve God as a minister!

Today, Christians desperately need to follow the example of Paul. Passionate faithfulness is not optional! Philippians teaches us that the most important thing in Paul's life was his faithfulness to God and God's mission of sharing the Gospel. I'd like to encourage you today to read Philippians 3 and ask yourself: what in your life is keeping you from sharing the message of God? What do you need to count as loss and throw away?

Today, I will...Make a list of things I need to "count as loss" and brainstorm how to do so.

Wednesday
Think About These Things

We live in a society dominated by anxiety. A Psychology today article published in 2008 by Dr. Robert Leahy asserts that 49% of the U.S. population has dealt with an anxiety-related disorder at some point in their life. Since anxiety and stress levels since 2008 have been on the rise, I'm going to go ahead and assume that the number has climbed to over 50%. I'm quite confident the rest of our country (who will never have an anxiety-caused mental illness) still struggles with anxiety on almost a daily basis.

Philippians 4 is a powerful chapter for the Christian about how to overcome anxiety. You are probably already familiar with Philippians 4:4-7, where Christians are commanded to rejoice and pray with thankfulness in order to receive the peace of God which cannot be understood. These are powerful verses that a Christian struggling with anxiety can't afford to overlook. However, when we as Christians think about overcoming anxiety, we also must consider Philippians 4:8-9 which reads in the ESV, *"Finally, brothers, whatever is true, whatever is honorable, whatever is just, whatever is pure, whatever is lovely, whatever is commendable, if there is any excellence, if there is anything worthy of praise, think about these things. What you have learned and received and heard and seen in me—practice these things, and the God of peace will be with you."*

Now, I understand there are faithful brothers and sisters that struggle with legitimate mental illness caused by physiological conditions outside of their control (like chemical imbalances in the brain) but I also know (the Bible tells me so) that much of the anxiety plaguing our society is because as a culture, we have rejected "The God of Peace" and the actions He wants us to take that produce peace. We live in a society that is permeated by sin, and anxiety and worry are a natural consequence of sin!

Today, I will...Think on the things of God and not sin. I will invite the God of peace and the peace that He brings with Him into my life.

Thursday
Be an Epaphras

It seems in his ministry, Paul prioritized preaching in large cities, probably because he could influence more people that way. However, Colossae was not a large city and it's almost unmentioned in history outside of scripture. The book of Colossians makes it clear that Paul had never traveled to the city of Colossae and it tells us the church there was established by a man named Epaphras. Not much is known about Epaphras except that Colossians 1:7 and 4:12-13 tell us that Epaphras established the church in Colossae, was native to the area, and seems to be a missionary working with Paul and financially supported by the church in Colossae by the time Paul wrote Colossians. We don't know how Epaphras was converted but some have theorized that while Paul was preaching in Ephesus, Epaphras might have traveled to the large city for business or vacation and heard Paul preach there, and returned home to share the gospel.

I tell you this because I think Epaphras should be a role model for all Christians. It's most logical to assume because of Paul's missionary patterns in the book of Acts that he'd have never traveled to Colossae and preached the Gospel. Therefore, the reason a church exists there is because Epaphras learned the gospel and preached it to his family, friends, and neighbors in his hometown.

I truly believe that for every Christian, there are people in your life that will only hear the gospel if you tell it to them. You probably have a friend or acquaintance for whom you're the only Christian they know. This was the case for a lot of people in Colossae but Epaphras stepped in and made a difference! What will you do? I encourage you to write down a list of five names that represent lost souls that you have the best chance (or only chance) to reach. Pray for those five people, and start to formulate a plan to share the gospel with them. It's your responsibility as a faithful believer: not the preachers, the elders, or missionaries. God gave it to you: go be an Epaphras to them!

Today, I will...Reach out to the people on the list I have made..

Friday
Truth Has Already Been Decided

There are so many interesting and powerful things in Colossians 2 for us to discuss today. However, there are three phrases I want to highlight, Verse 4, *"I say this in order that no one may delude you with plausible arguments."* Verse 8, *"See to it that no one takes you captive by philosophy and empty deceit, according to human tradition, according to the elemental spirits of the world, and not according to Christ."* Finally verse 23, *"These have indeed an appearance of wisdom in promoting self-made religion and asceticism and severity to the body, but they are of no value in stopping the indulgence of the flesh."*

Now Paul, like we discussed yesterday, was writing to a new church and the purposes of these passages was to keep them from being misled by false doctrine that on the surface seems like it makes sense but in the end is false. Not surprisingly almost 2000 years later, the church still faces the same problem.

There are a lot of ideas in culture, science, and religion that all sound good and wise but they are not! A prominent example of this in our society relates to sins of a physical and carnal nature. You can find a relationship/marriage/mental health professional that will make a "plausible argument," with the "appearance of wisdom" telling you that any and every type of perversion is not only acceptable but good for you. However, God has already warned us about the danger of these sins in His word and we should know that these experts are not trustworthy because their teaching is "not according to Christ."

Today's challenge: even though it is counter-cultural (maybe BECAUSE it is counter-cultural), remember that truth is not decided by compelling argument or popularity or appearances of wisdom—the truth has already been decided by God and revealed to us by His word.

Today, I will...Live in joyful, healthy, stable relationships in submission to His word.

Colossians 3-4
1 Thessalonians 1-3

Denny Petrillo

Monday
Therefore...

By ourselves, we are nothing. We are sinners, lost and falling short of God's glory (Romans 3:23). By ourselves, we accomplish nothing. The fruit of our lives will not be productive for the cause of Christ (Matthew 7:15-23). Yet when we are in Christ, Paul says we should "reach all the riches of full assurance of understanding and the knowledge of God's mystery, which is Christ, in whom are hidden all the treasures of wisdom and knowledge" (Colossians 2:2). A few verses later he declares "you have been filled" (Colossians 2:10). Filled? There is no room for anything else? Exactly! Why? Because you do not need anything else!

Our baptism into Christ (2:12) has both eternal and temporal consequences. It no longer is viewed as a solitary act that took place in our past. Instead, it was the beginning point to a different life — at least, it should have been the beginning point.

While not always visible in the English translations, Paul follows his point about our acceptance of Christ with several "therefore" paragraphs (each section begins with the same Greek preposition).

2:6-15 — Therefore, if we truly accepted Christ, act like it!
2:16-23 — Therefore, don't let anyone steal away your joy of salvation.
3:1-4 — Therefore, keep your head in the game! "Set your minds on things that are above" (v. 3).
3:5-11 — Therefore, destroy all thoughts that are unspiritual (vv. 5-9), and surround yourself with all thoughts that are Christ-like (vv. 10-11).
3:12-25 — Therefore, act like someone "chosen of God."

A few thoughts: God's plan is for us, each and every day, to reflect our relationship with Christ. The text in Colossians 3 should leap off the page and manifest itself in how we act, talk and treat others. It is the practical application that is crucial.

Today, I will...act like I belong to Christ, talk like I belong to Christ and manifest His love in my life.

Tuesday
Silence Is Not Always Golden

Today's Scripture Colossians 4:1-18

We frequently heard as children the saying "sticks and stones may break my bones but words can never hurt me." As time goes on, we learned just how untrue that saying was. Even Solomon noted that words "are like the thrusts of a sword" (Proverbs 12:18). Words are powerful tools, both for good and for evil.

Today we're considering Colossians 4. Think of this chapter in terms of the use of words on the lips of Christians.

First, those words can be found in prayer. In our prayers we express our gratitude (v. 2) and pray for God's workers (v. 3). We even pray for the gospel, that as it is preached it finds receptive hearts, and is preached clearly (v. 4).

Second, words need to be spoken with wisdom when in the presence of the lost (v. 5). We don't know if we'll ever have the opportunity to speak to them the saving message of Jesus Christ.

Third, words need to be "with grace" (v. 6). People are going to be more receptive to words that are said with kindness and sensitivity. No one wants to be badgered or berated. There is a correct way to talk to people (cf. Proverbs 15:23).

Fourth, we need to use our words to communicate to other brethren news of the work of God. Onesimus was going to "inform them" of what was happening. It is important that the people of God communicate with each other (vv. 7-9).

Fifth, we need to keep other Christian workers in our thoughts, prayers and discussions. People "out there" are putting everything at risk for the sake of the gospel. Equally, our local ministers are hard at work, "laboring earnestly" on our behalf. They use their words to pray for us. We should do the same for them (vv. 10-18).

A few thoughts: Let's all think about our words, and how those words impact the work of God. Silence is not always golden. We need to be ambassadors for Christ.

Today, I will…give careful thought to my words. Are they true, necessary, kind and helpful?

Wednesday
True and Genuine

There was something about the church at Thessalonica that Paul loved. This church, in so many ways, "got it right." Paul thanked God for them.

When he prayed for them, there were three aspects of their Christianity that stood out. Today, we should ask ourselves: "do these same attributes describe me as well?"

First, Paul was grateful for their "work of faith." Sometimes these are two words that we do not put together (probably because of some denominational ideas). Yet they most certainly belong together. A person might be able to talk the talk, where he or she sounds like a genuine Christian. Yet our faith is real when it is demonstrated. We should be busy doing the Lord's work. When we are, we know our faith is genuine (Ephesians 2:10; James 2:14-26).

Second, Paul was grateful for their "labor of love." We already identified that they were workers, but this word "labor" indicates an even more intense, difficult kind of work. They were not afraid to take on the tough, unpleasant jobs. What is even more impressive is that they did it out of love. This is agape love, where it is done out of a genuine, sincere concern for someone else.

Third, Paul was grateful for their "steadfastness of hope." In the Bible, "hope" means desire plus expectation. These great Christians were those who stayed the course despite great obstacles and opposition (v. 6). We can't be Christians some days and act like the world others. To be what God wants us to be, we need to maintain our hope every day. If we are not continually faithful, how can we have a legitimate hope?

A few thoughts: The Thessalonian church had a great reputation that went throughout the ancient world (v. 7). These brethren were true and genuine. No one would accuse them of being hypocrites. How about me? How do people see me?

Today, I will...consider how I impact the work of Christ in my life and associations. Am I genuine in my faith and consistent in my words?

Thursday
The Gospel Is Worth It

Today's Scripture 1 Thessalonians 2:1-20

Have you ever given much thought to what the apostles went through in order to preach the gospel? In this chapter we see clearly how they suffered and were mistreated (v. 2). They did not do what they did in order to receive glory from men (v. 6). They even worked secular jobs in order to not be a burden on the church (vv. 9-10). They did it because they loved people and wanted to bring this saving message into their lives (vv. 11-12). Their ultimate goal was to get people to "walk in a manner worthy of the God who calls you into His own kingdom and glory" (v. 12).

Their sacrifices were worth it. The people in Thessalonica accepted the message preached as the word of God, not some man-made doctrine (v. 13). As a result of their becoming Christians, Paul could proudly say that "you are our glory and joy" (v. 20).

This chapter brings to mind some important truths.

First, to those first century preachers, the "good news" of Jesus Christ was worth any cost or sacrifice. When we think about our own list of priorities, where is the gospel listed? Is it even listed at all? Jesus said that we needed to "seek first the kingdom of God" (Matthew 6:33). Are we doing that?

Second, despite the horrible things they endured, seeing others obey the gospel brought them unspeakable joy and satisfaction. Sometimes (many times?) we are not willing to go through the slightest inconvenience or embarrassment to share the gospel with someone else. Yet being instrumental in someone else's conversion to Christ is one of this life's greatest achievements. That person we led to Christ becomes our "glory and joy" as well.

Today, I will...remind myself how important the gospel of Jesus is to me and my life.

Friday
Abound In Love

Apparently the Thessalonian church received word that Paul, Silas and Timothy had suffered much trying to preach the gospel. Yet Paul had told them not to "be moved (disturbed) by these afflictions" (v. 3). He says proudly, "we were destined for this!" They even gave the church there an advanced warning that this kind of opposition and persecution was going to happen (v. 4).

Yet these three men were more concerned about the well-being of the church in Thessalonica than for themselves! They knew this was a young church, and were anxious to hear about how they were doing (v. 5). Specifically, Paul was afraid that two events might have taken place. First, he was afraid that "the tempter had tempted you" (v. 5). What does that mean? They feared that Satan had been successful in getting them to doubt the truth of the gospel message and its promises. Second, Paul and his companions feared that "our labor would be in vain" (v. 5). These three preachers had endured much to get the gospel to the Thessalonian brethren. It would be discouraging to hear that it was all a waste of time. Thankfully, Paul's concerns were unfounded. Timothy brought back word that the church was doing great, and standing firm in the faith (vv. 8-9).

Paul ends this chapter with some stated goals, goals that would be good for us to think about as we go about our day.

First, Paul wanted them to "increase and abound in love for one another" (v. 12). Do our brothers and sisters know how much we care about them? Have we expressed that love? Have we demonstrated it?

Second, Paul wanted them to increase in their love "for all." We need to develop a worldwide view and think about the lost everywhere.

Third, Paul wanted them to be "blameless in holiness" (v. 13). Jesus is coming. Maybe He will come today! We need to make sure we have our spiritual house in order.

Today, I will...think about how I demonstrate the love of Christ to others.

Week Thirty-Eight
1 Thessalonians 4-5
2 Thessalonians 1-3

David Morris

Monday

Life in Light of the Return of Jesus

Today's Scripture 1 Thessalonians 4:1-18

As chapter three closes, Paul mentions "the coming of our Lord Jesus with all his saints" (3:13). The Thessalonians doubted their dead would experience the glorious return of Christ, and Paul wants to comfort them.

Christians are motivated by Christ's return to live "blameless" lives. God's main concern is that His people be sanctified, growing more like Him (4:3). Specifically, the Thessalonians are to pay close attention to two areas of sanctification: 1) sexual purity, a major concern for Gentile converts, and 2) brotherly love. As they thought forward to Christ's return, the danger was to neglect their everyday responsibilities (4:11-12) instead of behaving in brotherly love.

Having established how to live in light of Jesus' return, Paul now moves to alleviate their fears that their loved ones will miss out on the second coming: there is no need to worry for when Jesus comes He will have the dead with Him (vs. 13f).

Paul uses an important term in 4:15, the word *parousia* (pahr-oo-see-uh). In the first century, the word came to mean the arrival of a ruler to a city where he is greeted with celebration and honor. Paul associates the word with the return of Jesus. Christ will re-appear coming down from heaven; Satan and his forces will be destroyed; believers will be reunited with their dead in the presence of Christ; judgement will be completed.

Jesus will arrive with the souls of the faithful. These souls are reunited with the resurrected transformed body (1 Corinthians 15:35ff) in a real, historical, reality-changing event. While Christians may sorrow when they lose someone they love (Romans12:15), those they love will not be excluded from the joy of Christ's return.

The happy certainty is that all saints continue "with the Lord forever" (4:17) and experience His glory. This is an amazing source of comfort not just for Paul's original readers (4:18), but also for us.

Today, I will...meditate on the glories of Jesus' return and the future reunion with my faithful loved ones.

Tuesday
A Thief in the Night

While Paul had previously taught the Thessalonians about Jesus' return during his visit, they were still worried about it. In chapter four, Paul addresses their worry over dead loved ones. In chapter five, Paul addresses the timing of Jesus' return.

Unlike so many in our modern age, Paul refuses to be lured into a discussion of setting dates for Jesus' return. Instead, Paul tells them that they have "no need to have anything written" about dates or times (5:1). The church already knew that nothing could be known about its timing from Jesus himself (Mark 13:32; Acts 1:7).

So, Paul is not identifying dates. He is describing "how" Christ will return. He does this with two vivid illustrations: 1) a thief who comes at night (vs.2), and 2) the suddenness of labor pains (vs.3). Both illustrate the unpredictability of Jesus' arrival.

Christians are to be "fully aware" of something: the return of Jesus can be known as accurately as the arrival of a thief. As we well know, thieves do not call your house ahead of time to let you know of the time of their arrival.

Paul calls the return of Christ "the day of the Lord." "Day" meant for them, "time" or "event." The phrase "Day of the Lord" describes a final divine intervention.

This day is a disastrous "sudden destruction" for the enemies of God (vs. 3). But for the Christian, Paul says they should not to be surprised but on guard (vss. 4–8). Part of this preparation is to "put on the breastplate of faith and love, and for a helmet the hope of salvation" (vs.8). Salvation in the Bible includes forgiveness but also has to do with the broader idea of rescue. Christians ready themselves for God's rescue, whenever it happens.

But our ultimate rescue rests on what God has done for us in the person of Jesus (vss. 9f).

Today, I will...encourage specific brothers and sisters in obtaining salvation (vs.11).

Wednesday
Marveling at Jesus

Today's Scripture 2 Thessalonians 1:4-10

Paul's second letter to the Thessalonians has a familiar main theme for them—the study of last things. Paul taught them that they are to live life in light of the return of Jesus (1 Thessalonians 4:1-18). But they are not to be afraid of it, because it is a day when God intervenes and rescues those who belong to Him (1 Thessalonians 5:1-11).

The opening of Paul's second letter makes it clear that living "blameless" (1 Thessalonians 3:13) matters and is rewarded. But those who are persecuting God's people will experience punishment (vss. 5-10).

Paul is proud of those who maintain their faith in the face of persecution. That kind of "steadfastness and faith" and "enduring" (vs. 4) is "evidence" that they will be "worthy of the kingdom of God" (vs. 5). Paul is saying to the persecuted, "I am bragging about you; your faithfulness shows God will rescue you."

But Paul also knows the Thessalonians wonder about persecutors who seem to escape punishment. So Paul highlights the judgment. This judgment takes place "when the Lord Jesus is revealed from heaven" (vs. 7). Jesus' return has all the awesomeness one might expect: the familiar "mighty angels" (vs. 7) and "flaming fire" (vs. 8) like many appearances of God in the O.T.

Jesus inflicts a repaying "vengeance" (vs. 6) on those who "do not obey the gospel" (vs. 8). The gospel is the story of Jesus and how He becomes the Messianic King. Persecutors are ignorant of God's character, that He is a revenger on those who harm His children.

Think about it: what greater joy could there be than to be in "the presence of the Lord and...the glory of his might" (vs. 9)? Conversely, what greater punishment could there be? To "marvel at" Jesus in His return is the greatest purpose and greatest pleasure of the Christians. Finally, we will see "the glory of God in the face of Jesus Christ" (2 Corinthians 4:4).

Today, I will...imagine the wonder and awe of seeing Jesus for the first time, and be strengthened by it.

Beware of Deceivers

This section is one of the most difficult to interpret in all of the Bible. Paul continues comforting the Thessalonian church over concerns they have about last things.

Paul wants them to not be deceived. History has taught us that when Christians ponder too much about the end times their beliefs and behavior becomes strange. Paul is working to avoid this, and we as modern readers should also pay attention to his warnings.

Paul is concerned they might think "that the day of the Lord has come" (2:2). They (and we) should know better, for the events of that Day are public and obvious (1 Thessalonians 4:16), since it is quite noisy and dead people are rising!

He thinks this deception may come from "a spoken word, or a letter seeming to be from us" (2:2). Apostasy was something the church already knew about. But this particular "rebellion" would be accompanied by a challenging figure opposed to everything about God. He is described five ways: 1) a "man of lawlessness" serving as Satan's prophet; 2) "the son of destruction" (2:3), referring to his destiny; 3) he "exalts himself" instead of God; 4) "takes his seat in the temple of God"; 5) "proclaiming himself to be God" (2:4).

Scholars have been widely divided over the identity of this person, from false Messiahs to the Papacy. The majority of scholars have seen this as a reference to persecuting Roman authorities who required Christians to pay homage to them as demi-gods (Daniel 11:36; Luke 21:20–22).

Whatever the right interpretation may be, we know the Thessalonians knew what Paul meant (2 Thessalonians 2:5). As for us, we must rest assured that in the end Christ will utterly defeat (vs. 8) all enemies. But there will sadly be those who will be so deceived by Satan that they refuse to be saved (vss. 9–12).

Today, I will...purify myself of anything that tries to take the place of Christ in my life. Christ is my King.

Friday
You Pray for Me, I'll Pray for You

As Paul ministered these letters to the Thessalonians, he has mentioned his prayers for them (2:16-17). As he comes to the close of this his second letter, he now asks for prayer from them for himself and his fellow evangelists (3:1ff). But, typical of Paul, he moves away from himself and back to a humble prayer for his friends in the church: "May the Lord direct your hearts to the love of God and to the steadfastness of Christ" (vs. 5). Paul believed in a very big God. He has full confidence that God's faithfulness will lead to his care for his own.

Both then and now, God's people need God's help. All those who seek to share God's word are in continuous need of prayer. Paul's own need arises from his continuous work as an evangelist.

What does Paul ask to be included in these prayers? Two things: 1) that "the word of the Lord may speed ahead and be honored" (vs.1); 2) that Paul and his friends would "be delivered from wicked and evil men."

God uses us in spite of our weakness to spread his word. The Thessalonians knew this: the gospel "sounded out" from them into surrounding areas (1 Thessalonians.1:8). Paul prays for the word, and not merely himself, to "speed ahead" because God alone gives the increase and He alone deserves the glory.

Sharing the gospel invites difficult situations, because "not all have faith" (3:2). Shouldn't we expect this? If they rejected Jesus, shouldn't we also expect rejection? Pray that the path of the gospel becomes clear.

Verse three forms the basis of the success of the Gospel, both then and now: "the Lord is faithful. He will establish you and guard you against the evil one" (3:3). Faithful God always sees his disciple-makers through; "I am with you always," Jesus said (Matthew 28:20).

Today, I will...pray, right now, that the Lord will direct me and my brothers "to his love and to Christ's steadfastness" (vs. 5).

Week Thirty-Nine
1 Timothy 1-5

Andy Connelly

Humility in Service

Today's Scripture 1 Timothy 1:12-17

It seems that all enjoy a good "rags to riches" story. That phrase usually references someone moving from poverty to riches, or from relative obscurity to great fame, often overcoming "insurmountable" odds. In his opening portion of his letter to Timothy, Paul writes as one who knows of such a story, but is actually speaking of himself.

As much of scripture shows, a hallmark of one coming into and maintaining a right relationship with God is humility, a recognition of the difference in his own weakness and God's holiness. Paul tells Timothy that he knows his own rags to riches story. Though he had quite a resume (see Philippians 3:4-6), he understood it was not enough. In addition, he states a passionate certainty that what Christ had done in him was much greater, stating: *"But whatever gain I had, I counted as loss for the sake of Christ"* (Philippians 3:7).

In chapter one and verse 12, we see how Paul's own recognition of weakness would become his platform as spokesman to the Gentile world. Not "sugar-coating" his own sins (vs. 13), Paul reminds Timothy that he himself is a sinner. In fact, Paul, in ignorance, was acting contrary to God's own plan and all the while thinking he was a man of God! One may then wonder why Paul was chosen to carry the greatest message the Gentiles would have ever heard. He answers that question in verse 16, saying it would be so that the mercy and patience of God might be on display through him.

Who may ultimately enjoy a rags to riches story of their own because you first approached them and told them your story? Like Paul, when you know your own story, counting it a privilege to bear His name in the face of your own past sin, God can use you also to bring great messages to others.

Today, I will...consider how to tell my story with Christ in hopes of showing others how they, too can be used for Him.

Tuesday
Calling Names

Today's Scripture 1 Timothy 2

In the fall of my sophomore year of college, in order to become part of a club that interested me, I went through a pledging period. As a part of my "demonstrated desire", I had to be prepared to rattle off many facts of all 37 "actives," those already in the club. Though this period lasted but two weeks, I can still repeat them all to this day.

Being able to call those names served to "save" me from certain trouble for that two week period. In 1 Timothy 2, Paul reminds Timothy and us that there are more names to call, for more important reasons, with consequences lasting an eternity. Paul begins chapter two by mentioning that prayers should take on some thought. The listing of four different words (supplications, prayers, intercessions, and thanksgivings) is not merely for repetition, but describing the different emphasis within each.

Moving from consideration of who should be included in prayer in verses 1 and 2, Paul shows that an expanded consideration of those needing prayer is pleasing to God (verse 3). Finally, it is pleasing because it is in keeping with His purpose which "desires all to be saved and come to the knowledge of the truth."

Notice that verse 4 closes with the singular emphasis of truth, evident in the words, the truth. That reminder ushers in the singular source of mediation between God and man, Christ Jesus, in verse 6. Our prayers should include a purpose of the expansion of the gospel. Is it possible that to expand the gospel's opportunity, we must expand first our prayers to include that emphasis? There is a group where God desires all names to be. Paul concludes this section of his letter in verses 7 and 8 by telling Timothy that this was his appointment as an Apostle, and should be our appointment in prayer.

Today, I will...expand my prayers for those in powerful influence that the gospel may have opportunity across the world.

Wednesday
The Greatest Group Purpose

Today's Scripture 1 Timothy 3:14-16

The Union of International Organizations website maintains information and statistics on over 68,000 groups around the world. Knowing not the number of individuals that represents, it does show the sheer volume of potential interests or concerns that draw people together from all over the world. Just imagine the thousands of people that give time, money, and honor to all of these groups drawing people from various nations and backgrounds together! Many of these efforts can be justly called "great."

Webster's Dictionary defines greatness as having these potential characteristics: being very large in size, prolonged in duration, more than ordinary, remarkable, impressive, and eminent. In every sense of these considerations, the Lord's church is truly and wholly great. It is great because of its author, its purpose, and its future. In considering the comparative greatness of God's great church to other groups that draw nations together in purpose, the church has no rival. Paul, writing to Timothy in chapter 3 of his first letter, urges him to remember and teach the greatness of God's body, both in purpose and destiny. In verse 15, he urges proper behavior of God's people as their opportunity to reveal the mystery of Christ to the world, just as He revealed the Father.

He reminds Timothy and all readers of the evidence of revelation for the certainty of our hope and the basis of available unity for people of all nations. Our Lord was indeed revealed in the flesh, and proven true by the Spirit. He was seen by the angels, and taught around the world even at risk of death because of the certainty of conviction. He has been believed as the chief cornerstone of faith as none other, and was taken up to meet His Father and seated at the right hand. The world has no greater group, and no higher purpose. Interestingly, in one alternative definition, Webster's defined great as "a generation removed from a relative." Isn't that great? Jesus our brother, and God our Father. The family of God.

Today, I will...praise God for the greatness of His church. I will call the leaders of the congregation I worship with and thank them for their service striving to lead the greatest organization in the world.

Thursday
A Disciplined Disciple

Today's Scripture 1 Timothy 4:7-16

Despite Peter's description of the church as a "royal priesthood" (I Peter 2:9), I suppose one of the more frustrating things in church leadership is to get an entire congregation to see themselves as ministers. The word "servant," however, seems to be more easily accepted as applied to every Christian. Throughout the New Testament, God's people are called to serve each other (Galatians 5:13) and to do so with a passionate spirit as they first serve the Lord (Romans 12:11).

As Paul writes to the younger servant, Timothy, he reminded him of the importance of two key ingredients in a fulfilling and effective ministry. The first ingredient, discussed in verses 7-12, is the importance of discipline. Paul urges a disciplined discipleship, mentioning at least three things. First, an effective disciple is careful to what takes his attention (vs. 7). There are so many things competing for our attention, and the effective servant sets his mind on things that "train for godliness." Paul then urges that he be disciplined toward long-term thinking (vs. 8-11). No doubt God's history will record far too many that started well in faith but were distracted over time by "here and now" thinking. Paul's third encouragement of discipline spoke to Timothy's example. He reminds the reader of the power and endurance of example, even from a younger Christian.

A second focus in discipleship is that of passion. In verses 13-16, Paul urges Timothy to fully "immerse" himself in two specific things. First, he says that effective ministry both starts and stays with scripture (vs. 13). It is the foundation of leading others to the right place. Next, he encourages an immersion in the gifts given to him by God (vs. 14), and being careful in stewardship not to neglect those things. Finally, Paul completes these ideas through the reminder that in the immersion of scripture and focus on the stewardship of his gifts, others are led to salvation.

Today, I will...not be distracted by the temporary, but will focus on my future.

Honoring the Body of Christ

The Lord's church should always respect its doctrine. Part of our doctrine involves demeanor, and in 1 Timothy 5, Paul gives instructions to the church regarding how we treat one another as a family, as the body of Christ. To begin, he reminds Timothy to teach the church that each member should operate with others in like mind as they would toward those in the most precious of relationships. He opens by comparing responsibilities and treatment toward the older as those toward father and mother, and to the younger as brothers and sisters (verses 1 & 2). Though it may not be as natural in our congregations to consider intergenerational responsibilities, it was never God's desire to be ignored, and leaves many opportunities of spiritual growth behind.

Moving further, Paul begins showing how the church seeks to take care of its own in the concern over widows. In verse 3, the church is instructed to be proactive in caring for their needs. In this section, the wisdom of God is shown in the specifics of how those needs are to be addressed by the church. In a series of examples in verses 4-16, Paul speaks to both the responsibility and reason for his instruction. He teaches responsibility in family (vs. 4), for the widows personal life (vs. 5-6), and for her age and opportunity. He gives reason for it in the next section. Verses 11-15 speak of certain spiritual dangers that can arise if some are left without any responsibility or expectation for care and a productive walk with Christ.

Our Lord loves His church. He desires for it to be both a source of care for its own as well as an attractive example to the world. We should honor this opportunity.

Today, I will...consider one way to honor the older members of my congregation.

Week Forty
1 Timothy 6
2 Timothy 1-4

Anthony Warnes

Monday
Godliness

Will you willingly follow someone you do not respect? Will you genuinely speak about someone you do not revere? Will you intentionally imitate someone that you do not think highly of? The easy answer to these questions is no. How wonderful it is to know that we can follow, speak of, and imitate our Lord with complete comfort knowing that He is worthy!

The items we speak of today boil down to one word: Godliness. Godliness encompasses a lifestyle of imitating the Lord based on a respect and reverence of who He is. If I am displaying godliness, I am displaying my knowledge and appreciation for Him. "Godliness" is found more times in 1 Timothy 6 than anywhere else in the New Testament. Here, Paul gives Timothy four insights to Godliness.

First, godliness is unwanted by some. *"If anyone teaches a different doctrine and does not agree with the sound words of our Lord Jesus Christ and the teaching that accords with godliness, he is puffed up with conceit and understands nothing."* (1 Timothy 6:3-4).

How sad to see individuals who previously lived a life for God, trade it in for a "shipwreck!" (1:19).

Second, godliness is misused by some. "...Imagining that godliness is a means of gain" (6:5). Do I ever look at my imitation of Jesus as my ticket to earthly prosperity? If so, I am performing correct actions, yet with wrong motives.

Third, godliness is valuable only under the correct conditions. "But godliness with contentment is great gain" (6:6). Do you want to have true gain? Try imitating the Lord while being thankful for what He has (and what He has not) given you. The gain promised is not in the form of money and fame, rather in the form of eternal life and the knowledge that I can have it!

Fourth, godliness is needed by all. "...Pursue, righteousness, GODLINESS, faith, love, steadfastness, gentleness." (6:11 emphasis mine). Chase godliness! Every day must be filled with the pursuit of these qualities of the Lord.

Today, I will...seek and appreciate godliness in my life.

Reminding the Discouraged

Today's Scripture 2 Timothy 1

Have you ever witnessed a servant of the Lord battle discouragement? Possibly the hardworking Christian is tired. Maybe the Christian is wearied with temptation.

Today we begin reading 2 Timothy. We gather through our reading that Timothy is discouraged. Possibly the attacks from evil men such as Hymenaeus and Alexander (2:17; 4:14; 1 Tim 1:20) had taken their toll. Maybe fatigue from constant work in the kingdom caused him to become stagnant. Whatever the reason might have been, Paul decided to write and encourage this discouraged soul. This encouraging process began by reminding Timothy of four truths.

First, Paul reminded Timothy of his prayers. *"I thank God whom I serve... as I remember you constantly in my prayers night and day"* (1:3). What a wonderful reminder for us as we try to minister to the discouraged. Pray for them! And tell them that you are praying for them! Remind them that you are mindful of them and that you are going before the Creator of the world on their behalf.

Second, Paul reminded Timothy of their closeness. *"As I remember your tears, I long to see you, that I may be filled with joy"* (1:4). Here, Paul reminds Timothy of the joy they bring each other when they are near and the sadness that ensues when they part. Remind your discouraged friend of the bond that you have because of the Lord.

Third, Paul reminded Timothy of his faith. *"I am reminded of your sincere faith"* (1:5). Sometimes during stagnant moments in our life, we need that push; "friend, don't you remember what Jesus has done for you? Don't you remember how you have lived out your faith?"

Fourth, Paul reminded Timothy get back to work. *"I remind you to fan into flame the gift of God..."* How many talents are squandered and how much work is unaccomplished because of the dying flames of discouraged souls? They need to be reminded of the great work that they are able to accomplish for God.

Today, I will...contact a discouraged soul and remind them.

Wednesday
The Unashamed Worker

Paul continues his epistle to Timothy by encouraging him to not be ashamed. Possibly he was ashamed of himself and felt inadequate to do the work of the Lord. Possibly he was ashamed of God because of the threat of persecution. Do we ever feel the same? This is not God's will for our lives.

"Do your best to present yourself to God as one approved, a worker who has no need to be ashamed, rightly handling the word of truth" (2:15). If we feel shame, let's push ourselves to become an unashamed worker for God. Notice three occupations Paul uses to illustrate to Timothy how to be an unashamed worker.

First, Timothy was to suffer as a soldier. *"Share in suffering as a good soldier of Christ Jesus. No soldier gets entangled in civilian pursuits, since his aim is to please the one who enlisted him"* (2:3-4). As an unashamed worker, I need to act like the selfless soldier who gives up comforts for others sake. As I am working through the scripture, I must obey my Lord as a soldier would obey his commander, even if earthly suffering follows.

Second, Timothy was to compete as an athlete. *"An athlete is not crowned unless he competes according to the rules"* (2:5). As I study the scripture I must follow what I read, for these are the rules of the race of life. The Word shows us how to live individually, how to treat others, and how to respect God.

Third, Timothy was to reap rewards as a farmer. *"It is the hard-working farmer who ought to have the first share of the crops"* (2:6). As we work through the word and apply it to our lives, even if suffering happens for following the rules of God, we will finish unashamed and rewarded before God.

Today, I will...work through a passage of the Word, knowing I can understand it (2:7). I will obey its rules regardless of the possibility of earthly suffering, knowing that I can stand before the Lord unashamed.

Thursday
Remember Your Roots

As we continue reading through Paul's pep talk to Timothy, we are struck with a contrast. On one hand, there will be evil men who will be striving for the loyalty of Timothy (3:2–5). On the other hand, Paul reminds Timothy to remain loyal to the message that several Christians have taught him.

The sinful world we live in also strives for our loyalty. As Paul encouraged Timothy, we must "Avoid such people" (3:5). Let us always choose our loyalties carefully, even when the world "creeps" into the church (3:6).

One of the ways we can do so is by remembering our roots. Who taught you the Word of God? Your parents? Your preacher? Your neighbor? For Timothy, his instruction in the Word started from Lois his grandmother and Eunice his mother (1:5). His instruction continued from Paul after meeting him in Lystra (Acts 16). Paul reminds Timothy, "You however, have followed my teaching, my conduct, my aim in life, my faith, my patience, my love, my steadfastness, my persecutions and sufferings..." (3:10–11). Paul tells Timothy, "continue in what you have learned and have firmly believed, knowing from whom you learned it and how from childhood you have been acquainted with the sacred writings..." (3:14–15).

How greatly would we benefit if we remembered our roots when we were tempted by the evil world?

First, by remembering our roots, we can be encouraged by WHAT we were taught. These memories should remind us that His Word which was spoken to us by others is "complete" and equips us "for every good work" (3:17).

Second, by remembering our roots, we can be encouraged by WHO taught us. Why do we get so caught up with impressing the world? Has the world shown us the way to heaven? Instead, let's be encouraged to live in the same manner as the individuals who cared enough for us to introduce us to His Word.

Today, I will...thank God for the individuals who taught me the gospel, and I will strive to plant gospel roots in others.

Paul's Last Will and Testament

What would you do if you knew you were dying in the near future? 2 Timothy is believed to be Paul's last epistle that he wrote before his death. The fourth chapter of this epistle serves as good proof towards that argument as Paul famously states, "...I have finished the race..." (4:7). As Paul wraps up his encouragement to Timothy, we see what Paul did with what he believed was his last months on this earth.

First, Paul charges Timothy to continue the process. As we remembered in chapter 3, Timothy was taught by his grandmother, mother, and Paul about the Lord. Now Timothy must do the same for others. *"I charge you in the presence of God and of Christ Jesus, who is to judge the living and the dead, and by his appearing and his kingdom: preach the word; be ready in season and out of season; reprove, rebuke, and exhort, with complete patience and teaching"* (4:1-2). Paul had even encouraged Timothy to pass on this charge to other "faithful men who will be able to teach others also" (2:2).

Second, Paul charges Timothy to continue for the finish line. *"I have fought the good fight, I have finished the race, I have kept the faith. Henceforth there is laid up for me the crown of righteousness, which the Lord, the righteous judge, will award to me on that Day, and not only to me but also to ALL who have loved his appearing"* (4:7-8, emphasis mine). How wonderful to know that we can be this confident.

Third, Paul charges Timothy to continue despite other's actions. Paul explains to Timothy how men such as Demas deserted him and Alexander harmed him. Yet as Paul sees his reward approaching, the actions of others will not affect him eternally. *"The Lord will rescue me from every evil deed and bring me safely into his heavenly kingdom"* (4:18).

Today, I will...continue like Paul by striving to have the same assurance of my salvation and show the same concern for others.

Week Forty-One
Titus 1-3
Philemon
Hebrews 1

Logan Cates

Monday
An Island Needing Elders

Today's Scripture Titus 1

Today we open our Bibles to the book of Titus. Paul is writing to Titus, his "true child in the faith" (1:4). What a special connection they must have had, similar to how we should feel with our own brethren. Written after I Timothy, Titus was left on the island of Crete (150 miles long) for the purpose of building up the church. It's clear there's a strong urgency in Paul's heart as he wrote to Titus pleading with him to, "put what remained in order" and also "appoint elders in every town" (Titus 1:5). One of their own said, "Cretans are always liars, evil beasts, lazy gluttons" (Titus 1:12). Yet there is great hope for ungodliness when Christians unite together!

Paul didn't give up despite the evil surroundings. He knew the greatest way to combat wickedness is to equip, appoint, uplift and establish shepherds to keep watch over the flock. Grab your highlighter and highlight all Titus was up against. What's the answer to those problems? Many were insubordinate, empty talkers, deceivers, teaching things they shouldn't teach. They professed to know God, but denied Him by their works (1:16). Paul even called them "detestable and disobedient." Do we face the same struggles today? What is the answer?

The solution is given in verse 9. It is such a powerful statement regarding the responsibility placed upon elders in the church. *"He (the elder) must hold firm to the trustworthy word as taught, so that he may be able to give instruction in sound doctrine and also rebuke those who contradict it."* The immediate goal is for the congregation to be "sound in faith" (2:13).

Today, I will...share in the same urgency as Paul in his love for the church. Let us honor and respect our Elders and pray for them and their families. Just as Christ said, we all must be a "city on a hill" (Matthew 5:14).

Tuesday
Grace Has Appeared To All People!

Today's Scripture Titus 2

Today we open our Bibles to Titus 2. You have a gift to share with the rest of the world. You have been given an overabundance of talents that will not only bless the church, but every individual you come into contact with. You can be an influence for good to someone. You can help someone direct their lives to be more like Christ. This is exactly what Paul is telling Titus to reveal to the men and women in the church on Crete.

In Titus 2:1, Paul reminds Titus that he is special because he must teach sound doctrine. He tells older men they are special because of their steadfastness, patience and self-control. He instructs the older women they are special because they can teach what is good and make a difference in the lives of younger women and children. Can an older woman truly make a difference in the lives of younger ladies and children? Can an older woman encourage younger women to love their husbands? Absolutely, we have seen it!

Paul informs Titus just how special women are. They should be submissive or respectful to their husbands, they get to be the queen of the home, and they can do all this showing kindness, integrity and dignity (2:3-5). He informs young men to be self-controlled, is that important? Then he concludes by saying the "grace of God has appeared, bringing salvation for all people" (2:11) but it's not just receiving grace. It's also what we do with grace. He said, "Training us to..." and he shows us a list of things to deny and live godly lives. Why? Because (vs. 13) "we are looking for that blessed hope and glorious appearing of the great God and our Savior Jesus Christ."

You are more valuable than you think! Influence others by your love for Jesus Christ!

Today, I will...see that I am special to God and I must use what I have been given to glorify God and bring others to Christ.

Wednesday
Reminded

Today we open our Bibles to Titus 3 where Paul had not fully completed his practical lessons in the previous chapter. He offers simple reminders for the Christians there on the island of Crete to shine brightly in Christian character regardless of who might be opposed to the teachings and how they respond. In our studies, it's as if we asked Paul, "How should we respond to those who are mean, hateful, evil-minded and stubborn when it comes to obedience to God?" Paul decides to first remind them where they once were in disobedience (3:3).

Don't we all need to be reminded of where we were without Christ? Anyone here in need of mercy? How much? Notice the entrance of God in verse 4, *"But when the goodness and loving kindness of God our Savior appeared, He saved us, not because of works done by us in righteousness, but according to His own mercy"* (3:4-5). Paul was quick to remind them how God was kind amidst our disobedience, so we ought to bear with those who are disobedient, malicious and even hateful.

There is never an excuse for those in Christ to respond as if they are not in Christ. Nor is there a place for arrogance or haughtiness since we were also in the same dark sinful state before we became Christians. They are admonished not to embrace in foolish controversies about the Law, perhaps questions having no answers. In regard to those causing division, they were to give warnings, in this case two. Then they were to simply avoid and reject those who are hatefully perverted for it brings harm to the Christian's character and the message of Christ. We reach a point when we must pull away from those who seek to divide because so much as at stake when the disease of division spreads.

Paul closes his writing with love, saluting those whom he cares for (3:12,13) and adding, "those who love us in the faith."

Today, I will...consider where I was before Christ and extend kindness to others.

Thursday
Pleading for Our Brethren

Today we open our Bibles to the book of Philemon. In the first few verses Paul begins with a prayer of thanks for the faith and love Philemon has shown toward all the saints (vs 5). Philemon is a wealthy slave owner and this letter is the shortest of all the letters sent by Paul, only 334 words. However, it answers so many questions about the practical side of Christianity working in the lives of people.

The reason for this letter is to plead for Phliemon to forgive Onesimus, a slave, receive him as a brother, and Paul even offers to repay Philemon for anything that was taken by Onesimus. There is a great love between Paul and Onesimus so much Paul wanted to keep him with him (vs 13).

Have you ever had anyone plead for you on your behalf? Have you ever known anyone that would write a letter to someone with you as the subject? Have you ever had anyone raise their hand and speak highly about you to others? Have you ever had anyone who knew your faults yet still desired for you to be close beside them? What about Jesus Christ? This book is a beautiful message of forgiveness and love and an example all Christians should see and live.

Would we ever consider loving our brethren so much that we call them our own? Would we ever plead for someone else to forgive our brethren even if it wasn't our business? Would we ever send a letter pleading, "accept him as you accept me" (vs. 17) or "if he has wronged you in any way, charge it to my account" (vs. 18)? Isn't this what Christ has done for each one of us at the cross?

Paul is intelligent in the way he composed and closed this letter, slightly urging with authority, "Don't forget you owe me yourself" and "I know you will do more than I ask."

Today, I will...consider the level of love and encouragement to my own brothers and sisters in Christ.

Friday
Christ Is Superior

Today's Scripture Hebrews 1

Today we begin our reading of Hebrews. As you begin the journey through this book, see the great blessing upon us: who Jesus Christ is, what He has done and how He is superior over all. The writer displays how God "spoke" (past tense) to "our fathers by the prophets" (vs 1) but now, "in the last days" He has spoken to us by His Son (vs. 2). The book opens displaying Judaism and the prophets of old, then reveals the superiority of what we have in Christ, even over the angels. The idea is to show the difference between the old and new covenants and you will see this throughout. I like to say, "when it comes to power and purification, My Lord is greater than all."

Do your best to notice phrases that might easily be overlooked and intensify your study by spending time on them. Verses like (1-3) must steal thirty-sixty minutes of your study. Such as "heir of all things," what does that mean? Or, "through whom also He created the world." Or, "upholds the universe by the word of His power" (vs.3). We truly see the magnificent power of God and also how He "made purification of sin" (vs. 3).

The rest of the chapter will have your fingers in Psalm 102, 104, 45, or Isaiah 61 as if the writer demands we look back. Prophets are excellent, angels are excellent, but Jesus Christ is and must be elevated over anyone. How glorious angels are, the ministering spirits our God created as highest of all His creatures. Elevated as they are, "which of the angels has God ever said, 'sit at my right hand?" (Hebrews 1:13). The Jews regarded angels as the most exalted of all creatures, yet there is a man who has been "given a more excellent name than they" (vs. 4). "To which of the angels did God say, 'You are my Son, today I have begotten you"? (vs. 5).

Today, I will...exalt Jesus over everything and make Him Lord in my life!

Week Forty-Two
Hebrews 2-6

Austin Johnson

Monday
Wafers or Pork Chops

You pick: lightly cheese flavored wafers OR grilled pork chops, mashed potatoes, and green bean casserole? It is an easy choice, right? Not for my son just a few months ago. We sat at the dinner table eating delicious food attempting to convince him of how much better our food was. He would begrudgingly try a few bites here and there. But if it were up to him, he would choose the lesser of the two foods! Sounds crazy, right? Pork, potatoes, and beans are so much better!

Hebrews is all about the fact that Jesus is better. Hebrews 2 proves this point by showing Jesus is better than angels, and it's not even close! Verses 9-10 say, *"But we see him who for a little while was made lower than the angels, namely Jesus, crowned with glory and honor because of the suffering of death, so that by the grace of God he might taste death for everyone. For it was fitting that he, for whom and by whom all things exist, in bringing many sons to glory, should make the founder of their salvation perfect through suffering."*

Jesus is better! No angel came in the flesh, suffered through temptations and pain, ultimately to be killed for our sins (2:10, 14-15). It is truly incredible what Jesus did to become like us so he could save us (2:17-18). But are there times where we choose the lesser of our two options?

We choose the wafers when we consider things of this world to be better than the Savior of the world. We choose the wafers when we allow trivial matters to trump our trust in God. We choose the wafers as we pursue academic and athletic excellence while settling for spiritual mediocrity. We call children crazy for their choices, but are we spiritually guilty of the same?

Today, I will...pray two non-mealtime prayers asking God to help me make Jesus a forethought instead of an afterthought.

Tuesday
Each One Reach One

Today's Scripture Hebrews 3:12-14

Who is the one who lifts you up when you are feeling down? Who is that person who you lean on for spiritual strength when your faith seems to waiver? Who is the one that can motivate you for service and sacrifice when your heart grows callous? Whoever that person is in your life, how much do you appreciate and care for him/her? I would imagine phrases like, "I don't know what I would do without him/her" or "They know just what to say" are flowing through your mind. These individuals have such an impact on others' lives!

Are you that person for someone else? If the answer to that question is anything but a humble "Yes," I want you to hear the words of Hebrews 3:13, "But exhort one another every day, as long as it is called 'today,' that none of you may be hardened by the deceitfulness of sin." Not only will our encouragement of others lift them up, it will also prevent a major issue—the hardening of their hearts (3:7-11, 12).

Hebrews 3:7-11 is a quotation from Psalm 95 that references Moses disobeying a direct command from God as he was influenced by the hardening of Israel's collective heart. Their generational disobedience "provoked" God because "They always go astray in their heart" (3:10). HEAR THIS: If it is true that my encouragement can positively affect someone else's actions, and someone else's actions can affect God, then my choice to encourage someone else or not has a direct effect on God!

A few thoughts: First, appreciate those people who have been spiritual rocks in your life because we do not make it easy on them from time to time. Second, oftentimes the best way to find encouragement yourself is by encouraging someone else. Third, by encouraging others to fight sin and pursue faith, we may help prevent the hardening of a heart towards the Living God!

Today, I will...find a brother/sister in Christ who needs spiritual encouragement and be that source of help in their time of need.

Wednesday
Jesus Knows

If you are waking up to read this devotional, pausing midday to peruse the words of a random person, or lying in bed at night, I ask you to stop and hear this—Jesus knows. Jesus knows the pressures from people in the community as they watch your every move. Jesus knows the heartache of loved ones leaving faith behind for corrupted coins. Jesus knows the battle of fighting fleshly emotions that appear unnoticed and unwanted. Jesus knows the struggle of relationships and expectations from without and within. Jesus knows!

Whatever our Wednesday weaknesses are, be uplifted by the presence of Jesus in our lives! "For we do not have a high priest who is unable to sympathize with our weaknesses, but one who in every respect has been tempted as we are, yet without sin." Incredible! Unlike the unapproachable and distant High Priests of old, Jesus has been positioned as the High Priest of our hearts, connected and close. Rip away the callous from your heart today and allow Jesus' position as High Priest of your heart to give you strength to be an obedient overcomer today (4:6, 11).

Notice the word "obedient" is italicized. God has done His part. Jesus has done His part. Others before us have faithfully done their part and now it is up to us, as individuals, to do our part. Obey. The "word of God is… sharper than any two-edged sword…discerning the thoughts and intentions of the heart" (4:12). God knows our hearts better than we do (John 2:23-25) and "all are naked and exposed to the eyes of him to whom we must give account" (4:13). Not only does Jesus know the help I may need, He knows the disobedience that may be present in my life. Change today and "with confidence draw near to the throne of grace" where God can help you in your time of spiritual need.

Today, I will…make a list of my greatest temptations and find peace knowing that Jesus suffered through them, overcame them, and gives me the ability to overcome as well!

Thursday
Spiritual Swamp Water

Today's Scripture Hebrews 5:11-14

Have you ever seen a pool in someone's backyard that has turned into a swamp? It was a slow process but eventually the crystal-clear water turned into a molded green and brown mixture of filth and debris. This happens when water stands still, alone and exposed to the elements of the world. Did you know the same thing happens to Christians who stand still, alone, and exposed to the elements of the world? The Hebrew Christians had become dull in hearing, were unable to teach others, and still needed to attend the elementary school bible class. Yikes! They had an issue that needed to be confronted. They were spiritually stagnant. Instead of moving and maturing, their faith had become spiritual swamp water.

Specifically, the Hebrew Christians were tempted to go back to Old Covenant Judaism leaving Jesus Christ behind. This regression was a temptation because they were not moving forward in faith. When people stop growing, it may be a slow process, but they start dying. Is your faith alive and growing or have you become spiritually stagnant? Spiritual stagnation could be shown by one who holds secret grudges, lives in the lowland of lust, constantly criticizes with negativity and backbiting or a host of other spiritual swamps.

A few considerations: Would you say that the past year of your life could be defined by faith formation and growth? Hebrews 5:12 calls our attention to the "oracles of God." Spiritual growth and maturity is based on growing in knowledge and understanding of the "word of righteousness" (5:13). This knowledge and understanding lays the foundation for Christian living (Matthew 6:33). Would you say that you are a mature Christian who is able to help and teach others or are you still in need of the elementary principles of God? Do not be spiritual swamp water!

Today, I will...ask a mature Christian friend to give me an important biblical topic to study and commit myself to it.

Friday
Taste and See That the Lord Is Good!

Today's Scripture Hebrews 6:9-12

If you have read this devotional book consistently to today I am going to make an assumption about you, you have "tasted the goodness of the word of God" as you have journeyed with Jesus and His word. Hebrews 6:4-8 speaks of a group of Christians who tasted the goodness of the word of God but chose to fall away. Going from salvation in Christ to separation from Him is painful to imagine. Verse 6 says that those who experience the goodness of God and still leave Him behind are "crucifying once again the Son of God to their own harm and holding Him up to contempt." Sad!

I want you to be able to repeat what the Psalmist said in 34:8, *"Oh, taste and see that the Lord is good!"* and 119:103, *"How sweet are your words to my taste, sweeter than honey to my mouth."* Let these words ring true in your life because you choose to turn tasting into practice and practice into peace. Taste God through His word and experience Him working through you in life. Allow that experience to motivate you to imitate those who have devoted their lives to the overflowing of faith in Christian living. This journey with Jesus will conclude with peace, in knowing that God is faithful and just and will not overlook your sacrifice and service.

"For God is not unjust so as to overlook your work and the love that you have shown for his name in serving the saints, as you still do. And we desire each one of you to show the same earnestness to have the full assurance of hope until the end, so that you may not be sluggish, but imitators of those who through faith and patience inherit the promises." (Hebrews 6:10-12)

Today, I will...pray that God will open my eyes to His work in and around me, taste His action, turn it in to my own action, and be at peace with my salvation.

Week Forty-Three
Hebrews 7-11

Richard Harp

Monday
Jesus Our Priest and King

Today's Scripture Hebrews 7

Today we begin our reading of Hebrews, continuing the book's theme that Christ offers a better covenant than the old law. This is realized through our advocate with the Father. Jesus, the Lion of Judah, is both our priest and king after the order of Melchizedek.

"For this Melchizedek, king of Salem, priest of the Most High God, met Abraham returning from the slaughter of the kings and blessed him, and to him Abraham apportioned a tenth part of everything. He is first, by translation of his name, king of righteousness, and then he is also king of Salem, that is, king of peace. He is without father or mother or genealogy, having neither beginning of days nor end of life, but resembling the Son of God he continues a priest forever." (Hebrews 7:1–3)

A king of Israel was placed on the throne because of the blood in his veins. A priest was also placed in his role because of lineage. These two bloodlines did not unite. Priestly king Melchizedek preceded the bloodlines, resembling the perfect Son of God.

Jesus is our priest and king of righteousness:

The Son was given the name Immanuel, which is translated "God with us." He represented the perfection of His Father on earth in the way that He taught and lived. He was in every way tempted as we are yet He was without sin (Hebrews 4:15).

Jesus is our priest and king of peace:

Jesus brought harmony to a world at war with God. We desperately need peace through His name. This peace is not a temporary treaty—it is set forever.

Not like the Levite, Melchizedek's parentage was insignificant, for he was called by God to be a priest. Similarly, Jesus also was called. Think of this, you, too, have been called to be a priest of God regardless of your background. Read 2 Thessalonians 2:14 and 1 Peter 2:9.

Today, I will...consider how to make peace through righteous interactions with those around me.

Tuesday
A New Covenant

Today we explore the book of Hebrews once more. The book's theme offers its original readers a reminder not to go back to the old law for Jesus offers the better covenant. This reminder has implications for you to hold to God's promise letting go of the world's deceit.

"For this is the covenant that I will make with the house of Israel after those days, declares the Lord: I will put my laws into their minds, and write them on their hearts, and I will be their God, and they shall be my people. And they shall not teach, each one his neighbor and each one his brother, saying, 'Know the Lord,' for they shall all know me, from the least of them to the greatest. For I will be merciful toward their iniquities, and I will remember their sins no more." (Hebrews 8:10-13)

The children of Israel had turned their backs on the God who led them by the hand out of Egypt (Hebrews 8:9). Their covenant from God was a promise they were born into. The Hebrews writer reminds us that Israel took God and His merciful covenant for granted. By forgetting His law and showing no concern for God, He gave them over to themselves. Through the new covenant a deeper and meaningful relationship with God can be realized. When God's Will soaks into the life of the Christian it alters behavior, and changes lives for the better. This change is because the word is written on the Christian's heart and thought about in their daily lives.

Because of this saturation in God's word under the new covenant, His children know Him. His children from the least to greatest in the land are known as those who love the word of God and are simply recognized by it. If God's children will remember and implement His word in their lives God will not remember their sin anymore (Vs 13).

Today, I will...consider how to love God through loving His word with more purpose and fervor than I did yesterday.

Wednesday
A Personal Sacrifice

Today's Scripture Hebrews 9

Today we continue in our study of Hebrews. The Israelites were not strangers to the continual practice of observances and writs to receive atonement. The epicenter for these writs was the temple. It was within the temple, in the Holy of Holies, that the priest would enter once a year with the blood of a sacrifice offered for his sin and the sin of the people (see Leviticus 16).

"But when Christ appeared as a high priest of the good things that have come, then through the greater and more perfect tent (not made with hands, that is, not of this creation) he entered once for all into the holy places, not by means of the blood of goats and calves but by means of his own blood, thus securing an eternal redemption." (Hebrews 9:11-12)

"Jesus is a high priest who entered the inner temple when He died on the cross. There He offered His own blood for all God's people before and after his death." (Hebrews 9:15-17)

Jesus is a high priest who entered the temple once for all time.

Matthew tells us that when He died the temple curtain was torn apart from top to bottom (Matthew 27:51). Thus the annual writ was fulfilled through our great high priest. No more do we offer up bulls and goats for our sins to be covered for a temporary atonement.

Before Christ, the high priest almost resembled an impersonal butcher preparing meat for the masses. He would be covered by blood but never shed it himself. Jesus' personal sacrifice for you and for me makes this sacrifice hit closer to home (read Hebrews 4:14-16). This could only have been accomplished through undying love for you. You are now able to love God through Christ in a personal way. "We love because He first loved us" (1 John 4:19). He calls you to follow Him personally (Read Luke 9:23-25)

Today, I will...consider how to love God deeper through personal sacrifice by taking up my cross and following His example for others I meet.

Thursday
Remaining Faithful

Today we persevere in our study of Hebrews. In chapter ten, perseverance is key to understanding our responsibilities in the Kingdom. Knowing what Jesus did for mankind in one day for all eternity means we serve Him faithfully daily.

"Therefore, brothers, since we have confidence to enter the holy places by the blood of Jesus, by the new and living way that he opened for us through the curtain, that is, through his flesh, and since we have a great priest over the house of God, let us draw near with a true heart in full assurance of faith, with our hearts sprinkled clean from an evil conscience and our bodies washed with pure water. Let us hold fast the confession of our hope without wavering, for he who promised is faithful." (Hebrews 10:19-23)

Since Jesus tore down the curtain of separation from God, we may approach Him through Jesus, our advocate. We are like priests coming before the Lord with His blood that is not our own (1 Peter 2:9). We may enter with confidence before our loving God when our once evil conscience has been washed clean (1 Peter 3:20-21). We must remain faithful.

Our service to God is unlike the Son's sacrifice. As royal priests we do not serve God once. We serve Him every day and this takes more than determination to remain faithful. In chapter 10 we see the severe consequence to turning our back on Christ is eternal separation from Him (vss. 26-31). But the Hebrews writer explains three important elements that make remaining Faithful possible.

God has faith in you (vs 23). God has given His faithful a responsibility to work together for the world (vs 24) and finally, God has established that worship to Him will bring encouragement to the faithful (vs 25).

Today, I will...seek to remain Faithful. I will ask God for help to reach out to one fellow believer I haven't spoken to lately and try to encourage them.

Friday
A Better Promise

Today, we carry on in our study of Hebrews. Often this chapter is referred to as the "Hall of Faith." The inductees into this hall remind us where our hope should be placed. They longed for and had faith in a promise that they never got to experience.

"Now faith is the assurance of things hoped for, the conviction of things not seen. For by it the people of old received their commendation..."

"These all died in faith, not having received the things promised, but having seen them and greeted them from afar, and having acknowledged that they were strangers and exiles on the earth. For people who speak thus make it clear that they are seeking a homeland..."

"But as it is, they desire a better country, that is, a heavenly one. Therefore God is not ashamed to be called their God, for he has prepared for them a city." (Hebrews 11:1-2; 13-14; 16)

These trusting trailblazers were the pioneers of faith. They were willing to be strangers and outcasts in search of a greater promise. They were looking for a heavenly homeland unlike the homes they left behind. They were motivated by faith, by a promise they would never see fulfilled. It is through them that God prepared the way for you.

As we saw in the last chapter, we are able to draw near to God through the blood of Christ (10:22). We have access to this promise, (sons in glory 2:10). How privileged we are to be able to reflect on the promise prepared beforehand. We see the providence of God through those who came before in this great hall of faith (1 Peter 1:10-12).

Unlike those who longed to see the promise but could not, we have seen the preparation process through the scriptures, the blessings at the cross, and the promise of being in glory with the Lord (Hebrews 11:39-40).

Today, I will...draw near to God in thanksgiving with a newfound appreciation of the scriptures that establish my Faith.

Week Forty-Four
Hebrews 12-13
James 1-3

Drake Jenkins

Monday
Cheering Section

It was Friday night—the lights were bright, the stands were full, the smell of hotdogs and fresh cut grass was in the air. It was football time. This Friday was different, though. This Friday for the very first time in his career, his maw-maw was in the stands. When he ran out on the field he peeked through the facemask of his helmet to find her. She was easily the loudest and most proud person in the stands. She was his person for that night. He played one of the greatest football games he had ever played, and even claims he could hear his maw-maw screaming, "that's my baby!"

"We are surrounded by so great a cloud of witnesses, therefore let us lay aside every weight, and sin which clings so closely, and let us run with endurance the race that is set before us." (Hebrews 12:1)

The writer of Hebrews wants us to know in chapter 12 that, we are not alone. The Christian faith is not easily lived out. Paul makes it clear in Romans 7:18-19, *"For I know that nothing good dwells in me that is, in my flesh. For I have the desire to do what is right, but not the ability to carry it out. For I do not do the good I want, but the evil I do not want is what I keep on doing."*

Being a Christian is hard—but you're not alone. You have a fan section cheering you on. You have people chanting your name in encouragement. And most importantly, you have Jesus.

Not only does the Bible tell us that we have a faith cheer section surrounding us, but we have the 'author and perfecter of our faith, Jesus.' You have Jesus cheering for you. You have Jesus chanting your name. You have Jesus calling the plays and putting you in the best position to win the prize. How?

Because Jesus has been where we are, *"Since then we have a great high priest who has passed through the heavens, JESUS, the SON OF GOD, let us hold fast our confession. For we do not have a high priest (JESUS) who is unable to sympathize with our weaknesses, but one who in EVERY WAY has been tempted as we are, yet WITHOUT sin...Therefore let us come before the throne of grace with boldness (confidence) that we may receive mercy and find grace to help in our time of need."* (Hebrews 4:14-16)

Today, I will...make it, because I have Jesus.

Tuesday
Our Big God

Many had the opportunity to grow up going to VBS, and Christian camp, and similar events. I remember specifically having a favorite song that was usually sung: "My God is so big, so strong and so mighty, there's nothing my God cannot do–for you." I love that.

We were learning about the omnipotence of God when we were 3 and 4 and didn't even realize it. Friends, God is HUGE. He can do anything. We serve a God who can create (Hebrew *bara*) everything from absolutely nothing (Genesis 1:1). We serve a God who can part the sea and make dry what was once, water filled (Exodus 14:21). We serve a God who can close the mouths of wild animals (Daniel 6:21-22). We serve a God who can bring life in the most unexpected and miraculous ways (Genesis 21; Matthew 1). We serve a God who gave sight to the blind and hearing to the deaf and words to the mute. We serve a God who cast out demons, drove out false teachers and raised the dead to walk again (Matthew 10:8). Praise be the name of our God.

And here is the good news about it all–This great and powerful God we serve, loves you–and is for you–and wants what is best for you. This great and powerful God we serve makes you a promise that He will "never leave you or forsake you" (Hebrews 13:5). The writer in this book reminds us that God is here to help us and not to harm us. My pawpaw had a saying, "God plus one is always the majority." So when life hits us (and life will hit you and shake you and stir you up) remember, "my God is so big, so strong and so mighty, there's nothing my God cannot do."

Today, I will...go forward boldly into whatever this day holds because of my big God.

Wednesday
Just Ask

There are some Bible passages that just don't make sense (at least at first glance). We hear them, we learn them, we can even quote them— yet they still are challenging to comprehend.

James chapter one has one of those verses. *"Consider it all joy when you encounter trails of all kinds in your life"* (James 1:2). No thanks! We don't like trials and tribulation. We run from problems. We are stressed by test. However, there is a reason for this beautiful passage: Jesus is a carpenter. Carpenters can't help but see things as they could be. Carpenters love raw materials. They love broken. Here is the good news, we are raw. We are broken. We don't have all the parts we need to be complete.....but Jesus is our Carpenter. Jesus doesn't see you for who you are but for what He can make you. What can I learn from this?

Number one, ask God for wisdom. *"If anyone lacks wisdom, let him ask God who gives generously to all without reproach"* (vs. 5). Friends, we need wisdom to get through the "various trials" and God is all about giving us what we need. The Proverb writer says, *"Blessed is the one who finds wisdom, and the one who gets understanding. For the gain from wisdom is better than gain from silver and her profit better than gold. Wisdom is more precious than jewels and nothing you desire can compare with wisdom."* (Proverbs 3:13-15)

Dr. Luke tells us in Luke 21:15, "For I give you a mouth and wisdom which NONE OF YOUR ADVERSARIES will be able to withstand or contradict." It seems to make more and more sense why King Solomon was so adamant about seeking this thing called wisdom. The Bible tells us that we need it to get through the trials and sufferings this world offers.

Number two, receive Gods wisdom. "But let him ask in faith, with no doubting" (vs. 6). Its one thing to ask, but you also must receive the gift in faith. Once you ask and receive Gods wisdom you will be able to keep yourself "unstained from the world" (vs. 27).

Today, I will...ask God for wisdom.

Thursday
Love, Love, Love

God calls us to stand out in such a way that we are different from the world (John 17). One of the greatest challenges that we face is that there is very little difference between those who claim Jesus is their Savior, and those who give their allegiance to this world. God calls for difference.

Is it any wonder that we are called to be the "lights of the world" (Matthew 5:14). Peter says "But we are a chosen people, a royal priesthood, a holy nation, Gods special possession, that you may declare the praises of Him who called you out of darkness and into His marvelous light" (1 Peter 1:9). We are to be different. The question is: how? How can we be in the world but not of the world? How can we be light in a place filled with darkness? How can we be holy, special, royal and priestly? The answer is always the same.

In Matthew 22 a lawyer comes to Jesus and asks Him, "what is the great commandment in the Law?" Jesus replies with the answer to all of our questions about difference. Jesus tells us how to be light in darkness. Here, Jesus tells us how to be royal and holy. In this answer Jesus even explains how people can distinguish between Christians and non-Christians, "Love the Lord your God with all your heart, soul, and mind, for this is the first and greatest commandment and the second is Love your neighbor as yourself" (Matthew 22:37-38; c.f. James 2:8). That's it. Love. Love God. Love people. Love Love LOVE!

When you love you don't show partially toward people. You don't see rich-poor, black-white, male-female, you see a soul who needs the love of Jesus (James 2:1-13). When you love you don't try to justify sin and test God, you do everything you can to live under the law even in imperfection. When you love, you don't try to claim and then ignore the opportunities and gifts God has granted you. You, by faith, work to become the best person God has called you to be. Love is everything. Love changes everything. God is love (I John 4:8) and He needs us to be love for Him.

Today, I will...strive to treat all I meet with the love of God and without partiality.

Take A Moment

Today's Scripture James 3

"Sticks and stones may break my bones, but WORDS will never hurt me." Have you ever heard that before? I hate to call out a nursery rhyme, however, this is a big fat lie. There have been many times in my life thus far, where I would much rather someone throw a stone or rock at my face than throw words.

Words are unique. Words can make us or break us. Words can hurt us or heal us. Words can cause great solution or cause great problems. Words are blessings and cursing. Why? Because so many people have trouble controlling what is said. The Bible tells us that human beings (top of the food chain) have tamed "every kind of beast and every kind of bird, and reptiles and even sea creatures but NO ONE can tame the tongue" James 3:7-8).

So how can I improve? The Bible says in James 1:5 "If anyone lacks wisdom, you should ask it of God who gives generously..." One way to learn better to bridle ours tongues is to seek wisdom. We must be wise in thought so we can be wise in word. We get so caught up in wanting people to hear our opinion or our reaction or our response, that we forget to (with meekness) listen and reflect and meditate on others. James goes on the say, "You must be quick to hear — slow to speak, and slow to become angry" (vs. 19). My maw-maw used to tell me that God gave me two ears and one mouth for a reason. In wisdom we learn to control our first thoughts. Some of the wisest and most well-spoken people I know, are also the slowest to respond in conversation. Why? Because they have learned to "bridle their tongues."

Today, I will...take a moment. Take pause. Let it sink in. God knows you have so much to offer, but instead of lashing out, or criticizing, or belittling, take a moment to wisely listen. Then your words may be filled with "pureness, and peace, and gentleness, and mercy, and good things" (vs. 17).

Week Forty-Five
James 4-5
1 Peter 1-3

Kevin Kasparek

Monday
Father, Hold Me Close

Have you ever been overwhelmed? Sometimes we are overwhelmed because of all the things the world is throwing at us. But then there are other times when the reason we are feeling overwhelmed is because of the choices we have made.

It is so easy to get caught up in the current of life today. Our culture is so effective in putting opportunities in front of us. Some of those opportunities are wonderful blessings, but then there are others that although they might appear to be something positive, they actually prove to be harmful to us, and they take us away from our Heavenly Father.

When that happens we start making poor choices and we become someone we do not want to be. We turn our focus inward, and we start feeding our selfish appetites. We begin to look at other people as a hindrance, an obstacle to overcome, even as an enemy. James would say, we are friends of the world.

It is good to have friends, but we have to be careful with that relationship. Friendship suggests agreement, fellowship, respect, and loyalty. We have to be careful because friends have an influence on us. That is why Paul wrote, "Bad company ruins good morals" in 1 Corinthians 15:33. Our selfish culture can have a devastating influence on us. And if we become friends with the world, James tells us we make ourselves "an enemy of God" (James 4:4).

In the depths of our hearts, that is not what we want. We get so busy. We get so involved in the day to day aspects of life, it is easy to lose our way. James offers us a way back. He wrote, *"Submit yourselves therefore to God. Resist the devil, and he will flee from you. Draw near to God, and he will draw near to you."* (James 4:7-8)

Today, I will...look for opportunities my Heavenly Father has provided to be compassionate and loving. Please Father...hold me close.

Tuesday
Wait For It!

Today's Scripture James 5:7-11

As a rule, people hate to wait on anything. Sometimes it seems stoplights are installed at the most inconvenient locations just to test our patience. And who has not gone to the doctor at the appointed time only to wait for an hour before the doctor can see you? We buy microwave ovens because we want our food in seconds instead of hours. And who takes the time to write a letter, and mail it and wait a week or more for a reply when you can send a text message and receive a reply within seconds? We hate to wait...on anything.

And now, we find ourselves waiting on the Lord to return. And He seems to be taking His own sweet time. When we look at our world today and witness the blatant disregard for God and righteousness, we may be asking ourselves...what is He waiting for?

Members of the early church were actually expecting the Lord to return in their generation. But James tells them they must have patience. He reminds them of the farmer who must wait for the harvest. In that time of waiting necessary things are happening, the early and late rains must fall.

And he reminds them of the patience of the prophets and of the steadfastness of Job. And then he writes, "...and you have seen the purpose of the Lord, how the Lord is compassionate and merciful" (James 5:11). You see, actually, the Lord is waiting too. He is waiting for people to turn and come to Him.

It becomes hard to wait when things do not happen according to our schedules. We get frustrated and we grumble. James encourages, "You also, be patient." As believers, we live in that 'in-between' time. The Lord has returned to the Father, and we wait for His return. We wait patiently therefore, knowing, necessary things are happening.

Today, I will...let my faith shine, not in glorious deeds done, but in my patience with others and with myself, as my God works all things together according to His purpose.

Wednesday
Reborn

Ever traveled to a foreign country? How strange it is to leave what was familiar and comfortable and step into a place where you know where nothing is, you know nothing of the culture, and you cannot ask because you do not speak the language. It is like you stepped into a new world.

And yet, when one becomes a Christian, that is what they experience. They leave what was familiar and comfortable and they enter a place that seems so strange.

The apostle Peter wrote his first letter to a people driven from their homeland because of their faith. They literally are in a different place. They do not know the people, they do not know how people do things, and they may not be able to speak the language. But Peter reminds them that in spite of the way things look, they are not outcasts, they have in fact been reborn, children of God.

He tells them, "since you have been born again, not of perishable seed but of imperishable, through the living and abiding word of God" (1 Peter 1:23). And since they are His children, they are to leave behind all that was familiar. He describes it as, "the passions of your former ignorance" (1 Peter 1:14). And the new place in which they find themselves is called, 'holiness'. "Be holy in all your conduct, since it is written, "You shall be holy, for I am holy" (1 Peter 1:15-16).

What does Peter mean when he says, "be holy?" Is he suggesting we should become some super-religious person looking down our nose at everyone else? And the answer is, no. To be holy is simply to be something other than what is common.

We are reborn by an uncommon seed and uncommon blood. The result is an uncommon person. A person who lives, not to put others down, but to show others the way.

Today, I will...enter the world as a stranger, and I will offer the world an uncommon life, for I live in the sphere of God.

Thursday
You Are Special

Do you remember that pretty little girl you really wanted to date, but when you asked her out, she said no. Or there was that great looking guy you really wanted to impress, but he acted as if you did not exist. Or you might recall applying to the college of your dreams, only to receive that letter which said, 'I'm sorry, you do not meet our standards." Or maybe you have had the experience where the boss came in and said,'"we no longer need you."

To be rejected is an incredibly painful human experience. Painful because it is human nature to want to fit in. It is normal to want to be accepted and valued by others. Acceptance by others provides solid footing for our self-esteem. It affirms who we think we are. But when the acceptance is not there, when we are rejected, we may start to think we are nothing of value.

God wants you to know...you are special.

The apostle Peter wrote to believers who had been "grieved by various trials," their faith had been "tested." And then he described them as being "rejected by men." This world can be a cruel place. Unbelievers mock those who seek to honor God with their lives. The life of a Christian is often not an easy life to live. But God wants us to remember our value is not determined by what the world thinks of us.

As Peter reminded his readers, *"But you are a chosen race, a royal priesthood, a holy nation, a people for his own possession...Once you were not a people, but now you are God's people; once you had not received mercy, but now you have received mercy"* (1 Peter 2:9-10).

It is an amazing reality! God chose you to be His! He values you that much.

Today, I will...walk in confidence knowing my Heavenly Father loves me and chose me to be His own.

Friday
You Are Being Watched

A current threat in our society is identity theft. Identity theft happens when someone takes your private personal information from various forms of documentation and uses that information to their own advantage. In essence, they steal your identity. They become you. If the stolen information is connected to financial properties it can be a costly nightmare.

And so, we are warned; 'you are being watched.' We have to be on the alert. We have to be vigilant. But sometimes, being watched can be a good thing.

In his first letter, Peter addresses a very sensitive issue. He writes to encourage wives who are married to men who are not believers. That home can be a very difficult place for a believer to live. But then he essentially tells the wives, 'you are being watched.' Their husbands are watching. So he encourages the wives to have lives of "respectful and pure conduct" and "a gentle and quiet spirit" (1 Peter 3:2, 4). The hope is the husband will be won to the Lord by what he sees in her life.

Peter is talking about the power of an example. In this case, the power of a life that seeks to honor God.

As we go through each day we find ourselves surrounded by all kinds of people. Chances are, most of those people will be unbelievers. What do they see in us? We do not live with all of those people, but perhaps we work with them. Maybe we go to school with them, or we live next door to them. Perhaps we belong to the same club or the same civic organization. And, they are watching us. What do they see?

There is so much anger in our world today. So much violence. So much abuse. So much disrespect. The Christian has an extraordinary opportunity to provide the world with a wonderful alternative lifestyle.

Today, I will...refuse to contribute to the angst in our world. I will share peace and civility with everyone I meet.

Week Forty-Six
1 Peter 4-5
2 Peter 1-3

Paul Shero

Monday
Good From Suffering?

Today's Scripture 1 Peter 4:1-19

What possible good could come from suffering? How in the world can I face suffering with joy? (1 Peter 4:13).

Most of what we know about suffering we learned from the world. Namely, suffering hurts and should be avoided. But in this chapter, Peter tells me some things about suffering that makes it possible to survive; even thrive.

He teaches me that when I cease to sin, it will hurt (Vs. 1). Sin hurts us when we do it and it hurts us when we stop. The claws of satan are in so deep that tearing free is painful. The pain of repentance always accompanies the joy of salvation. Sometimes there is painful retaliation from those in darkness (Vs. 4). I must always remember the end is near (Vs. 7). Judgment is coming.

These are serious times. We have a lot to do, so limp if you need to and crawl if you must. But above all, be faithful. There is judgment ahead, but there is also glory ahead. Remember, this is my opportunity to glorify God (Vs. 11). It all began with God and it ends with God.

Peter tells me not to be surprised (Vs. 12). It will probably get worse. This test is necessary and should not surprise us. Jesus suffered and when we suffer in His name, we have fellowship with Him (Vs. 13). This is where we are refined and made into His image.

Peter also tells us not all suffering is noble (Vs. 15). There is no glory when we suffer because of our sin. But when we suffer as a Christian, well, "that will be glory, glory for me."

One last thought. When we suffer as Christians, we are in the hands of God. God has all power and God is also faithful. He will not let us down.

Today, I will...put myself into the hands of God. I will submit myself to whatever He has for me. I want to have fellowship with Jesus and to become like Him.

Tuesday
Humble, Through Suffering

Today's Scripture 1 Peter 5:1-11

As if suffering were not enough, now Peter says I must be humble. Not only as a worker but also as an overseer. Even if, maybe, especially, I have a position of authority, I must be humble.

There are bad motives for leadership (Vs. 3). These must be avoided. Especially arrogance, which will disqualify me. When I seek the crown, I lose. But when I serve Him humbly, the Chief Shepherd (Jesus) crowns me in glory (Vs. 4).

This rule of humble service also applies to those who are a little lower in the church organization. I demonstrate humility by my subjection (Vs. 5). Peter tells me to be covered up in humility. This is not only a good idea, it is God's will. The proud are opposed by God. The humble receive grace (Vs. 5). When I humble myself, I submit to God's timetable. I trust Him to do the exalting at the right time.

My submission to God is also demonstrated by how I handle my worries. When I give Him my anxieties, I am giving Him my trust (Vs. 7). And I trust Him because He cares for me.

Peter warns me that the times are dangerous (Vs. 8). The devil is near. He is like a lion waiting to eat me. I know what satan can do. I know what I must do. I need to remember what God will do. In verse 10, Peter promises that my humble suffering will be rewarded with glory.

In the meantime, God will restore me. When an old table is restored, it is brought back to its original like-new condition. God can and will do that for me. This is His seal or mark that makes me His.

God will strengthen me. Paul said, *"I can do all things through Him who strengthens me"* (Philippians 4:13). God will establish me. I am standing on firm ground. My roots are deep. My backing is from God. I know all this because He is in control (Vs. 11). He even says Amen or "so it is."

Today I will...submit with humility to God and lean on Him and not myself. To God be the glory.

Gifts

Today's Scripture 2 Peter 1:1-8

Peter lets us know what God is doing for us. He says that God has given us all things that pertain to life and godliness. If we need it, He has provided it. We don't need to go anywhere else.

He has also given us precious and very great promises. God promises us we can partake of His divine nature. We are being offered the opportunity to become like God.

He then promises us that we can escape the corruption that is in the world. Sin is dirty. When we sin we become dirty. No soap we can make will clean us. But God promises us to clean us and protect us from the contamination of sin. And He will sanctify us to be like Him. These are wonderful gifts of grace that God offers.

Then Peter tells us what we must do. This list, in verses 5-7 are called the Christian graces or the building blocks of a Christian life.

The Beatitudes, in Matthew 5 are arranged in a similar way. Think of a staircase. One step is supporting the one above which supports the one above it. They are in a proper order. If you haven't taken the first step, you cannot get to the next step. Our Christian life starts with faith and only then will we move up. We all want to be the godly brother who is full of love. But before you can be that person, you have to tackle knowledge and self-control.

We are grateful that God has presented this task in steps. We should develop the habit of saying "What is the next step?" Maybe the next step is faith. Without it, we cannot please God. So, we hear the word of God; think about it until we believe, then we are ready for virtue. There will be no real virtue without faith.

He promises us that if we do this, we will never be ineffective and unfruitful.

Today, I will...begin the practice of asking "What is the next step?"

Thursday
Bridge Out

Today's Scripture 2 Peter 2:1-22

Peter takes the gloves off when he warns us about false teachers. What we believe affects who we are. Bad doctrine produces bad lives. Not everyone tells the truth. Liars will lie.

Peter says they are sly about their motives (Vs. 1). But the effects of their lies are destructive. When they have run their course, they end up denying our Lord. As if this was not bad enough, Peter tells us many people believe the lies they tell (Vs. 2). This cycle of sensual appetites feeds on those who believe these lies and produces more appetites. False doctrines are lifted up and truth is blasphemed. Often the motivation is greed (Vs. 3) so people lie to get what they want.

It seems there is no stopping them. But there is God. God is sovereign. No one gets away with this arrogance. Angels didn't (Vs. 4). The word in Noah's day didn't. Sodom didn't. God knows; God is sovereign. God judges those false teachers. God will rescue the righteous.

These liars are arrogant before God. They think sin is trivial and truth is a matter of opinion. They speak about things they don't know and make promises they can't keep. But the truth is...sin is no small thing. Sin kills us, corrupts us and enslaves us. These liars can't deliver on their promises. They are on a slippery slope and sure destruction is waiting for them.

But God is God. He has always been God and always will be God. His word has always been true and always will be true. God cannot lie. God is in charge and He will judge the liars. God will also rescue the righteous.

This scripture is a little upsetting. It seems so blunt. It seems like Peter is shouting at us. Why would a loving God be so blunt? Well, because He is a loving God.

It makes a difference what we believe and who we listen to. Remember what happened to Adam and Eve when they listened to the serpent? Think of this chapter as a "Bridge Out" sign. Plain and to the point. Because the message is important.

Today, I will...check what I hear against the Word of God, which is true.

Friday
God's Day-Timer

Not everyone believes the Word of God. Some are bold in their denial. They say things like "It's been over two thousand years since He said it. Nothing has happened yet!"

We need to remember there have always been guys like this. Even in Noah's day. They learned too late that God's Word is always sure. God has said this world will be burned up. Don't be disturbed by the fact that it has been a long time since He said it. God does not operate on daylight savings time. He does not work on our schedule but on His. Time, as we know it, does not control God.

Instead of thinking of God as slow, we should think of Him as patient. He is waiting for people to repent. Is He waiting for me? But His patience will one day be exhausted (Vs. 10). One day will be the last day. Judgment will come. It will be a surprise. The material world will end and we will meet God.

So, what should my reaction be right now? (Vs. 11). What should I do? How do you prepare for something like this? How do you get ready for the last day? Peter says we have to wait but while we wait there are somethings we should do. He even made us a little list.

In verse 14, He says while we are waiting, we can work on cleaning up our lives. Not just tidy up, but a deep cleaning. If your life was a house, you move the refrigerator to clean behind it. There are little dirty places we have gotten use to and overlook. No more. We are going to see God so this blemish must go. He also tells us we can wait in peace and work on relationships with those around us.

Then He says stay away from lies. How? Fill yourself with truth. Keep growing; keep learning. Stay ready. He is coming.

Today, I will...ask myself, "Am I ready for His return?" I will start the cleaning right now.

Week Forty-Seven
1 John 1-5

Robert Johnson

Monday
What a Fellowship

Today's Scripture 1 John 1:3-4

The letter of 1 John is encouraging to study on several different levels, whether you look at John's use of words like know and love, or some of the phrases that repeat through his letter. John wants us to have a full and complete joy that comes from our fellowship with God and with each other. This phrase seems to imply that it's possible to be a Christian, but not experience the full measure of joy that should come from knowing God. John wants the best for his readers, including us today, and that best includes having the joy of the Lord.

There is a natural progression in what John is saying; we have fellowship "with the Father and his Son Jesus Christ," which means we share fellowship with all who are in fellowship with God. That unity with God and each other should be a source of joy in our lives. Sin is an often-used tool of Satan to rob us of joy, to try to substitute something less for what God works through His will in us. God offers us so much more, however, than we can imagine.

John reminds us what we have with him in Christ. *"But if we walk in the light, as he is in the light, we have fellowship with one another, and the blood of Jesus his Son cleanses us from all sin."* (1 John 1:7)

There is great joy in the fellowship we have with each other. There is joy in knowing God longs to forgive us. *"If we confess our sins, he is faithful and just to forgive us our sins and to cleanse us from all unrighteousness"* (1 John 1:9). God offers us so much more than what life without him could be.

Today, I will...find joy in the relationship I share with others in Christ.

Tuesday
Trust and Obey

In 1 John 2, the apostle John talks about the central role of obedience in our faith. Our spiritual survival depends on our willingness to obey the directives that come from God. It has truly been said you can obey God without loving, but you can't love God apart from obedience. John reminds us that our spiritual progress depends on our willingness to do what God wants. We know God desires nothing but the best for us, which means we must get out of our own way, so to speak. Jesus himself told us if we are to follow Him, we must deny ourselves and take up our cross daily (Luke 9:23). For God to accomplish our salvation, we must trust him to work His good purposes in and through us.

Being sure of our fellowship with God is based on the life we live in Him. The term "keep" means to be attentive to, to fulfill one's duty, to perform one's task watchfully and attentively. Such an obedience proves the reality of our love. Our life in God and love for God are integrated; it's not a function of lip service but life service (John 14:15, 21). John affirms that the obedient Christian grows in the love of God, until that love is mature, or complete. Divine love is made complete in the person who obeys the word of God. The proof of love is loyalty to Christ and the life He commands us to live. *"Whoever keeps His word, in him truly the love of God is perfected. By this we may know that we are in Him"* (1 John 2:5).

To have a genuine relationship with God, to know that we know of His life and love, we must trust and obey His will. This is walking in the same path Jesus walked for us. This is how our love for God is perfected. This is how we truly know we know Him.

Today, I will...show my love for God in doing my best to live for Him.

Wednesday
Being Like Christ

When John writes, "what kind of love," he is literally saying, "Of what soil is this love." The term was used by Greeks before the writing of the New Testament to mean of what country. John uses this term to remind us God's love is like no other kind of love we could know. One way we know this unique love is that we are God's children now; "such we are" (1 John 3:1). What a blessing it is to be able to call God our Father, and know how that speaks of His love, care, concern, and promises for us. As our Father, God is blessing and disciplining us for our spiritual well-being, that we might reflect His image in our lives today (Ephesians 5:1).

Being God's children now also speaks about tomorrow. In 1 John 3:2, John tells us, *"We know that when He appears we shall be like Him, because we shall see Him as He is."* Consider what John tells us in this verse about God; He will appear, we will be like Him, and we will see Him as He is. What glorious promises God offers us! As Jesus prayed in Acts 17:24, *"Father, I desire that they also, whom you have given me, may be with me where I am, to see my glory that you have given me because you loved me before the foundation of the world."*

John tells us, for this to happen, we must reflect His image today. John summarizes the transformation of character that Jesus offers us today with the word "pure." Spiritually, the term speaks of being clean morally, inwardly; being pure means having the attitude of heart needed to live the consecrated life Christ calls us to live in Him. The motivation for a pure and holy life is a deep comprehension of the love of God. The more we know His love for us, the less likely we'll be to live an impure or sinful life.

Today, I will...remember all God has waiting for me in eternity.

Thursday
Love One Another

Today's Scripture 1 John 4:20-21

If you listen to people talk, you learn we "love" lots of things. We use the term for food, movies, friends, sports, and many other things, but do we really love those things or just have great affection for them? True love is rare in this world, but it shouldn't be rare among Christians. John reveals to us the logical flow of God's love from Himself to and through us to others.

Loving each other can be hard to do, as we sometimes allow our biases and emotions to override the love of God we should show each other. John tells us that truly loving each other shows integral aspects of our relationship with God. It shows we are walking in the light (1 John 2:9-10). It shows we have passed out of death into life, life together in Christ (1 John 3:14). It shows we truly love God, for we can't genuinely love others if we don't first love God (1 John 4:11).

How do we love one another with the love of God? We should love sincerely. Jesus asked, "For if you love those who love you, what reward do you have? Do not even the tax collectors do the same?" (Matthew 5:46). We should love sacrificially. *"We know love by this, that He laid down His life for us; and we ought to lay down our lives for the brethren."* We should love personally. *"No one has ever seen God; if we love one another, God abides in us and His love is perfected in us"* (1 John 4:12).

True love is love that is expressed in real actions that impact real people and real needs. It is how God has loved us through Christ. No one who has seen the love of God shown through the cross, through the life and death of Jesus Christ, lives a life of selfishness. If we show a genuine love for each other, we find genuine life in Christ.

Today, I will...try to show God's love by helping others.

Friday
Overcome the World

Today's Scripture 1 John 5:1–4

When Nicodemus came to Jesus by night, he wanted to know more about Him. Jesus, however, knew what Nicodemus needed. *"Jesus answered, 'Truly, truly, I say to you, unless one is born of water and the Spirit, he cannot enter the kingdom of God'"* (John 3:5). Paul described how we as the church are sanctified by the washing of water with the word (Ephesians 5:26). When we come in obedience to the gospel, and our sins are washed away by the blood of Christ in immersion, we have stepped away from the world, held captive by the power of the evil one. Satan, however, does not want to let go. The temptation to sin is real and something we must contend against.

In speaking of false teachers, John wrote, *"Little children, you are from God and have overcome them, for He who is in you is greater than he who is in the world"* (1 John 4:4). Similarly, we can be successful in overcoming temptation. Faith is the means by which we can overcome sin and live a dedicated life for Christ. Never underestimate what we can do by faith. Scripture says, *"In all circumstances take up the shield of faith, with which you can extinguish all the flaming darts of the evil one"* (Ephesians 6:16). Our faith is based on the word of God (Romans 10:17), which is the sword of the Spirit (Ephesians 6:17). Faith enables us to have a conviction of the eternal, of giving us substance to our hope (Hebrews 11:1). The righteousness of God is revealed in faith, and from beginning to end, we live by faith (Romans 1:17).

How powerful faith is! Victory comes through our Lord Jesus Christ (1 Corinthians 15:57), who dwells in our hearts by faith (Ephesians 3:17). Living a life of faith strengthens us in godliness, reminding us there's more to life than today, assuring us that heaven is worth it all. "For we walk by faith, not by sight" (2 Corinthians 5:7).

Today, I will...trust God and his word in living my faith in Christ.

Week Forty-Eight
2 John
3 John
Jude
Revelation 1-2

Craig Evans

Monday
One Subject

Today's Scripture 2 John

There is an old preachers' story (which means you have probably heard it before and it may or may not be true) about a preacher who always preached every sermon on baptism. At first, the congregation loved his enthusiasm for baptism, but after a while, they wanted him to preach on other subjects. The Elders talked to him and encouraged him to preach on other subjects. They asked him to preach a series of sermons from Genesis, for they knew there was no baptism in Genesis. The first Sunday the preacher began with an overview of Genesis beginning with the creation, Adam and Eve, and the fall of man. Then he began talking about Noah and the Flood. He said, "The flood is a story about water which brings me to my subject today...baptism." When confronted after services by the Elders, they asked, "Why do you speak on baptism for every sermon?" He responded, "When everyone here is baptized, I'll preach on something else."

John the beloved apostle, spoke of one subject repeatedly: love. In John's writings, John; 1, 2, 3 John, and Revelation, he uses the word love 79 times. John writes about the love God has for us (John 3:16-17), the love we are to have for God (John 14:15), and the love we are to have for one another (John 13:34-35).

John writes in 2 John 5-6, *"And now I ask you, dear lady—not as though I were writing you a new commandment, but the one we have had from the beginning—that we love one another. And this is love, that we walk according to his commandments; this is the commandment, just as you have heard from the beginning, so that you should walk in it."*

John ties our love for Jesus and our love for one another to our keeping his commandments. I wonder if the Elders had confronted John about constantly preaching on love if he would have said, "When everyone loves one another, I'll preach on something else."

Today, I will...thank God for his love for me and show God's love towards someone else and tell people of God's love for them.

Tuesday

That Guy

When people visit your congregation, what impression will you leave upon them? Some may talk about the singing, the preaching, or the friendliness, But many will leave and talk about that one person who made an impact on them whether it be good or bad. Many people will make up their entire opinion about a congregation and Jesus based on that one person they meet. How will they feel, and what will they tell people after visiting your congregation?

In the book of 3 John, John mentions two very different men, Gaius and Diotrephes. Gaius made a difference in the kingdom through his hospitality, love and generosity. He had such a powerful impact on people that news made it all the way back to John, and John praised Gaius for his walking in truth. Gaius made such an impression that people made sure John knew about it.

Diotrephes also made an impression on those who visited the congregation, and they also took a report back to John. Diotrephes is remembered for his selfishness, arrogance, and the opposite of hospitality...his hostility. This attitude was not only toward visitors, but toward his own church family.

The apostle John was known even in his old age to have one simple sermon, "little children love one another." Let me ask you again, not just what is your congregation known for, but what are you known for. It is said that people may not remember what you said, but people will remember how you made them feel. After people were in Gaius' presence they left feeling loved. After they left Diotrephes presence, they felt unloved. John said people will be known for their love.

Have you ever heard the phrase, "Don't be that guy?" Usually the phrase describes someone who is rude, annoying, aggravating, hateful, or arrogant. John in 3 John gives us a person to imitate and another to not imitate. When it comes to Diotrephes, please Don't be that guy.

Today, I will...examine my own life and see if I am more like Gaius or Diotrephes.

Wednesday
Jude Is That Friend

Today's Scripture Jude

In a group of friends, you will find many different personalities. Many times, there will be ultimate optimist who makes the best of any situation, the pessimist who rains negativity on everything, the encourager who will always build you up, and then there is the blunt friend. The one you ask when you really want the non-sugar-coated truth. The truth may hurt, but you know you need to hear it.

Jude is that friend. Jude wanted to write a letter to build up the church about the common salvation all have in Christ, but he spends the short letter condemning and warning against false teaching. Jude knew while persecution of the church was rampant, the most dangerous threat the church faced was false teaching. Christianity's biggest threats are not from the outside but the inside.

What was the false teaching that Jude warns about? He tells us false teachers abused the teaching of God's grace to justify their sexual immorality, and they denied the lordship of Jesus and reject his authority. Simply put they want the blessings of Jesus, His grace and forgiveness without submitting to Him as Lord and King. He reminds the readers of God's judgement of cities of Sodom and Gomorrah that were not only punished in this life with fire and brimstone but are punished with eternal fire. He encourages the faithful to maintain their faith by keeping themselves in the love of God and waiting on his mercy and showing mercy to others.

Jude's blunt letter is filled with imagery and illustrations that to some may seem confusing, but there is a simplicity to it. Those who reject the lordship of Jesus Christ will spend eternity in fire, and those who remain faithful spend eternity in the mercy and love of Jesus.

I am thankful for Jude's message of warning, but also of the charge he gives us to remain faithful to Jesus. Jude is the friend we all need.

Today, I will...be thankful for those who are honest with me and I will submit my life to the Lordship of Jesus.

Thursday
Aloud

For many, Revelation is one of the scariest books in the New Testament. It is filled with apocalyptic language, stunning visuals, and at times difficult to understand imagery. Some want to make it a book of prophecy with all the fulfillment of these prophecies during our lifetime, it seems they have not read when John tells us in Revelation 1:1, *"The revelation of Jesus Christ, which God gave him to show to his servants the things that must soon take place."*

While some preachers preach and writers write on it often, others stay away from it except for the occasional reference to be "faithful unto death (2:10), to not be lukewarm (3:14), or the description of Heaven as a place with no tears, sorrow, pain, grief or death (21:4).

John tells the readers there are blessings associated with Revelation. In Revelation 1:3 John writes, *"Blessed is the one who reads aloud the words of this prophecy, and blessed are those who hear, and who keep what is written in it, for the time is near."*

There is one word that is overlooked in this verse, and it is the word "aloud." John tells the readers to read this book aloud. It is for public reading and teaching, and the reading should be given close attention to through active listening, and the listening becomes evident as the words of this book are not only read and listened to, but obeyed. If all the book of Revelation is read, listened to, and obeyed how much more will this be a blessing to the reader?

The reader will know the power of God, the love of Jesus, the necessity of a church family that loves God, the reality and pain of persecution, the victory of Jesus and his disciples over this world and Satan, and the promise of Heaven. The reader will be blessed with a love for God, a faith that will endure persecution, and a longing for the eternal presence of God in heaven. What a blessing!

Today, I will...not only read God's word, but I will listen carefully to his word, and obey it.

Friday
Report Cards

Today's Scripture Revelation 2

There are few things that cause more anxiety than being evaluated. Ask any student who has been given at test, a professional who has gone through their yearly job performance review, a restaurant that has had the health inspector visit, or any construction site that has had a visit from the building inspector.

Our schools are built on a system of evaluation: daily work, tests, papers, and projects are all graded and a report card is given every six to nine weeks. As a child, I remember assignments and tests returned to me with red smiley faces on them. As I progressed in my education, I received papers and tests back with so much red ink I thought my teacher may have hemorrhaged to death.

I had an instructor in college who used the Harbrace System of grading essays and papers that had seven deadly sins of writing, and each mistake would cost you a letter grade. In a ten-page term paper I made four mistakes and received a D. That instructor was strict.

It is one thing to have a term paper or job performance graded, but can you imagine your congregation being graded by God? Revelation chapters 2 and 3 contains God's report card on the seven churches of Asia. God tells the church at Ephesus while they are known for their stance on the truth, they have left their first love and He called for them to repent. God knows the faithfulness of the church at Smyrna through their poverty and tribulation, and encourages them to maintain their faithfulness to the point of death and promises them a crown of life. God warns the church at Pergamum of following teachings other than the truth and calls them to repentance. He praises the church at Thyatira for their love, faith, service, and patient endurance but charges them to repent from allowing paganism to infiltrate their congregation.

When God's grades church He praises the good, calls out the bad, and tells them what they need to do be right. I don't know how the churches responded to His grading of them, but I wonder if God were grading your life, what would you brag on, and what would He tell you to change.

Today, I will...use God's word to honestly evaluate my walk with God and I will celebrate His faithfulness, and will correct my deficiencies and thank God for His goodness and mercy and walk toward Him.

Week Forty-Nine
Revelation 3-7

Tommy Haynes

Hot and Cold Churches

Have you ever attended a congregation that totally impressed you? Have you visited some that repulsed you by their coldness? Most of us have. Jesus knew churches like this, and spoke to seven of them. Among these seven churches were two that were on fire for the Lord, and five that He threatened.

The church in Sardis was asleep. Jesus calls them "dead" (Revelation 3:1). The church in Philadelphia had only a "little power." Christ used that power to send them through an "open door"(3:8) of opportunity that He was confident they would seize. The church in Laodicea was like so many churches today who rest on their past, and no longer do much. They had become lukewarm and repulsive to the Lord (3:16).

When we observe some of these symptoms in our own congregations (both good and evil) we need to point them out. We also need to encourage progress in our ministries, and become part of the cure for either dead works or ministries half-done. We do not want to be like the generation that followed Joshua, who did what was right in their own eyes and did not finish the conquest (Judges 1-2:10).

We built an addition onto our house when I was a teenager. My dad used the lumber out of an old house we dismantled, and used the good stuff in the construction. When my parents decided to sell the house many decades later, the inspector asked my father who built the addition. My dad told him he and his sons did it, and he remarked, "This is the most overbuilt place I have ever seen. Everything is above code." Isn't this the way we should be in the work of the Lord. Sardis and Laodicea were dead and dying when it came to the Lord's work. Only Philadelphia was on fire for the Lord. We must make sure that we are on fire every day!

Today, I will...examine my heart (2 Corinthians13:5), and make sure I am really on fire for the Lord.

Tuesday
Around the Throne

The concept of an "open door" appears in Revelation (Revelation 3:8; 3:20; 4:1). Philadelphia had a door that was opened by the Lord to expand their ministry. Now Jesus opens the door to heaven so John can see.

What John observes is the throne of God in heaven. There is unimaginable beauty all around this throne and twenty-four more thrones for the elders who sat there. There is sound, flashes of lightning, seven torches burning, and four special creatures: a lion, ox, man, and an eagle. Instead of the seraphim of Isaiah's vision (Isaiah 6), these four creatures have six wings and are flying and shouting a similar praise, "Holy holy, holy, is the Lord God Almighty. Who was and is and is to come!" When these creatures fly and shout, the twenty-four elders fall down and cast their crowns before Him who sits on the throne, and they shout praise as well (Revelation 4:9-11).

Have you ever opened a door and had your breath taken away by something awesome on the other side? Can you imagine John's reaction when this door opened? We sing the song, "How Beautiful Heaven Must Be" and Jesus here gives us a small taste.

Some have said, "If all heaven is about is singing and worshipping all the time, then what is so great about it?" The fact is we know little about heaven. The picture God gives us is so amazing it is hard to conceive. We should all want to go there so that we can meet Jesus and praise God in person, before His breath-taking throne. The Bible depicts heaven as rest (Matthew 11:28; Hebrews 4:1) and as Paradise (Revelation 2:7; 22:1-5). Neither of those things is boring. When I was a boy, I was amazed at the colors of the castle in Wizard of Oz. That cannot begin to compare to heaven.

Today, I will...spend some time trying to envision the throne room of my God, and then spend time in prayer thanking Him for allowing His Son to prepare that place for me (John 14:1-6).

Wednesday
A New Song

Revelation four through nine take place in heaven. Everyone in heaven is upset because no one can open the scroll with seven seals. Jesus appears as a Lamb who had been slain. When He takes the scroll, all in the throne room fall down before the Lamb and sing this new song:

"Worthy are you to take the scroll and to open its seals,
for you were slain, and by your blood you ransomed people for God
from every tribe and language and people and nation,
and you have made them a kingdom and priests to our God,
and they shall reign on the earth" (5:9-10)

This wonderful song is about the worthiness of Jesus to open the scroll, revealing its contents, because Jesus was crucified on our behalf, and ransomed all who come to Him. We have been richly blessed by His payment for our souls in that we are made into a kingdom, we have become priests, and we shall reign on the earth (1 Peter 2:5-10).

In what sense do we reign on earth? First, we are made royal through the blood of Christ. We have been adopted (Ephesians 1:5). This places us in the Royal Family of God, and makes us spiritual rulers on the earth. Second, as Christians we have had our eyes opened to the truth about what this life is about, and how to live it. This gives to us the keys to the kingdom (Matthew 16:19) by means of revealed scripture that opens the door of understanding. Third, we reign on earth because the decisions we make effect the lives around us. We have the Gospel. Proclaiming the Gospel either saves men or repels them.

We have been ransomed. Jesus paid for our sins. Satan, the kidnapper, has lost his grip on us when we obey Jesus and walk away from sin.

Today, I will...sing the new song by taking charge of my life, living as a member of the Royal Family of heaven.

Thursday
How Long?

Today's Scripture Revelation 6:9-11

When facing trials that endure for a while, we have a tendency to say and to ask God "How long?" We want the trial to end so we can get back to a smooth and easy way of life.

God has not promised us that life here will be easy. Paul's accounting of things that happened to him during his ministry is both amazing and frightening (2 Corinthians 11:22-29). All of the apostles with the exception of John, died violent deaths (Mathew 24:9; Luke 21:16; John 16:2; 21:20-24). There is often a high price to pay when you stand up as a witness (ear witness) for Christ.

While few are paying the ultimate price of death today, we cannot know what the future holds. In the middle of persecution, we all want relief. Jesus records for us that those who were witnesses for Him in the first century, and martyred, were crying out "How long?" We are in good company when we also ask "How long", however, it is a very human question.

The Bible does not say that God gave them an answer. God instead, gives these martyrs a white robe, and they were told to rest until the number of all those who died in like manner, was complete. We notice that these who are asking "How long?" are no longer suffering. They are asking on behalf of those whom they left behind on earth, knowing the struggle was not finished. There is no selfishness here, and the Lord does not rebuke them for asking.

If anyone ever understood human suffering, it is Jesus. The unjust treatment, the constant ignorance of Who He is, and the misdirected concepts men had in His day of the kingdom, all led to His own death. When we face fiery trials, we can turn to Christ who understands and can comfort. He can also give us patience to endure.

Today, I will...pray about spiritual peace and tranquility that can come even in trial, and I will patiently wait on the Lord.

Friday
God Knows His Own

Today's Scripture Revelation 7:1-17

The seventh chapter of Revelation has caused much confusion and been the victim of terrible misinterpretation. In actuality, it is a very comforting passage giving great insight into our God who is described by John in another letter as "love" (1 John 4:8).

Some religions use the "144,000" to try to claim that the "inner sanctum" of heaven is full. Revelation is designed to hide the truth from the enemies of God (in the first century this was Rome), and to reveal the truth to God's people. Numbers as code for various concepts was known to the Hebrew people, and was passed down to the church by means of Jewish Christians. The 144,000 is simply a multiple of 12 and 10 thus meaning numerous and complete. There are clear signs that this is not literal as there is no tribe of Dan or Ephraim listed, and Joseph never had a tribe. Joseph's two sons Ephraim and Manasseh were given a tribe. God wanted us to know that this is not a literal number, but a symbol for the large number who will be in heaven.

Another proof of the figurative nature of this number is that following this section (7:1-8) John is shown that these are not the only ones in heaven. There is another group in heaven that "no one could number… "(vs. 9). This conclusively proves that the 144,000 are not the only ones in heaven.

The real bottom line of this chapter is that God knows all those who have suffered for Him. These had come out of the "great tribulation" (vs. 14) and have had their robes washed white in the blood of the Lamb.

God knows us. This is one of the greatest truths in scripture. Through Jesus, He also understands us and forgives us (John 1:14; Hebrews 4:15-16). This is the embodiment of grace, and our hope to be a part of God's innumerable heavenly family.

Today, I will...read Psalm 139 along with this chapter to strengthen my confidence in God knowing who I am.

Week Fifty
Revelation 8-12

Barry Grider

Take Heart, Christian...Judgment Is Coming

Today's Scripture Revelation 8

Most Americans are avid football fans. As one of those "fanatics" I have experienced the great anticipation of entering a stadium shortly before a kickoff. The moment the game begins is near, but it can seemingly take forever because of the anticipation of the moment.

While living on earth the Christians are filled with the hope of eternal life (Titus 1:2). Biblical hope is expectation with anticipation. We fully expect to go to heaven and we can hardly wait.

The longing for heaven floods our souls for various reasons. First, we long to be with the Divine Godhead. Second, we look forward to being reunited with the faithful children of God, including our loved ones who died in triumphant faith. Third, it will be a blessing to be released from the baneful burdens of this life.

The trials, tribulations, and temptations that beset us can often lead to discouragement, distress, and despair. We know Jesus is coming again, and there will be a judgment. Despite the inequities of life, God will settle all scores (Romans 12:19). Yet we still cry "O Lord-how long?" (Psalm 6:3).

Revelation eight is a reminder that saints ought always to pray. *"And the smoke of the incense, with the prayers of the saints rose before God from the hand of the angel."* (Revelation 8:4)

Often we feel as if the forces of evil are going to win. But the message of Revelation eight is an admonishment to keep on praying. Just as God heard the Children of Israel in bondage in Egypt and the persecuted saints during the first century, he hears the faithful and today will avenge the elect.

Today, I will...not fear what the Devil and wicked men try to do to me. I will watch and pray for the Lord is coming.

Tuesday
It Pays To Know Your Enemy

Today's Scripture Revelation 9:1-6

When Elizabeth Kalhammer answered an ad in a newspaper during the early days of World War II, she did not realize until later for whom she would be working. She was hired as a maid at the Berghoff retreat of none other than Adolf Hitler. Since his hideaway was nestled deep in the Bavarian Alps, Mrs. Kahlhammer did not realize the impact the fiendish fuhrer had inflicted upon the world until after the war ended. For many years she refused to even talk about the job because she was so ashamed she had been an employee of Hitler.

When Satan slithered into Eden he came as an intruder. This earth was made for man, not for the Devil. He is a powerful being, even though his power is limited. He is the one who is responsible for the entrance of sin into this world and its accompanying sorrow.

It pays to know your enemy which is the Devil (1 Peter 5:8). In Revelation 9, he is described as one who has been "given the key to the shaft of the bottomless pit" (vs. 1). Evil exists in our world and concurrently with it pain and suffering. Sin's impairment is likened unto the sting of a scorpion. Paul says, "The sting of death is sin" (1 Corinthians 15:56).

How does the wicked one sting today? Many are brought under his control through addiction, apathy, adversity, arrogance, and anxiety. Their lives are miserable and are often cut short. While death may seem like the best alternative, it is not. In the 1951 musical "Showboat," deckhand "ol Joe," played by the great baritone singer William Warfield, sang the classic "Old Man River." Among the lyrics are as follows, "I'm tired of livin' and scared of dyin'." That may well describe most people in our world today. Sadly, many know something is not right with their lives, but they have never considered the source of the problem.

Today, I will...keep my eyes on my enemy but cling to my God.

A Rainbow In the Cloud

As a boy, I remember our congregation would occasionally sing a very upbeat hymn, written by Alton Howard, entitled, "There's A Rainbow In The Cloud." The lyrics of the chorus were as follows:

> *There's a rainbow that is shining,*
> *There's a rainbow in the cloud;*
> *When life's race is run, and the victry's won,*
> *There's a rainbow in the cloud.*

The imagery of a rainbow is always connected with the promises of God. Following the flood, God said to Noah, "I have set my bow in the cloud, and it shall be a sign of the covenant between me and the earth" (Genesis 9:13). The imagery in Revelation 10:1 is of a mighty angel with a rainbow atop his head. The scene envisions a message of hope. It is a message that has been fully revealed in its scope and promise. It is the judgment of this writer that such a passage describes the completion of New Testament revelation. The hope of the gospel is now fully known and can be understood. Hence, that "into which angels long to look" (1 Peter 1:12), may be known by all.

Man cannot save himself. We need a Savior and that Savior is Jesus. Throughout biblical history God was unfolding His divine plan to save a sinful race. At just the right time in history, a time ordained by God, Jesus was born (Galatians 4:4). While God may not be confined by time, with Him, timing is everything. After Jesus suffered and died and rose again, he commissioned His disciples to carry the gospel to the uttermost parts of the world, which they did. Now we have completed revelation. All those who want to be saved can be saved. Just as a rainbow offers a promise by God, so does the gospel. Those who accept the gospel find it sweet. Those who reject the gospel find it bitter.

Today, I will...gladly follow the gospel of Jesus Christ as I ever look above, seeing the rainbow in the cloud.

Thursday
The Victorious Christ

Today's Scripture Revelation 11

In 1743, England's King George II heard a performance of George Frederick Handel's "Hallelujah Chorus" and could not contain himself but had to stand until its conclusion. It has become customary since that time for entire audiences to do the same. The hymn is based upon the following passage, *"The kingdom of the world has become the kingdom of our Lord and of his Christ, and he shall reign forever and ever"* (Revelation 11:15).

Later his great-granddaughter, Queen Victoria, upon hearing the majestic hymn, "All Hail the Power of Jesus' Name," would set aside her crown in deference to the King of Kings and Lord of Lord's. Her great-great-grandaughter, Queen Elizabeth II, the present monarch, has no doubt stood at attention hundreds of times during her long reign, as the strains of "God Save the Queen" lauded her majesty. However, as her ancestors have so admirably demonstrated there really is only one sovereign, the Lord Jesus Christ.

Revelation 11 clearly sets forth the fact that Jesus has won the victory over sin, death, and the grave. Though the enemy tried his best to thwart God's plan and bring to naught the seed line of the Christ, such could not be accomplished. God said to David, *"When your days are fulfilled and you lie down with your fathers, I will raise up your offspring after you, who shall come from your body, and I will establish his kingdom"* (2 Samuel 7:12). Man cannot subvert the plan of God. Jesus made clear to his disciples that he was going to establish His church, which is His kingdom, and he said, "the gates of hell shall not prevail against it" (Matthew 16:18). Jesus went into the realm of death and came back out again. He ascended to the right hand of His Father, where He rules and reigns over His kingdom.

Today, I will...rejoice to be a citizen of the kingdom of Christ and will ever live to bring glory and honor unto my King.

Friday
The Defeat of the Enemy

Today's Scripture Revelation 12

There is nothing that Satan can do to the saints of God unless we give him such power. We have this assurance in Christ. Satan, though still wielding a powerful influence, has been defeated. Not long after man sinned in the garden, God confronted the Devil, and said, *"I will put enmity between you and the woman and between your offspring and her offspring; he shall bruise your head, and you shall bruise his heel"* (Genesis 3:15). A war will rage for the souls of men. One in that battle will be victorious and the other will receive a fatal blow.

In Revelation 12 there is the description of a glorified woman who represents the redeemed of the ages. God has always had a people. Such is called a remnant. Since Satan hates what God loves, he especially despises those redeemed by the blood of Christ. He will persecute them and if possible he would destroy them. Satan takes delight in those who follow him but is filled with fury and wrath toward those who oppose him.

Satan is motivated out of his great hatred for God. His mission is to destroy man and his method of accomplishing this is the lie. He is a sophisticated, subtle and smart being. However, he is also sordid in his behavior and actions. This diabolical creature will tempt a man to sin against God and if the man gives in to the temptation he will point a finger of accusation against him. He is identified as the "accuser of our brothers" (Revelation 12:10), but one who has been cast down.

At one time Satan decried God's faithful servant, Job, and surmised that Job's faithfulness was only because God had blessed him. However, Job would not turn his back on God, even when the Devil tried to destroy him. Friends, we do not have to give in to the Devil. Jesus has won the battle of the ages.

Today, I will...confront my enemy, the Devil, and because of Jesus I will be victorious.

Week Fifty-One
Revelation 13-17

Kirk Brothers

Monday
Who Can Fight Against It?

Today's Scripture Revelation 13:1-4

The theme of Revelation is "Victory in Jesus." One might outline the book as follows:

Chapters 1-3: Christ Oversees His Churches
Chapters 4-11: Christ Opens the Book
Chapters 12-20: Christ Overcomes the Dragon
Chapters 21-22: Christ Opens the Gates.

The chapters we will look at over the next few days are from the section that highlights Christ's defeat of the Dragon and his minions. Revelation 12:9 makes it clear that the Dragon is Satan (or the Devil; cf. Rev. 2:13, 24; 3:9; 12:2, 7; 20: 2, 10). The following chapters introduce the servants of the Dragon:

The Sea Beast (13:1)
The Land Beast (13:11)
The False Prophet (16:13; 19:20)
The City of Babylon (14:8; 17:1ff)

The chapter we are considering today focuses on the sea beast and the land beast. The land beast serves the sea beast and makes the earth worship him (13:12). Both beasts serve the dragon (13:4).

"Beast" commonly referred to an oppressive world power that was persecuting God's people in apocalyptic literature (which Revelation is). When we compare Revelation 13 with Daniel 2 and 7 we see many similarities. The most dangerous beast of Daniel 7 is the great beast of Revelation 13. Daniel says that the great beast he forsaw is a fourth kingdom from the kingdom of Babylon, the kingdom of Rome. This is the very empire that was persecuting the Christians who first read Revelation 13.

The first readers of this letter felt overwhelmed by the power of the beast, the Roman government. Their fears are embodied in the cry, "Who can fight against it?" (13:4). John is reminding them that there is a Savior who can fight against it. We have the luxury of not being persecuted by our government but we need to remember that governments do not always serve God. Will we?

Today, I will...put my trust in my God, not my government.

Tuesday
Fallen Is Babylon the Great!

Today's Scripture Revelation 14:6-8

We were introduced to the Sea Beast and Land Beasts in Revelation 13. Both serve Satan (the Dragon). The Sea Beast is the Roman Empire and the Land Beast likely refers to Roman religion, which "makes the earth and its inhabitants worship the first beast" (13:12). We meet another of Satan's minions in Revelation 14: Babylon the Great (cf. also Revelation 17, 18). The city of Babylon represented one of the great empires that had tormented the people of Israel. Babylon had invaded Judea on multiple occasions and carried the children into captivity. Many of these captives were held in the capital city of Babylon itself. The name "Babylon" became a symbolic name. In Jewish literature, it was used (along with "Edom") as a code word for the city of Rome (cf. IVP New Testament Background Commentary). This is likely how John uses it here in Revelation 14.

Many early Christians, who read Revelation shortly after it was written, would been facing persecution for their faith at the hands of the Roman Empire. The city of Rome itself represented the eye of this terrible storm. Rome was also a source of great immorality as she "made all the nations drink the wine of the passion of her sexual immorality" (14:8). Many Christians died in this evil city. Others faced the most horrible of tortures. Think of what it would have meant to the early Christians who read this letter when they first saw or heard, "Fallen, fallen is Babylon the Great!" W.B West, a great teacher of the book of Revelation, would tell his students, "Look at the book of Revelation through first century glasses." We often consume ourselves with what this book might reveal about our future but spend too little time considering the impact it would have on those who first read it. For them, it was a message of hope. The great city of Rome, the source of so much pain, would fall!

Today, I will...picture the day when the forces of evil have fallen.

Sing a New Song

Today's Scripture Revelation 15:5–8

Numbers were important in the Jewish culture. One of the most important numbers in this book is the number seven. It is found 52 times. It plays an important role in the layout of the book. In chapter five we have the book with seven seals. The was symbolic of information that was sealed up and then revealed. Jesus was revealing things to come and John was to write it down. Chapter eight reveals seven angels with seven trumpets. In Israel's history, the trumpet sounded as they marched into battle and as a warning. The latter is probably the symbolic meaning of the trumpets in chapter eight.

This brings us to chapter fifteen and the seven bowls of wrath that are being poured out. It is interesting that these bowls of wrath are also called plagues. When one looks at the details of the plagues in chapter 16, there are many similarities to the plagues in Egypt as recorded in Exodus (first, second, sixth, seventh, ninth are also found in Revelation). These plagues are a reminder that God is a God of justice and that those who rebel against him will face his wrath.

 One of the best-known statements in Revelation is found in this chapter: "And they sang the song of Moses" (15:3). There are two songs that Moses is known for. One is the song in Exodus 15 on the shores of the Red Sea as the army of Egypt lay floating nearby. The other is in Deuteronomy 32 as Moses was on the doorstep of eternity and the children of Israel were on the doorstep of the Promised Land. Both songs speak of God's greatness and his deliverance of his people. They also speak words of warning to those who rebel against the Lord. These songs were designed to praise, teach, and warn. It is a reminder of all the songs we sing what have powerful messages. I wonder if we are listening.

Today, I will...pay closer attention to the songs I sing in worship.

Thursday
The Battlefield

Today's Scripture Revelation 16:16

Shiloh national battlefield is 30 miles from my house. A Civil War battle was fought there on April 6-7, 1862 resulting in 2,300 casualties. It is now a national park with thousands of visitors each year. When you say the word "Shiloh" in west Tennessee, the first thought for most people is "battlefield." The same would be true of Gettysburg, Mannasses, or Fort Sumter.

Revelation 16:16 represents another of the well-known verses in the book of Revelation. Countless words have been spoken and written in an attempt to explain it. Some translations use the word "Armageddon" here but "Har-Magedon" is the best spelling. We do not know where this place is. Some believe that it is referring to the valley between Mount Megiddo and Mount Carmel in north-central Israel. It was known in the ancient world as a great battlefield. Many such battles are recorded in Scripture. This is the place where...
...Deborah and Barak defeat Canaanites,
...Gideon defeats Midianites,
...Saul defeated by Philistines,
...King Ahaziah died from Jehu's arrows,
...Josiah is killed by Pharaoh Necho.

Remember that book written in symbols and symbolic language. The battle referred to is not a literal battle. The armies described cannot fit in the literal valley near Megiddo. Jesus is using it to symbolize the great victory he will have over the Dragon and all his foot soldiers, the enemies of God's people. The primary focus of Revelation is on Jesus victory over the Roman Empire and the force behind the Roman Empire, Satan. The battle in Revelation was not much of a battle. The victory was swift and complete.

We need to remember that we are in a great battle. Paul said, *"Put on the full armor of God, so that you will be able to stand firm against the schemes of the devil. For our struggle is not against flesh and blood, but against the rulers, against the powers, against the world forces of this darkness, against the spiritual forces of wickedness in the heavenly places"* (Ephesians 6:11-12).

Today, I will...remember that the battle belongs to the Lord.

The King of Kings

We learned of the fall of Babylon in chapter 14. Chapters 17–19 give us further details concerning its wickedness and fall. The fact that Christ's revelation spends so much time focusing on its fall, means that it is very significant. When reading chapter 17, one is struck with not only the evil of Babylon but her beauty. She was "drunk with the blood of the saints, and with the blood of the witnesses of Jesus" (17:6).

I wonder if some of the Christians who first read this book thought of the blood of friends that had been shed in the great Coliseum in Rome. Babylon, the great harlot, was clothed in purple and scarlet, gold, precious stones, and pearls. Rome was a majestic city that enjoyed the wealth and culture of the world. Her power and beauty was impressive. Rome had used her power to crush God's people but judgement was coming.

Even as John wondered at the majesty of Rome, an angel began to describe her demise. He started with a reference to the destruction of the beast that she served. The one who "was, and is not" (17:8). Doom was coming. The forces of evil would wage war against the Lamb, "*and the Lamb will overcome them, because He is Lord of Lords and King of Kings, and those who are with Him are the called and chosen and faithful*" (17:14).

Recent years have been filled with stories of the atrocities of ISIS and other radical groups. There are many who would seek to destroy all that is good and holy in the world. There are nations who seek to conquer with no regard for others. People with power and money use their wealth and position to take advantage of others. At times, it seems that these forces of evil are allowed to do their will unchecked. We need to remember that there is only one true power in the universe, the King of Kings.

Today, I will...remember who is really on the throne.

Week Fifty-Two
Revelation 18-22

Neal Pollard

Monday
Bye, Bye Babylon

Babylon once stood as the center of the world, conquerors of all people including God's chosen ones. While God used them as His instrument to correct His children, they were a wicked nation that would eventually be overtaken by the Medes and Persians (Daniel 6:30). John uses Babylon, a powerful but wicked people, to describe Rome. In New Testament times, they, like Babylon before them, ruled the world but were destined for the same end. In Revelation 18, an angel reveals the coming downfall of the Roman Empire. Judgment language is found throughout.

Rome was guilty of evil (Revelation 18:2), idolatry (vs. 2), bad influence (vs. 3), immorality (vss. 3,9), sensuality (vss. 3,7,9), and sin (vss. 4-5). Thus, the angel warns that "in a single hour your judgment has come" (vs. 10). God warns foreign merchants and seafarers away from her, and warns citizens within her of the empire's ominous end.

Meanwhile, numbered among the inhabitants of the empire were God's people. His simple message for Christians was, "Come out of her, my people, lest you take part in her sins, lest you share in her plagues..." (vs. 4). The church was not the nation. It was found within its boundaries, but God wanted it distinct. In fact, God was acting on behalf of His people who had suffered at her hands (vs. 24).

What a balancing act we find ourselves faced with today, especially those of us living in the United States. We hope and pray for our leaders to seek God's will, for her wealthiest and most powerful citizens to fear Him. While we hold out that hope and seek to share this hope with our society, we still hear God's clear call to us to not conform to this world (Romans 12:2). Instead, we are to "go out from their midst" in the sense of living spiritually sanctified lives (2 Corinthians 6:17).

Today, I will...remember that the holy God has called me to be holy in all my conduct (1 Peter 1:15), hoping to show someone the better hope that's available.

Tuesday
Victory In the Midst of Defeat

Today's Scripture Revelation 19

Today, we see as stark a contrast as is revealed anywhere in the Bible. As thorough as the defeat of Rome is, as described in chapter 18, the victory for Christians is as complete. The focus is shifted from the troubles of earth to the triumphant sounds in heaven. There is incredible praise directed at God's character, judgment, and reign. Four times, a hallelujah chorus goes up to Him. Imagine the thunderous sound of a great multitude united in praise!

This victory is pictured with the illustration of intimacy, as the saints are the bride betrothed to Jesus, the perfect husband. The church is dressed in pristine garments of "fine linen," acts of righteousness. Yet, He appears as a triumphant king and victorious warrior. This banquet is about winning as much as it is about a wedding. The overriding message is that Jesus forms the winning side, and the world is thoroughly defeated by Him.

Do you ever feel like the Lord's side is losing? The world seems to have all the assets, power, attention, and influence. At times, it seems that the message of salvation is hopelessly drowned out by the noise of ungodliness. But it is not so! Victory awaits. Eternal salvation is the gift, and the giver is "King of kings and Lord of lords" (Revelation 19:16). While Rome's final demise is the focus of John's contextual message, we can conclude that our spiritual adversary will be eternally vanquished, too. It will be a horrible day for those who joined sides with the Adversary (see Revelation 12:9), but it be a happy day for those of us who have Jesus as King. We will join that deafening throng who fall down and worship God. Whatever scars we won by walking through this vail of tears will be salved by the gentle shepherd who rides the white horse of justice. My call is to keep focus on this fact!

Today, I will...keep my eye on "the prize of the upward call of God in Christ Jesus" (Philippians 3:14)!

Wednesday
The Thrown and the Throne

Today's Scripture Revelation 20

A dramatic shift occurs between Revelation 20:6–7. John turns from the present, where he referenced the ultimate fall of the Roman Empire and spiritual preservation of first-century Christians (Revelation 1:1–3) to what takes place after this (1:19; 4:1).

In verses one through six, we see martyred souls awaiting Christ's vengeance on the wicked. In verse seven through the end of the book, we get a glimpse of the end of all things. Two words can describe the end— "thrown" and "throne." Satan and his followers will be "thrown" into the lake of eternal, punishing fire (vs. 10), Death and Hades are thrown in the lake of fire (vs. 14), and anyone not found in the book of life is thrown there, too (vs. 15). This is the fate John wrote to warn everyone to avoid.

Contrast this with the "great white throne" (vs. 11). Coupled with the concept of Christ reigning in the first part of the chapter, it seems clear that it is Jesus who occupies this throne of judgment. It will be a terrifying day for the unprepared, but judgment serves to vindicate as well as indict. The sentence for the acquitted is, "Blessed and holy is the one who has a part in the first resurrection" (vs. 6).

As we struggle with meeting earthly obligations, carry various burdens of responsibility, guilt, and pain, and as sin "clings so closely" (Hebrews 12:1), we cannot forget how this ends! John is about to end his book with a bang, but leading up to that he puts the focus on the book of life along with the other books. If I can keep my focus on the victory, I will enjoy something more spectacular than I can imagine. Here it is: *"The one who conquers will be clothed thus in white garments, and I will never blot his name out of the book of life. I will confess his name before my Father and before his angels!"* (Revelation 3:5)

Today, I won't...be thrown by life; I'll focus on the throne of life!

310

What John Saw and Heard

Breaking down Revelation 21:1-8 exegetically, we observe what John saw and what John heard. First is what he sees. He sees a new heaven and new earth, a thrilling sight first described in Isaiah, promised by Peter in 2 Peter 3, and seen now by John in the context of unending reward here in verse one. It is different from the present heaven and earth (2 Peter 3:10-11). He also sees the holy city coming down out of heaven from God, having been made ready (2,10ff; cf. John 14:1-3). Second is what John hears. From a booming voice from the throne, John hears a six-fold promise. There is a promise of relationship (vs. 3), relief (vs. 4), renewal (vs. 5), refreshing (vs. 6), residence (vs. 7), and refuge (vs. 8). For a beleaguered, persecuted people, this hope and promise had to be the spiritual salve they so needed in order to keep going.

How often do you think about the promise of heaven? While John uses highly figurative language to describe it, decorated with jewels and precious metals, it is encased in the "glory" of God (vss. 11, 23-24, 26). The God that has led and protected us in this life will dwell among us in the place He will have made ready for us. Living here in the Rocky Mountains, I never cease to marvel at the beauty on this earth. I have seen it looking down from Mount Arbel at the Sea of Galilee in Israel, at the fertile steppes of eastern Ukraine, gazing at the Pacific Ocean from Mount Maunganui in New Zealand, and drinking in the amazing views of the Ngorogoro Crater in Tanzania. God made a beautiful world for us to enjoy in the brief, tumultuous existence on earth (Job 14:1). What He is preparing is infinitely greater!

As I see what John saw and hear what John heard, I am anxious to experience the reality of heaven!

Today, I will...start thinking more about heaven and worry less about the things of this world!

Friday

Coming Soon! Come, Lord Jesus

Today's Scripture Revelation 22

After a second description of heaven, Jesus wraps up the incredible revelation to the apostle John. Three times, as He concludes, He tells him, "I am coming soon" (Revelation 22:7,12, 20). It is not a threat. It is a hopeful promise. It is as if He is saying, "I know you are going through so much, but hold on! I am coming soon." Maybe you have anticipated the homecoming of a child or going home to see a parent. The anticipation mounts with every passing mile.

Seeing the coming Lord meant a blessing for the obedient (vs. 7), reward for the one doing well (vs. 12), and blessed assurance to the one waiting and longing (vs. 20). Isn't it interesting that the coming Lord tells everyone to come to Him. He says, "The Spirit and the Bride say, "Come." And let the one who hears say, "Come." And let the one who is thirsty come; let the one who desires take the water of life without price" (vs. 17). He knows He is coming again. Before that moment, He invites us all to come into a relationship with Him.

No, we don't know the exact moment of His coming (Matthew 24:36), but we want Him to come as quickly as He can. We are exposed to the kind of people Jesus refers to in verse 15. We have struggled to overcome being that kind of person ourselves. We have tried to stay on biblical center (18-19). We have tried to practice righteousness and holiness (vs. 11). But, we cannot wait until the battle is over and the victory is won.

Through this wonderful, two-chapter odyssey, we see death dying, cemeteries ceasing, morgues becoming moot, and funeral homes fading. We cherish the ultimate "out with the old and in with the new." We hang on because we know how the journey ends for the faithful. We can become very attached to this world, but we know the world to come is infinitely superior. So, we say with John, "Come, Lord Jesus."

Today, I will...live in anticipation and expectation of His manifestation (1 Corinthians 16:22)!

Order additional copies of this resource at:
thejenkinsinstitute.com/shop
or
tji@thejenkinsinstitute.com

Find more information on the One Word study at:
onewordstudy.com

Other titles available from The Jenkins Institute:

The Living Word: Sermons of Jerry A. Jenkins
The Glory of Preaching
Before I Go: Notes from Older Preachers

Thoughts from the Mound
More Thoughts from the Mound
All I Ever Wanted to Do Was Preach
I Hope You Have to Pinch Yourself

The Preacher as Counselor
Don't Quit on a Monday
Don't Quit on a Tuesday

Five Secrets and a Decision
Centered: Marking Your Map in a Muddled World

Me, You, and the People in the Pews
From Mother's Day to Father's Day

A Minister's Heart
A Youth Minister's Heart
A Mother's Heart
A Father's Heart

Free Evangelism Resources by Jerry Jenkins:
God Speaks Today
Lovingly Leading Men to the Savior

To order, visit thejenkinsinstitute.com/shop